# Studying Plays

## Mick Wallis and Simon Shepherd

### Fourth Edition

BLOOMSBURY ACADEMIC
LONDON · NEW YORK · OXFORD · NEW DELHI · SYDNEY

BLOOMSBURY ACADEMIC
Bloomsbury Publishing Plc
50 Bedford Square, London, WC1B 3DP, UK
1385 Broadway, New York, NY 10018, USA

BLOOMSBURY, BLOOMSBURY ACADEMIC and the Diana logo are trademarks
of Bloomsbury Publishing Plc

First edition published in Great Britain by Arnold in 1998
This edition published in 2018 by Bloomsbury Academic
Reprinted by Bloomsbury Academic 2018

Cover design: Liron Gilenberg | www.ironicitalics.com
Cover image © Susan Detroy/EyeEm

A catalogue record for this book is available from the British Library.

Library of Congress Cataloging-in-Publication Data
Names: Wallis, Mick author. | Shepherd, Simon author.
Title: Studying plays / Mick Wallis, Simon Shepherd.
Description: Fourth edition. | London; New York: Bloomsbury Academic, 2017.
| Includes bibliographical references and index.
Identifiers: LCCN 2017025093 (print) | LCCN 2017028824 (ebook) | ISBN
9781350007352 (ePDF) | ISBN 9781350007345 (ePub) | ISBN 9781350007321
(pbk.: alk. paper) | ISBN 9781350007338 (hardback : alk. paper)
Subjects: LCSH: Drama–Explication.
Classification: LCC PN1707 (ebook) | LCC PN1707 .W32 2017 (print) | DDC
808.2/–dc23
LC record available at https://lccn.loc.gov/2017025093

ISBN: HB: 978-1-3500-0733-8
PB: 978-1-3500-0732-1
ePDF: 978-1-3500-0735-2
eBook: 978-1-3500-0734-5

Series: Studying …

Typeset by Deanta Global Publishing Services, Chennai, India
Printed and bound in Great Britain

To find out more about our authors and books visit www.bloomsbury.com
and sign up for our newsletters.

*For Connie, Graham and Reg, with love*

# CONTENTS

Words in **bold** are in the Glossary, along with other useful words.

# ACKNOWLEDGEMENTS

Thanks are due to Mick Mangan and Terry Stevenson for their expert advice; to Drama Section students at Loughborough University for helping develop these materials in class; to Simon Donger and Simon Stephens for information about key productions; to Christopher Wheeler for his patience, good humour and constructive criticism in getting the first edition of the book published with Edward Arnold; to Elena Seymenliyska for seeing the second edition into print; and to our editors at Bloomsbury Academic for producing the third and now fourth editions.

We owe a debt, too, to Manfred Pfister. We have acknowledged his direct influence several times in this book. In addition, however, his example of systematic analysis, so assiduously conducted in *The Theory and Analysis of Drama*, has guided our own independent enterprise as a whole.

## A note on texts

In preparing a book like *Studying Plays*, there are significant choices to be made about which playtexts to use as examples. The attempt to represent the full variety of drama runs the risk of many of them being unfamiliar to most readers. Confining the list to the most known – the 'canonical' texts – runs the risk of uncritically affirming the canon. We have, in fact, taken the option of returning continually to about a dozen plays, some at least of which we guess will be known to a substantial number of readers. We do this to make the book more accessible, more immediately useful, though in all cases we provide sufficient plot outlines and other details for our analyses to work on their own account.

# 1

# Getting started

In Shakespeare's *A Midsummer Night's Dream* (1594) there is a famous comic scene which shows a group of workmen rehearsing a play. Shakespeare invites his audience to feel superior to them, because they have been reading their script incorrectly. They make a mess of staging it because what they don't know is that reading a play is a special skill. The purpose of this book is to help the reader develop that skill, whether they are reading the play for study or pleasure, or dealing with it on the rehearsal floor.

There is nothing arcane or magical about this skill. If you have tried analysing novels or poems you will be using the same careful attention to words when you read a play. What often goes wrong with analysis of plays is that people try and imagine what is not there, inventing past lives for characters and dreaming up stage business. But, at base, you simply need to read, closely and rigorously, everything that is in front of you. At the same time, you also have to be aware that a play is a different sort of written object from a novel or poem and therefore you are attending to text that does different things. We describe those different things over the course of this book.

Compare the activity of reading a play with that of reading a novel. The novel is designed to address its audience directly: open it and we have everything we need in front of us. But a playtext addresses its ultimate audience indirectly; it is a set of instructions designed to be interpreted by theatre makers who will then stage the play before its own audience. Whether we are reading in the study or in rehearsal, then, we are dealing with a very specific object with a very specific job to do.

The playtext is, if we think about it, quite a strange – incomplete – object. Our aim here is to help our readers recognize this; but at the same time to show how exciting the activity of reading plays can be when the signals they contain are recognized for what they are. That, we hope, will contribute to more pleasurable reading, more productive study – and exciting productions. So we are on a journey to discover more about the relationship between the two sorts of 'play' – the script and the performance.

# Reading the play

## Play as pretext

Let's begin by thinking about texts. A text is something that invites itself to be read. The printed play is obviously a text, and we have already used the word 'playtext'. Another term for playtext is *dramatic text*, and this is commonly paired with the term *theatrical text*. This in turn is an equivalent term to 'production' or 'performance'. The notion of the theatrical text is especially useful because it emphasizes the fact that the stage is itself 'read' by the audience. Both the page and the stage invite some sort of reading. The dramatic text is read on the page, the theatrical text is read by an audience from the stage.

Now, we have already raised two things in relation to the dramatic text. First, we have stressed the importance, as we read a play, of bearing in mind the role of the dramatic text in scripting the theatrical text. Second, we have raised the fact that the dramatic text therefore necessarily has an indirect relationship with the theatre audience. But how can we get into the habit of seeing both that connection *and* that indirectness as we read? How can we think usefully in general terms about how the play which we read as a script relates to the play which we see as a performance? A useful way of thinking about this is to consider the dramatic text as a *pretext* – something that comes 'before' the thing the audience actually 'reads' in performance, the show. The dramatic text is 'previous' to the theatrical text.

To get to grips with what the notion of pretext implies for the relationship between page and stage, let us begin by thinking laterally – sideways – for a moment. Almost anything can be a pretext for a work of art. Suppose we compose a piece of music in response to a painting. The painting is our chosen pretext for the music. Suppose it is a figurative painting – one depicting human figures. Suppose it depicts a woman in distress on a bridge. If we composed simply in response to this literal content, our use of our chosen pretext would surely be impoverished. What about the colour range, the feel of the painting's own composition or design, the quality and rhythm of the brush strokes? By attending closely to the specific features of the painting *as a painting*, we are more likely to make a better piece of music. It is not a question of slavishly following the original; rather, responding to it in its own *specificity* enriches what we make.

We might instead, of course, use the painting as a pretext for a piece of theatre. Or, say, in place of the painting we use a piece of sculpture, or a poem. In each case, there will be features specific to the medium of each that will – if we plan to make full use of our pretext – influence what we come to make on stage. Consider the bulk and feel of the sculpture; the sense of space in the poem. And, say, we made a piece of theatre in response to a novel. Most novels have 'scenes', nearly all contain dialogue and conduct a story. We could make a play that more or less reproduced them. But how much better if our production somehow echoed or played with the vigour or the weightiness of the narration, its attitude to events, its own 'voice'.

And what if we choose to use a playtext as the pretext for our piece of theatre? And suppose again that the playtext deals with human figures in recognizable scenes in the grip of events that constitute a story. Shall we merely retell the story and re-present the characters on stage in our own way? Or shall we discover and enrich our own way by responding to the playtext in its own specificity – that is as a text that *itself* points forward to activities on a stage? What we come to make is entirely up to us. But we shall gain much if we are wise to the specificity of our pretext as we create.

When we read realist novels, we 'stage' them in our heads. And when we read plays we do much the same. Each invites such a staging, in fact. But the play has a real stage in mind, not just a private imagination. We lose so much of what plays have to offer us if we read them as if they were novels, whether privately or in rehearsal. They are special kinds of text, indeed special kinds of pretexts. For they are *designed to function as pretexts*.

Clearly, recognizing dramatic texts as designed pretexts will help us get more from them in our role as readers of plays in books. But will it on the other hand threaten to stifle our creative responses in our role as theatre makers? Some theatre makers make the assumption that the text is their enemy, because it requires actors simply to repeat words written for them rather than to express themselves as individuals. The text is seen to be a mechanism for control exercised by an absent author. Genuinely new and democratic theatre is made, these people think, by liberating themselves from text. But actually this is to make mistakes about both its function in production processes and its nature as a special sort of text. Let's think in another way for a moment about that word 'pretext'. Sometimes we use the word as a synonym for 'excuse': so-and-so used such-and-such as a mere pretext for doing what they really wanted to do. And some people complain that modern productions of old plays often use the original text only as a pretext in that sense – that they are somehow being 'unfaithful' to the original. This is not a position we take. So much good theatre has been achieved precisely by reworking, adapting or 'refunctioning' plays from the past; and we could only be fully 'faithful' to the original if we reproduced its original staging conditions, and brought the original audience back from the dead. Theatre is not a museum; and anyhow most modern museums are more interesting than this. But recognizing the dramatic text as something that is designed to function as a pretext helps us, as it were, see the brush strokes in the painting, feel the space in the poem, imagine the touch of the stone. And these are great cues for making our own art in response.

## Production, reception, determination

So, then, the first thing to realize when we open a playtext is that the words in front of us are not designed to function in the same way as the words in a novel or poem. The words are designed to become a performance. We readily talk about 'the production'. And, while we are apt to talk, say, about 'our' production of a particular play, what we have already established suggests that we should pay attention to the ways in which dramatic texts themselves are involved in the business of *production*. But how do they produce a performance? At a basic level they do so by instructing not only what is to be said but how it is to be said, to whom, in what context, with what actions and in what space. The words of the playtext in front of us contain a great deal of different sorts of information; they are issuing a lot of instructions for the production of a performance. We shall soon begin the job of showing how these instructions operate.

For now, however, let's continue thinking in general terms about how we approach this strange object, the dramatic text. Many people do in fact begin reading a play in the same way as they begin reading a novel or a magazine. They are curious to know what the story is, they want to follow it through as it unfolds. Without an author, a narrating voice, to guide them, as there is in a novel, they tend to set about extracting the main outline of the story for themselves. The places where that seems stated most clearly tend to be chunks of dialogue which are usually spoken by the important characters. So their eyes skate over the other bits, which seem less relevant. In particular, they often leap completely over the bits in italics, which seem to be instructions only of relevance to actors and designers.

The attention to dialogue, rather than to other elements of the text, will also be reinforced if you are studying the play mainly as a filmed production. In these circumstances the only bit of the author's text which is more or less accessible is the dialogue and possibly the setting. The way you look at the setting and how characters move in it will be controlled by the camera movements, as required by the director. So too your focus on particular characters, and even the importance you attach to what they say, can be controlled by the camera, as it lingers over or pulls away from them. When you are watching the filmed play, then, you are watching at least two texts: what the author has scripted and what the director has scripted (as seen mainly through the camera activity). If you want to see for yourself what sort of staging the author has scripted then you have to return to the written text and look not just at the dialogue but at those bits in italics.

These are described, and usually dismissed, as stage directions. But, as we hope to demonstrate, much of the dialogue also contains directions. Indeed, it is very rare that we read what someone is saying without at the same time also being given the information about how it is to be said. It is the second part of that reading process (learning about the 'how') which has to be learnt as part of the discipline of studying plays. This is the point at which we face the fact that because the words of a playtext are designed differently and function differently from the words of a novel, so they need to be read differently.

The dialogue in front of us is busy doing a lot more than telling a story. It is, as we have said, creating images, movement, a stage world. And the stage directions are every bit as important as the dialogue in scripting what is to happen on stage. Let us then summarize the relationship between the written thing, that strange incomplete object, the playtext and the performed thing, the show with real people and spaces, the production. Our summary, shown in Figure 1.1, is in the form of a diagram (Figure 1.1).

Note that in Figure 1.1 we have favoured the use of 'dramatic text' and 'theatrical text' over 'playtext' and 'production', to foreground the fact that there are two sets of reading going on, or at least implied. For, even in the absence of an actual stage production, the dramatic text produces the sense of one. Just as part of the productivity of a novel is its suggestion of scenes in the mind of the reader, the major *productivity* of a dramatic text is its scripting of what might actually happen on a stage. Note – might happen. We can say that each dramatic text contains an *implied* theatrical production. The implied production is written in the dramatic text; often it is said to be *inscribed* there. (And when it becomes an actual production this also takes a textual form – the stage manager's 'book', the designer's plans, the director's notes all may be read as text.) The actual content of the theatrical text – what exactly happens on stage – depends on the creative choices of the theatre makers. But whoever has written the words of the dramatic text has imagined them as a performed event. They have not been written to exist on the page; they have been written to help *produce* a theatrical text through the work of others.

The word 'production' comes to us readily, and we just suggested one way in which we can make it even more useful to us, through the idea of productivity; we shall return to it later in connection with the audience. But there is another very useful term for us here, and that is **determination**. We have said that the dramatic text helps produce the theatrical text. We might say that it provides one of the 'frames' for the making of the show. And this is one important sense of the word 'determination'. So we can say that the dramatic text is one of the determinations on the theatrical text – the show – alongside the work of the director, designers and so on. There is no such thing as the solely correct production of the play. All sorts of different interpretations in different societies can happen. But the dramatic text offers to determine each – through its inscription of an implied production.

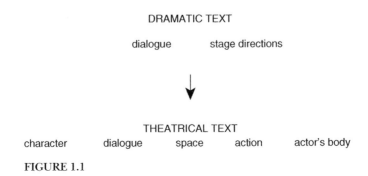

DRAMATIC TEXT

dialogue        stage directions

THEATRICAL TEXT

character      dialogue      space      action      actor's body

FIGURE 1.1

DRAMATIC TEXT

IMPLIED
PRODUCTION

*production*                                        *determination*

THEATRICAL TEXT

RECEPTION

FIGURE 1.2

But what happens in the theatre? Where and how, for instance, is meaning made? A text has no meaning in and of itself. If we speak of a theatrical text, then the meaning of that text is made in the act of its being read by each member of the audience. The show ultimately means what it means to its audience. The audience has a key role in the production of meaning in the theatre; it is one determination on the production of meaning there. This sort of emphasis, on the *reception* of texts, developed strongly in English Literature studies in the1970s. Thus, we can diagram as in Figure 1.2.

Now, we have in a very short space introduced a number of terms: dramatic and theatrical text; pretext; production and productivity; inscription; determination; reception. If any of these terms are unfamiliar, they will become familiar through their use in your own discussion or writing. We introduce them because they are useful – and especially useful for thinking about reading plays.

Chapters 2 to 6 are organized around the five basic elements of the theatrical text, as it is shaped, scripted, 'produced' or 'determined' by the dramatic text, that we identify in Figure 1.1. In those chapters we shall set out methods and terminology for analysing the dramatic text in relation to these elements. We have consciously drawn examples from across the historical range, in order to introduce you to different sorts of text. Inevitably some of these examples will be unfamiliar so we suggest you look them up online to read a synopsis and discover when they were written. Before you get on to those chapters, however, we want to push a bit further with our exploration of the relationship between playtext and performed text. In order to do that, we'll look at a couple of examples.

## The playtext into performance

Imagine a stained-glass window in a Christian church, in which a chaste young woman, the type of woman who is a virgin until marriage and faithful to her husband thereafter, kneels and prays to God. The stained-glass window shows us the image. We are interested in her as a picture which signifies innocence, rather than in the details of her life.

And now imagine the same image made by a performer on a stage. As she kneels, she speaks:

> Here I kneel.
> If e'er my will did trespass 'gainst his love,
> Either in discourse of thought or actual deed,
>
> ...
>
> Comfort forswear me!
>
> ...
>
> I cannot say 'whore';
> It does abhor me now I speak the word;
> To do the act that might the addition earn,
> Not the world's mass of vanity could make me.

These are lines spoken by Desdemona in Shakespeare's *Othello* (1602–4, 4.2.152–65). The young bride has been accused by her husband Othello of being unfaithful. We can take the lines as evidence of her guiltlessness and purity, and of her pain at being wrongly suspected. But, if we also note that she is kneeling, we start to see that Shakespeare is here constructing a formal picture, an emblem, rather like that in a stained-glass window. As we get better at this, we might also see – and find ways to describe (as we show later) – how the very rhythm of the lines which open and close the speech produces a stillness on the stage.

But let us look a little more widely. Also on stage are Desdemona's servant Emilia, and her husband Iago, Othello's right-hand man, who has deceived his master into suspecting Desdemona. While Emilia is agitated and suspects foul play – 'I will be hang'd if some eternal villain ... Have not devis'd this slander' (ll. 131–4) – the villainous Iago feigns innocence and tells Desdemona, 'I pray you be content' (l. 166). Indeed, Desdemona's lines just quoted are made in the same speech which she begins, 'O God! Iago, / What shall I do to win my lord again?' (ll. 149–50).

What we have, then, are two pictures, one inside the other. Inside is the emblematic Desdemona, pure and innocent. But the total stage picture is of Iago manipulating Desdemona into her posture of defeat, and revelling in it. Surrounding the emblem of innocence is the emblem of villainy and deception. This double emblem is part of the way in which this scene produces meaning for an audience.

Here, then, is clear evidence of the importance of remembering always that the dramatic text is a script for activity on a stage.

Let us now turn our attention to another woman with a dodgy husband, Nora in Ibsen's *A Doll's House* (1879), the play which we shall be coming back to throughout this book. We are well into the third and final act. Nora has a secret – that she forged her dying father's signature in order to secure a loan, which she then used to take her seriously sick husband away on convalescence. He has been ignorant of this fact and Nora knows that knowledge of it would anger and disgust him, probably destroying their marriage. But a man called Krogstad knows the truth and has written a letter to Nora's husband, Torvald Helmer, spilling the beans. Nora knows this. Helmer has just carried his mail into his study:

> NORA: (*wild-eyed, fumbles around, seizes* HELMER'S *cloak, throws it around herself and whispers quickly, hoarsely*). Never see him again. Never. Never. Never. (*Throws the shawl over her head.*) Never see the children again. Them, too. Never. Never. Oh – the icy black water! Oh – that bottomless – that – ! Oh, if only it were all over! Now he's got it – he's reading it. Oh no, no! Not yet! Goodbye Torvald! Goodbye my darlings!
>     *She turns to run into the hall. As she does so, HELMER throws open his door and stands there with an open letter in his hand.*
>
>                                                                  (p. 92)

Helmer is indeed furiously angry. When Nora tries to explain herself, that she acted out of love, Helmer tells her, 'Oh, don't try to make silly excuses.' And when she becomes still more agitated and says, 'You're not going to suffer for my sake. I won't let you' – sharing with him her suicidal thoughts – he snaps back,

> Stop being theatrical (p. 93).

We might be inclined to look at Nora's speech and think that this is just a bit of old-fashioned, melodramatic, over-the-top writing. Yet, if we note how it stands out from the rest of the play, if we note Helmer's own comment about theatricality (other translators have him say, 'Stop being melodramatic'), and if we look at the stage directions concerning the cloak and shawl, we start to see something much more interesting going on.

As will emerge later in our account of the play – and, we hope, in your reading of it – Nora is indeed being 'theatrical'. She is living her life just now *as if* it were a melodrama, or a play with a melodramatic drive to it: a happy and just conclusion will, she imagines, suddenly emerge by some miracle out of desperation. Nora wants both to kill herself – to make a huge sacrifice – *and* to have Helmer stop her from doing so because he loves and values her. But life is not like that.

There is more than this. Ibsen lets the audience also imagine it is watching a play that works like a melodrama. Nora's speech and actions will at first have been taken at face value (even if they might have sounded a little old-fashioned) as the depiction of a desperate woman. Helmer's riposte to her breaks into this sympathetic response from the audience, and 'frames' the moment as melodrama.

Then, a little later on, Krogstad relents and returns the only evidence of Nora's guilt – an IOU – to the couple, torn to shreds. Helmer is beside himself with joy: 'Nora! No – I must read it once more. Yes, yes, it's true! I'm saved! Nora, I am saved!' (p. 95). Indeed, the play could quickly end hereafter. The crisis has passed. But Nora has learnt her lesson. Her husband cannot hear her love. What they must do is sit down and talk. And eventually she leaves, famously slamming the offstage street door.

What Ibsen does, then, is not only show that Nora has been locked into a 'theatrical' frame of mind. He also shows that Helmer *and the audience* have been locked there as well. What have they been doing sitting there in the auditorium anyway? Waiting for a happy end? Life is not like that. As readers of the play we would miss all of this startling challenge if we were merely concentrating on the story of Nora's development.

Our two examples have taken us into quite complicated territory. They do not simply show how the written playtext instructs a performer to move or to deliver lines, or how a stage picture is created as a context for those lines. They focus on the activity of the audience watching, reading the stage. And, even for a relaxed audience, this is far from being passive. Reading the stage is an activity. But our examples also show how the attitude of the audience is itself being shaped. *The dramatic text steers the theatre audience into a particular mode of reception.* In the case of Desdemona, the audience is encouraged to regard her in two ways – as the emblem of a virgin and as a real woman falsely accused. In the case of Nora, the audience is encouraged to adopt a somewhat sentimental attitude to her, and then, rather challengingly, Ibsen shows them how false this attitude is. This task of steering audience **reception** is one of the key considerations of the dramatic text.

Where has this taken our argument about the dramatic text? We have suggested so far that the playtext *produces* the performance, in the sense that it carries information which can be used by the acting company in constructing a performance. Now we are suggesting – in addition – that the playtext seeks to *produce an attitude* to the performance: its pictures are designed to lead the audience towards particular sorts of interpretation. By manipulating the audience's recognition of melodrama, and by subverting expectations derived from different sorts of drama, Ibsen was challenging the fantasy solutions offered by other sorts of drama in favour of a drama which shows life as it 'really' is.

So the production is not necessarily a stopping-point, and it may push the audience somewhere new: to new thoughts about 'emblem' or 'melodrama', for instance. So we are here talking about ways in which dramatic texts *negotiate* sense-making with their ultimate audience, or at least script ways in which such sense is to be negotiated.

# How does reading performance happen?

If an audience responds to something as realistic, and then discovers it's melodrama, this implies that audience members bring a certain amount of knowledge about drama with them into the theatre. More than that, it implies that they agree to respond to the play according to how they think the play wants them to respond. If it looks like pantomime, you start to respond to it as pantomime (and you don't shout 'Look out behind you!' when you're watching *Hamlet*).

This readiness of an audience to respond appropriately is called *convention*. The root of the word 'convention' is to do with agreement (see R. Williams 1968: 12–16). When we watch Renaissance dramas we acknowledge the convention that asides cannot be overheard by others on stage; or, at grand opera, we agree to the logic that a heroine dying of tuberculosis can still sing hideously high notes. Shakespeare's mechanicals in *A Midsummer Night's Dream* (3.1) got themselves in a particular pickle because they were in a muddle about conventions. Their script required that a lion appear. But they did not know how to present the lion in the story without frightening the ladies (and to frighten their audience may have cost them their lives). They had to find a means of showing a lion which would be taken seriously as a lion without being taken so seriously that people were frightened.

Conventions are in fact very handy, and no performance is ever without them (for, at the minimum, we agree to let the performance happen on the stage without walking onto that stage uninvited ourselves). We respect the convention in order for the thing to happen in the first place.

But it also has to be said that conventions change. We no longer use the aside, or look for emblems. What past audiences accepted, present audiences may find unacceptable. We often use the word 'conventional' to mean something which is old-fashioned, where the conventions have gone past their use-by date. Nevertheless, all performances work with conventions – it is just that some conventions feel old and hence noticeable, while others that are contemporary don't seem to be conventions, just natural. And when new conventions are coming into being they might feel strange, difficult, unintelligible. Ibsen's audience may well have found melodrama old-fashioned, a residue from the past; but they may also have felt that his new conventions, the conventions of Naturalism, were presenting them with shocking or inexplicable material: the door slam became notorious. To us, by contrast, the conventions of Naturalism feel like a residue of the past as we head towards other sorts of theatre. But, as you'll note from television dramas, Naturalism is still being used. We can make sense of this situation, first, by adopting the terms given by Raymond Williams (1977) – residual, dominant, emergent (where the 'dominant' are the set of conventions most preferred at the present); and then we can acknowledge Williams' point that all three sorts of convention can be seen in use at any one moment. Thus in the Desdemona extract we saw how the creation of an emblem (a medieval practice) coexisted with the new Renaissance writing of psychologically complex characters. You could try observing similar coexisting conventions on a night's television.

So the way that the dramatic text establishes and manipulates the conventions of the theatrical text can in turn question or challenge an audience, or indeed give them pleasure. When we watch those mechanicals rehearsing, we find them funny not only because of their mistakes about how to do a play but also because the play they are rehearsing is itself old-fashioned. Now, if a reader or an audience had no knowledge of conventions, they would be ignorant of this whole context to the lines spoken by the mechanicals. And the experience of reading the play, in whatever respect, would be not just thinner but also rather wrong-headed.

## Shaping the dramatic text

Let us lastly think a little more about just what it is that we are holding when we hold the text of a play. We have discussed the productivity of the dramatic text and its role in negotiating convention. If we think the same thought in the other direction, it becomes obvious that the texture of any one dramatic text is determined by the theatrical – stage – conventions it aims to manipulate. A Doll's House bears the marks of the stage conventions Ibsen was grappling with. A skill we can develop is to 'see' those stage conventions as we read the play.

But the play we hold is usually also more than an author's script for theatrical production. Especially in the case of earlier plays or plays in the 'canon' – those that have become the dominant texts in academic study and are given a special place in the culture – the printed play is something quite different from the version used to make the first production. Editors have intervened; different versions have been collated (as especially with Shakespeare); the thing has been adapted or tidied up for scholarly study or a general readership (see p. 13 below). Understanding the status of the playtext you are handling is important.

# Stage directions

As we noted at the start, readers often skip over stage directions rather fast. But stage directions work with the dialogue to script the implied production. And it is this that we should get into the habit of reading. Even as we make our own production, the way dialogue and stage directions together shape the implied stage is every bit as important as character or story – as materials that we then work on, with or against to make our own show.

## What do stage directions do?

Stage directions script a variety of things. In the short extract from A Doll's House, for instance, there are instructions regarding facial expression, vocal delivery, gesture and basic actions, costume, 'kinesics' (moving about the stage), 'proxemics' (blocking – positioning of characters), space and props.

*STAGE DIRECTIONS*

scenic arrangements                    actor(s)/characters

lay-out of stage                       delivery of dialogue
furnishings                            bodily state
props                                  emotion
                                       proxemics (blocking)
                                       kinesics (movement)

FIGURE 1.3

Figure 1.3 sets out the various functions of stage directions. You may want to adjust or add to it.

# What is the relationship between the stage directions and the dialogue?

Since dialogue not only contains a story but also makes directions for action, character and space, it is often assumed to be the most important of the two elements which comprise the dramatic text – it seems to have more bearing on the production. The preferential treatment of dialogue over stage directions is institutionalized in the practice which refers to *Haupttext* (German for 'main text') and *Nebentext* ('ancillary text') in place of dialogue and stage directions respectively (these are the terms of Roman Ingarden, which are explored in Aston and Savona 1991). But this is actually a partial, and thus misleading, version of the relationship between stage directions and dialogue.

In many cases stage directions work in conjunction with dialogue, explaining it: such stage directions may be called *conjunctive*. But there are some plays, such as Beckett's *Acts Without Words 1* and *2* (1958,1960), where stage directions have completely replaced dialogue. In other plays dialogue is suspended for long passages: thus, in all of Act 3 scene 3 of Galsworthy's *Justice* (1910), the unjustly imprisoned Falder roams distractedly about his prison cell, the box-like **proscenium** stage transformed from familiar living space to a place of mute entrapment.

Stage directions can, then, take precedence over dialogue. But they can also act in tension with or against dialogue. These sorts of directions may be called *disjunctive*. Manfred Pfister (1988: 48) provides a good example, again from Beckett. *Waiting for Godot* (1955) ends with the following exchange:

VLADIMIR: Well? Shall we go?
ESTRAGON: Yes, let's go.
(*They do not move.*)

The same contradiction between their intended actions and what they actually do is scripted to happen at each act end. Its repetition drives the point home: we assume in life that intention leads to action, and we expect to see this affirmed on stage, but Beckett refuses.

## Implicit stage directions

We have already suggested that dialogue contains 'implicit' stage directions, and we have seen an example: when Shakespeare gives the Desdemona actress the line, 'Here I kneel', he indicates quite directly that the speech is to be played kneeling.

It was common practice in Renaissance plays to embed the stage directions in the speeches, to have people say how they were moving and where. With this in mind if you look at the opening of *Hamlet* (1601), you will observe that the characters tell us what the image is: "Tis now struck twelve', ' 'Tis bitter cold', 'Have you had quiet guard', 'good night' (1.1.7–11).

Once you get used to looking for the implicit directions in Renaissance plays, you will find them in many later sorts of drama. The custom of writing fairly full stage directions only began in the nineteenth century. And even since then, many directions are still embedded: in Libby Mason's *Double Vision* by the Women's Theatre Group (1982) this exchange takes place: 'Shh, I'm watching. It's educational. Leeds United.' 'Oh God, he's so patronising.' (p. 37). The dialogue tells us not only that they are watching television, but also that, as it goes on, it is a quiz programme. There is no other stage direction.

## The changing importance of stage directions

If you look at the opening of *Hamlet* in the edition by Hibbard (1987), you will find this at the top of the scene: '*Enter Francisco, a sentinel, who stands on guard. Enter Barnardo, to relieve him.*' This direction has been invented by the editor. He has done it to make the play easier to read. Even at the cost of interfering with Shakespeare's text, he wants the play to look like a proper playtext would look in 1987.

What has happened between Shakespeare's time and the editor's is that plays have turned into books. Shakespeare could count on the fact that his actors would be used to picking up the implicit stage directions. Many plays until well into the nineteenth century were written on the basis that actors would automatically note not only these directions but also the conventions within which acting and speaking were to be done (someone who specialized as a melodrama villain would know the sort of walk and gestures that were to be supplied, much as a session musician knows the harmonic arrangements that are required). When, however, dramatists wanted their play to be done differently, when they wanted to resist the regular treatment that the actors would have given it, they needed to supply stage directions to insist on precise detail: '*This speech is not to be spoken in a tone implying hardship*' (Robertson, *Caste* 1867: 144). In stage directions of this sort, you can see a tension between the dominant and the emergent conventions (as we described them earlier), between what the actor would normally do and the new thing the dramatist wanted.

This tension between actors and dramatists became very apparent in the late nineteenth century, when a group of writers who were trying to 'reform' the drama found that commercial managements were not interested in their serious and political plays. Lacking much prospect of frequent commercial production, they published their plays to be read as books. This meant supplying sufficient information to make them easily readable by people who were novel readers rather than actors. Thus if you look at a play by one of these new political dramatists, George Bernard Shaw, you will find not only detailed descriptions of the action but expressions of opinion that seem much more than a direction to actors: thus, '*Externally he is pretentious, booming, noisy, important. Really he is that obsolescent social phenomenon the fool of the family dumped on the Church by his father the patron*' (*Mrs Warren's Profession* 1902: 227). The same sort of thing appeared years later: a character note describes '*that middle-class womanhood, which is so eminently secure in its divine rights, that it can afford to tolerate the parliament, and reasonably free assembly of its menfolk*'. This is John Osborne, *Look Back in Anger* (1956: 39). The stage direction has turned into a supplementary and mostly unperformable part of the text. Shaw's prefaces to his plays became as famous as the plays themselves (and *Mrs Warren* was published as a book about four years before it was performed). This tradition continued in the work of Edward Bond, whose plays were accompanied by poems which are published in the programmes for the performance. The provocative or unperformable stage direction now functions as part of post-realist drama (see **pp. 182, 188**).

Thus from the sort of stage directions, their presence or absence, their quantity and content, you can deduce something of the conditions prevailing when the play was written, and the play's relationship to dominant conventions.

## Reading the design for the performance

As a conclusion to this chapter we can return to, and enlarge on, the way that the dramatic text scripts the stage – and the way in which we can read that scripting.

In the late twentieth century there was a significant shift in the way that companies approached the production of theatre shows. Rather than start from an already-written script, the company would generate its own material through the process of devising. In many cases the devising was and is done by the actors, but where scenographers or sound and light designers were members of the company, there were moves towards exploring how the main creative development of a show could come not from the movement and speech of actors but from the design of sound or stage images. Such a process of creation can be described as 'design-led'.

Since our concern here is with the study of plays – the already-written scripts – the activity of devising is not directly relevant to this book. But the idea of a 'design-led' approach to a project may be something that we can use in circumstances other than devising. All too often sound and visual images are regarded as accessories, ornamentations, bolted onto the primary work of the drama, which is assumed to be the activity of the actors. They are regarded as effects and atmospheres, whereas the written words are seen as the core text. A design-led approach, by contrast, conceives of sound and light and the visual organization of the stage as having their own coherent shapes, following a logic from one scene to another, manipulating the audience's response to what they experience on the stage, if not actually making meanings in their own right. In other words, sound and visual organization are, as much as words, texts.

A design-led approach to the study of a play may thus encourage us to see how the printed script contains several elements of pretext. Awareness of how these different elements operate will enable us to show more fully how a play does its work. The problem, however, is that scripts don't seem readily to yield up this information. As we note in the previous section conventions for writing stage directions vary over the years in relation to different sorts of theatre practice. Long and detailed stage directions appeared at the very end of the nineteenth century as part of a bid by authors to take more control over the production of their plays, at a time when it was conventional for actor-managers to concentrate their attention on spectacle to the exclusion of the written text. But even at this date there was no such thing in the theatre production process as a lighting designer or a sound designer, although there were scene painters and stage engineers. Those designer roles are mid-twentieth-century inventions. Dramatists did of course imagine their plays as sonic and visual entities, but there was no standard language, no set of terms, for writing about sound and light. The consequence is that, if we want to make a design-led analysis of a script, we have to be ready to hunt around for our evidence.

Let's try to do that with a text from a period which had none of the modern equipment of visual and sonic management, let alone its terminology. *Macbeth* dates from around 1606 but, from its opening requirement for a storm, we know that it is a visually and sonically imagined piece. In order to suggest how we might gather information about its various design suggestions, as a first step towards showing what these layers of pretext do, we have taken the opening sequence of the play (if you are using a text which has anything more than minimal stage directions, then you need to check that these are not editorial additions to what Shakespeare wrote).

This sequence comprises nine scenes, up to and including the dramatic climax of Duncan's murder. For the purpose of the exercise, we have attempted to note every indication as to the organization of visual or sonic arrangements. At the same time we have largely ignored everything the characters say, except where it is relevant to these arrangements.

Sound is usually fairly obvious, either mentioned specifically in stage directions or in characters' speech. Visual arrangements are initially less so. Clearly specifications about props or costumes have a visual element, but so too we can find requirements about the relationships between bodies. As an obvious case, a hierarchical procession or a tableau of people deferring to one another are each visual organizations of the stage. Such relationships between bodies can be organized as a contrast between group and individual, and they can be expressed through specified gestures. Thus a requirement that a group of people enter or exit together, as opposed to a single entry or separate exits, can provide both visual and sonic organization. There is a strong visual contrast between a stage filled with bodies and one with a solo performer, and the space around those bodies can also be made to seem orderly or frightening, strange or domestic, from how the bodies interact with it (we shall develop these points in more detail later in the book). So too a group makes very much more sound than does an individual, through its feet crossing the stage and from its costumes and the props it carries. Costume can be a powerful source of sound: one of the characteristic effects of Royal Shakespeare Company productions in the 1970s was the swish of cloaks across the floor. This was the sound of 'classical' drama.

We have noted two other sets of details that bear on visual effect. These are the differences between characters who are familiar and those who are unfamiliar, and those who are recognizable as opposed to unrecognizable. A character can be unfamiliar but recognizable as a type – you may not have seen him before but if he's got a crown on his head he's recognizable as a king. These two sets of differences can provide pictures with, at one extreme, familiar figures in roles that are clear, and, at the other, people who not only are unknown to us but whose function and role we cannot determine. The latter case will give us a stage which is a lot more visually, and thus perhaps intellectually, unsettling.

Here are the elements that comprise the visual and sonic arrangements of the first nine scenes of *Macbeth*.

1. [Act 1] Thunder, lightning; enter three witches; unfamiliar characters but recognizable role?; they speak as 'we three': unison, verse; exit three persons.

2. Alarum within: enter king plus three persons and bloody man (unfamiliar but recognizable roles): verbal text supplies requirements – 'what bloody…', 'Say to the king…'; exit king plus five persons (without bloody man), king instructing another.

3. Thunder; enter three witches (familiar); place marked: 'How far is't called to Forres?'; exit four persons, 'Come friends'. No witches at exit.

4. Flourish; enter king plus three persons (familiar): bodily gestures: 'My liege' 'humbly take my leave'; exit seven persons: 'let's after him'; flourish.

5. Enter woman with letter, reading (unfamiliar, unrecognizable?); exit two persons.

6. Hoboys, torches; enter king plus seven persons plus attendants (unfamiliar persons are Macduff and attendants); place: 'This castle'; exit king plus seven plus attendants plus Lady M: gestures: 'Give me your hand', 'By your leave mistress'.

7. Hoboys, torches; enter sewer and servants, carrying dishes and 'service' (unfamiliar, recognizable); place: 'Why have you left the chamber?'; exit Lady M and M (no servants).

8. [Act 2] Enter two persons with torch (one familiar, one not: Fleance); sword: 'Take thee that too'; sword: 'Who's there?' Enter two with torch (M plus servant: familiar); exit two [with torch?]; exit one [with torch?]; 'bid thy mistress ... strike upon the bell'; exit one: 'the bell invites me'.

9. Enter one (familiar: Lady M); place: 'Who's there?' [within?]; 'Hark'; enter one (familiar: M), with bloody hand(s) and daggers: 'Didst thou not hear a noise?' 'Did not you speak?' 'Hark'; after five lines note bloody hand(s): 'sorry sight'; after 26 lines note bloody hand, then note daggers; exit Lady M with daggers; knocking within: 'Whence is that knocking?' Note bloody hand(s); enter Lady M with bloody hands; 'I hear a knocking' 'Hark! More knocking' 'Wake Duncan with thy knocking'; exit two.

What can we read off from this as to *Macbeth*'s design for, and use of, visuals and sound?

1. Very obviously, the quietness of Lady Macbeth's first entrance contrasts with all that has preceded it. She is the first person to enter alone. So too she is an unfamiliar character, and also possibly, at first, unrecognizable, in that we may not be sure what her social role is. This is the first time these two elements have been brought together, and the first time a scene has started in silence. There is, then, not simply a designed emphasis here, but also a somewhat unsettling one.

2. After this scene the sound returns, but now marked as interior or domestic. The hoboys make a mellifluous sound and accompany ceremonies of hospitality. Then there's silence. The stroke on the bell comes out of apparent silence, from elsewhere. Although expected, this is a different sort of sound from any we have heard. It has a less 'natural' relationship to the activity on the stage and, perhaps more importantly, it breaks in upon the apparent silence. Two effects follow from this: the silence becomes fragile and a sense of offstage space is generated. Both of these effects will return, more intensively, in the next scene. Thus the murder scene is designed sonically in such a way that the stage in front of us feels risky, with unknown space somewhere beyond.

3. The Lady Macbeth scene [5] is the first in which a character is required to hold an object. Thereafter there is quite a lot of carrying, principally of torches. Scene 8 introduces a sword that comes on and goes off. This amounts to a bit more than having us become conscious of the passage of objects around the stage. It also shows what people are doing with their hands, and into this pattern the courtesies between king and hostess [scene 6] also fit. This works its way through, in design terms, to the entry of bloody hands in scene 9, and then the climactic doubling of the number of bloodied hands.

4. The power of that murder scene arises in large part from sonic and visual design. We have noted that design elements lead up to it, getting our responsiveness ready. In sonic terms the Macbeths are required to begin the scene listening for noise which apparently isn't there. This has two effects. First it makes the actors respond to the space around them as if they were no longer in control of it, as if it were an environment impinging upon them. This leads into the second effect. The listening is a listening to the whole space, which includes the auditorium. The audience is woven into the management of noise and silence. And while most audiences nowadays watch in silence, and often stop their habitual rustling at this moment, the scene still works – and works well – where an audience is a lot noisier. For what happens then is that the Macbeths' attempts to cling onto the security of silence make them look both fragile and odd. Into this tension the introduction of an altogether new sort of sound – knocking – has a very violent effect.

5. The visual trickery of scene 9 is a parallel to the sonic oddness of the Macbeths. Hands and objects have been activated and an audience may well have become alerted to them. So they may well (we can only ever guess at what audiences really do) notice the bloody hands and bloody daggers straightaway. But the scene requires that the Macbeths delay before remarking on these things. Up to this point there had been a straightforward functional relationship between props and persons: a letter is held and read, torches are carried, a sword is handed over. In this scene bloody daggers are not noticed by the person who carries them. They may be on stage but they are not acknowledged. This suggests a curious dislocation between character and material object – and the power of that dislocation is marked in the problems that directors and actors sometimes have with playing the scene as it's written. The red hands are both a part of the person's body and yet at the same time unnatural. One consequence of the repeated noticing of them later in the scene, together of course with the blood effect on them, is that the hands seem to change status: they seem to become less functional, not available for carrying or even polite gesturing, a bit of the body that has become alien. The bloody hands, alien things that they are, also testify to human power, namely the ability to kill.

This exercise can be done for any play, and any sequence. It's often most interesting for those plays which apparently have next to no stage directions. We hope that by taking you through it we have suggested some of the richness, the layering, of the dramatic text and at the same time flagged up some of the topics we shall consider in the chapters which follow.

# 2

# Characters and persons

## Expectations about character

Many of us who are interested in drama would say that this is part of our more general interest in people. It is in plays that we can extend our reflection on human action in a variety of circumstances. There is indeed a rich variety of characters to admire, pity, blame, suspect or be curious about. For some of us, especially setting out on a study of drama at school or college, this 'interest in people' is quite securely grounded in a forceful notion of what a proper stage person should be. It seems to be common sense that an adequately scripted character is a 'fully rounded' one, that our encountering the character on stage should be just like our encounter with real people in daily life.

We expect, for instance, to be able to place them as a recognizable social type; but also that they have hidden depths to their personality that will only gradually become apparent to us. Similarly, we expect that their motives will only gradually become discernible, as we match their actions to their words and learn to hear the implications of what they say as much as the surface content. We expect that the story of their past has some bearing on their behaviour in the present. And we expect them to adapt to changing circumstances, to develop.

As in life, our response to a dramatic character may be to judge them. We might scan the playtext (or review the performance of the play) for evidence of the character's motivations, to solve the riddle of their behaviour, to find the fatal flaw of character or crucial choice of action that brings about their fate, if unhappy.

But this set of expectations clustered around the idea of the 'rounded character' is in fact a fairly recent one. It only became fully established in the early years of the twentieth century. It is quite specific to Western culture.

One of the things we shall do in this chapter is to unpick what we mean by a dramatic 'character'. What do stage persons do, and how? What might 'roundedness' consist of ? What other conventions of character are there?

In other words, we shall be suggesting what questions – for all of us as *analysts and performers* of the drama – are most pertinent to ask about dramatic character. The sorts of question we suggest will not be ones about blameworthiness or virtue, or whether the characters are properly rounded or not. This need not deny that many plays do indeed invite the judgement of the *audience*: our question will be how, and on what terms? And neither need this shift of emphasis deny our own interest in people. That interest will not only be justified, but also enriched by the questions we all come to ask. To start, it will be useful to continue our account of the Ibsen play.

# Three aspects of dramatic character

Recall from Chapter 1 that Krogstad knows Nora's guilty secret and so holds power over her. One of the critics who saw the first production in Copenhagen complained: 'That his makeup bore evidence of the mark of Cain did not surprise me; it is of course traditional at the Royal Theatre to reveal to the audience at once who you are.' (For initial press reactions, see Marker and Marker 1989.) He complains, then, that this is an old-fashioned sort of stage person: one who is obvious from the start. The character is too simply drawn for him. Moreover, it is based on a racial stereotype, and one that has become a regular feature of too many plays – the stage Jew as villain.

The basic complaint, then, is about the character's *conception*. Krogstad had been conceived too simply, and conceived on an unacceptable basis. *Character conception* is our first aspect of character.

If Krogstad was conceived too simply for the critic, the implication is that, for him, a complex characterization is the best standard. But some characters are simpler than others. We can think of 'simple' and 'complex' as two ends of a sliding scale.

To establish our other two aspects of dramatic character, let us consider what many had come to feel was 'old-fashioned' by 1879. The 'well-made play' is a formula commended by Eugène Scribe to fellow writers and audiences alike in Paris in 1836. Scribe's maxim was that people went to the theatre to be entertained rather than to be improved, and that by picking out elements from past models of dramatic writing – from ancient Athens through the Renaissance to melodrama – it is possible to arrive at a formula for the delivery of such entertainment: simple action, easily recognizable characters, intrigue and secrets, points of crisis and entanglement, a just conclusion. (For a consideration of the well-made play in England, see Taylor 1967.)

The well-made play is driven by the plot. At its most basic, the characters are mere devices – like the characters in a video game now – placed there to make the plot work. These 'stock' characters – ones easily taken down from the shelf, held in stock for repeated use – merely serve the plot. The **monological** characters of melodrama had easily found their way into

Scribe's formula. Yet of course one aspect of even complex characters is their function in the plot. Nearly all characters move the action on in some way or another.

So an important aspect of the vast majority of stage persons is their *plot function*. This is our second aspect of dramatic character.

Now, in Ibsen's play, it turns out that Krogstad has himself committed a misdemeanour in the past, one not dissimilar from Nora's forgery. Since then he has been treated as a social outcast. It has been very difficult for him to find work. His plight contrasts with Nora's outwardly comfortable position. In the play's design, he is a *foil* to Nora – a point of comparison. And there is a second foil in the play. In the first act Nora's old friend Mrs Linde returns to town after a long absence. Because of circumstances beyond her control she has had to become a very independent person. Her life has not been easy. As Nora in the course of the play comes to strive for her own independence, our knowledge of Mrs Linde acts as a point of reference for what that might imply.

If a character is being used as a foil, this is purely for the audience's benefit. We do not have foils in real life, because there is no audience. A character's function as foil is specific to the fiction. It is part of its formal design. Our third aspect of dramatic character is *formal function*.

We can find more formal functions in *A Doll's House* – aspects of character which are specific to the 'rhetorical' dimension of the play, the way it 'speaks to' its audience. Take Mrs Linde. In her first long conversation with Nora, we learn about Mrs Linde herself, but Ibsen uses the scene to develop and reveal to us Nora's own attitudes and give us hints about her past. We learn about Nora through her dialogue with her friend. The character Mrs Linde is, then, being used here as a *confidante* – the person to whom the **protagonist** speaks privately and in earnest, thus revealing their inner thoughts to the audience. And Dr Rank is in the position of the *raisonneur* – the regular character of the nineteenth-century Parisian stage, often a doctor, who explains things, makes sense of the situation, reasons things out for the sake of characters and audience alike.

Apart from the brief period of stage Naturalism – and leaving aside conventions dominant in TV and film drama – theatre has always had recourse to characters serving a directly formal function. To foils, confidantes and *raisonneurs*, we can add choruses and narrators. These sorts of character remain important in theatre today – because there is always a live audience to be explained to.

From our discussion of the Ibsen play, we have drawn out three aspects of dramatic characters in general:

- *Character conception* – from stereotype to psychological complexity.
- *Plot function* – how the characters serve the plot.
- *Formal function* – characters or aspects of them specific to theatrical communication: narrators, confidantes, foils, etc.

Note that these are *aspects* of character and not separable types. Any one stage person will combine at least the first two. We shall explore these three aspects further below.

## Mapping characters

A useful way to begin the analysis of a play is to draw up a 'family tree' of the main characters. What relationships do they bear to one another? Figure 2.1 makes a start on *King Lear*.

While it may begin with actual family ties, our diagram goes on to map out the characters in terms of their given 'value' in the drama. Very roughly, then, we have separated out forces for good from forces for ill. Note, too, that our map shows the groups of characters involved in the plot strands centred on Lear and Gloucester respectively.

At a more detailed level, we can map out significant similarities and differences between characters. We might, for instance, consider that each of

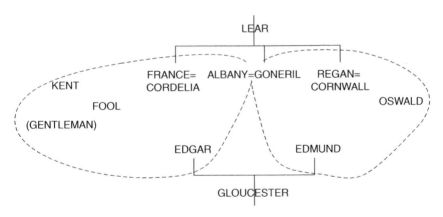

FIGURE 2.1

| | Cordelia | Kent | Edgar | Fool |
|---|---|---|---|---|
| sacrifice | fatherly love/power | king's love/power | embraces absolute poverty/feigned 'madness' | stays with Lear/risks unwelcome honesty |
| redeeming qualities | loyalty/Romance figure/'Christ' at end | loyalty/yeoman values | basic humanity/ Romance chivalry at end | popular wisdom/ truthful/sense out of nonsense |

FIGURE 2.2

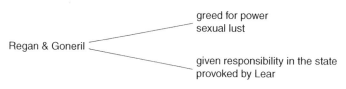

FIGURE 2.3

these characters makes some sacrifice which contributes to Lear's eventual coming to rest. So each makes a sacrifice and each has some sort of quality that helps redeem Lear, as Figure 2.2 illustrates.

We have placed them in rank according to social order and have started to sketch out the sort of sacrifice and redemptive quality associated with each. This is just a beginning. When we look a little more closely at our map and the play, other shapes will emerge. Our simple table above might for instance prompt us to think more about 'value'. So Kent reduces himself, but comes to represent traditional yeoman values, the very stuff of Renaissance 'Englishness'; Edgar as Poor Tom is basic humanity without social organization; Cordelia both quickly becomes a figure from Romance (see the way France speaks of her in the first scene, 1.1.250 ff.) and at the end speaks like Christ (4.5.15–17; 23–4). The characters set these values to work within the play.

Similarly, we might choose to map single characters or character groups. We might come to think it too simple merely to categorize Regan and Goneril as 'forces for ill'. It is clear that their father has been belligerent and headstrong. We might start with something like Figure 2.3.

If we read more about Renaissance culture, we find that women in all sorts of art and reference, including plays, sermons, tapestries, paintings, fables and other stories, were often stereotyped into one of two positions, very crudely that of the 'virgin' and the 'whore', so we might want to develop a map according to the headings in Figure 2.4.

One task of commentary on the play is to see to what extent Shakespeare uses this virgin/whore **binary** in the actual design of his woman characters, as well as what other characters say about them. In making such a commentary we have to remember that other characters speak from a point of view which is not necessarily the dramatist's own.

None of what we have sketched out here provides the 'answer' to what the play means or to what any one character fully means. But it begins the work of modelling how the play, through its characters, *produces* meaning for its audience. It looks at what the play *sets in play*, how it sets up the theatrical text to be read by the audience.

| Lear's vision (and who else in the play?) | Cordelia, Regan, Goneril virgin-whore | Shakespeare's vision (what the playtext 'says') |
| --- | --- | --- |
|  |  |  |

FIGURE 2.4

# Developing the aspects of dramatic character

## Character conception

In this subsection we develop further our notion of character conception.

### Mode and basis

The critic who complained about Krogstad thought that the character had been conceived too crudely, that it was a theatrical stereotype (the villain), and that it was based on a racial stereotype (the wicked Jew) as well. He wanted something more complex.

In fact, Ibsen progressively reveals Krogstad to be a complex personality: not only does he feel terribly wronged, and is able to speak about this persuasively; he also resumes a tender relationship with Mrs Linde. Both what that critic felt was missing and in fact what Ibsen seems later in the play to supply is Krogstad as a complex character based in some psychological truths.

So, taking the cue from our example, we can usefully make two distinctions. The first is between simple and complex characters – let us call this the *mode* of character conception. The second is between the mode and what it is based on, what underlies it. So let us call this the *basis* of the character conception (see Figure 2.5).

### Variety and combination of basis

Characters almost always 'stand for' or act as representatives of something in a play.

They may typify a *social class* (Willy Loman in Miller's *Death of a Salesman*) or a *moral position* (Bonario in Jonson's *Volpone*), for instance. They may represent a *fundamental drive*, like greed (Volpone in *Volpone*). In other plays by Jonson, such basic drives are conceived in terms of the scheme of **humours** developed earlier by medieval physicians. Furthermore, 'Volpone' derives from the Italian word for 'fox'; other predatory characters in the play have their names derived from words for vulture and raven; Mosca, from the Italian for fly, is very quick and feeds off decay and waste. The characters are based in animal *fable*. Or the most important thing about a character in the play might be their behaviour, the choices they make in life – that is, they may stand for a particular sort of *ethic* (Antigone, who insists on a proper funeral for her brother who

FIGURE 2.5

has died in a fight; and her royal father Creon, who resists this because it will displease the gods and bring the city into disrepute, in Sophocles' *Antigone*). The character Amalia in Cherríe Moraga's *Giving Up the Ghost* (1984) is an 'earth-mother' figure. Representing both Chicano (Mexican) culture and nurturing, she is conceived in *mythic* terms – she brings into the play what are felt to be eternal qualities especially associated by some feminists with women, and felt by them to be suppressed in dominant Western cultures.

Recognizable values and opinions, human qualities and situations, are set to work in these plays through the bases of their character conceptions. The character 'mobilises' these qualities, sets them to work in the play.

Character basis cuts across distinctions between different modes. We tend to distinguish characters in complex mode from simple ones on the evidence of their *psychology*: we witness the workings of their thoughts and emotions as they unfold in the changing circumstances of the action. But it is perfectly possible to have a psychological basis for a *simple* character – someone who clearly typifies a certain sort of 'mind-set' – especially in comedy. Alan Ayckbourn's comedies are full of such creatures.

Psychology is not only, or even necessarily, the basis for complexity. Characters may, for instance, be *ethically* complex – consisting of conflicting behaviours and their justifications for that behaviour. Antony and Cleopatra in Shakespeare's play are both good examples of ethical complexity.

Equally, we may be able to see a number of different bases all strongly at work in a character. Volpone is a good example – he is a moral type, conceived in terms of both *humour* and animal *fable*.

Let us review what we have established in this subsection so far. We have identified, in alphabetical order, the following bases of character conception: *ethical*; *fabular*; *fundamental drive*; *humoural*; *moral position*; *mythic*; *psychological*; *social class*. This list is not, of course, exhaustive. It is what our examples threw up for us. When reading or rehearsing a play, a first question needs to be, what are the bases of conception of the various character conceptions? You will find your own words and phrases. We have listed more terms of our own, in our own language, in Figure 2.6 below.

Let us make a couple of clarifications. By 'historical' basis for a character, we do not simply mean that the character is drawn from history as a source. You could make all number of stage characters out of the records of Robert J. Oppenheimer's life, for instance – a tragic hero, a sad clown. But, in Kipphardt's documentary play, the character appears as historical record. If we note that the play also invests the character with an ethical basis, we can start to unpick how it works. Similarly, some modern plays use ancient myth as the source of their characters, but do not use them mythically. Sartre's play *The Flies* (1942) uses the Greek myth of Orestes to make an image of Nazi occupation of France.

What we have called 'mythic' and 'universal' bases are quite similar. Maybe they are the same thing. If we were writing an essay about both Toller's *Masses and Man* and Moraga's play, we would need to spend some

**cultural** Sam and Willie *vs.* Hally in Fugard's *'Master Harold' ... and the boys*;
**discursive** speaking from a particular sort of position, e.g. a pessimist, Marxist, royalist (see below, p. 40);
**emotional** Katherina in Shakespeare's *The Taming of the Shrew*;
**epochal** from a distinct 'time' in relation to other characters, e.g. Kent and Cordelia in Shakespeare's *King Lear*;
**formal** basis confined to the play's rhetorical aspect, e.g. narrators, chorus;
**generic** stock types, e.g. the wicked squire in melodrama; or typical of another genre than the main one of the play (e.g. Cordelia);
**historical** e.g. Oppenheimer in Kipphardt's *In the Matter of Robert J. Oppenheimer*;
**pastiche** quoted from a different genre, e.g. the Gods in Brecht's *Good Person of Setzuan*;
**pathetic** designed to move the audience, e.g. Laura in Williams' *The Glass Menagerie*;
**poetic** i.e. representing a poetic force, like Nemesis, e.g. Death in *Everyman*;
**psychological** late Naturalism, but also e.g. Mathias in Lewis' *The Bells*;
**social** prejudice race, class, gender stereotypes;
**'universal'** archetypes, e.g. Man and Woman in Toller's *Masses and Man*.

FIGURE 2.6 *More descriptions of character bases.*

time thinking about what we meant by each. Identifying the bases makes us clarify our commentary and analysis.

Note also that some bases are interdependent with the other two aspects of character besides conception that we noted on p. 22. What we call a 'formal' basis here corresponds to a character's 'formal function'. A character with a 'generic' basis – the stock type – is likely to be there to serve the plot.

Lastly, let us note that there need not be a single basis for any one character conception. This will usually only be the case for very simple characters. We can expect to find a variety of bases – though one of these might, in our understanding of the play, appear to be the *dominant basis*.

## Variety and combination of mode

We began by distinguishing between just two modes of character conception – simple and complex – and by then suggesting that we can see these as two poles of a *continuum*. Some characters are simpler than others. Meanwhile, out of our table of bases there have emerged some *specific sorts* of simpler character: archetype, stereotype, type. We shall meet another specific mode – the 'personified abstraction' – on p. 41.

An *archetype* is a character standing for something held to be universal. So, Woman is a character supposedly representing the essence of womanhood.

Even though archetypes are always open to challenge, we usually think of them as being conceived of without malice or deliberate prejudice. Dealing in *stereotypes* is usually felt to be a much more blameworthy activity: if characters are consciously conceived as stereotypes, this must involve some degree of aggression. Yet sometimes theatre allows such aggression in the name of health – as in moral and political satire.

We might talk of social *types* and moral *types*. When we do, we implicitly point to the wider world beyond the theatre. The theatre is one place among many – including, for instance, journalism, TV news, gossip, sociology, religious parables – where we cluster different people together into convenient groups in order to think about the world and our culture. A type – which can surely be a good thing or a bad thing, depending on how it is used – is simply a representative of one such perceived cluster.

Brecht tends to deal in types (e.g. Pelagea Vlassova in *The Mother*), though he insists that his theatre is there to demonstrate that people can *change*. 'Type' rather suggests fixity. So the mode of the relatively simple characters in Brecht's plays might better be described as *model*. Brecht is not alone in creating characters which are there to be considered, pondered over from a critical, curious distance. A model is both a replica of something and something that we can 'model', meaning 'reshape'. In Brecht's theatre, actor and audience imaginatively reshape the character – they see how adaptable it is to different circumstances, how it might have taken different decisions. This is meant to replicate our own choices in life.

So we have now generated, as well as our sliding scale from simple to complex, a list of specific modes: *archetype*, *model*, *stereotype* and *type*. You may find that you want to add more.

Given that any character might have a number of bases, it may well be that the mode of the character is simple in some respects and complex in others. While Pelagea Vlassova, Brecht's *Mother*, is ethically complex, many find the character to be based on a very simple gender stereotype – albeit probably unconsciously on Brecht's part. Shakespeare's characters Othello and Cleopatra are both quite complex in psychological terms. But there is plenty of evidence in *Othello* and *Antony and Cleopatra* that Shakespeare sets up scenes to play off stereotypes (which he may or may not have agreed with) of women and black people against one another (see e.g. Wallis 1995).

## Plot function – actantial analysis

In some instances (much farce, for instance), it is clear that the main function of the stage persons is to serve the plot. Even when this is not the case, the functioning of the plot can be seen as 'calling up' the need for characters – even very rounded ones. Thus Rosencrantz and Guildenstern need to be invented to get Hamlet to England.

A useful conception here is that of *actantial analysis*. Deriving from a study of Russian folk tales, this model is especially relevant to *quest narratives*. A useful and brief account can be found in Aston and Savona (1991: 36–42). Basically, the idea is that there are various functions to be fulfilled by the characters in order for the narrative to operate. For instance, there needs to be a hero (called the 'subject of the quest'), an object of the quest (what is being sought by the hero – maybe a lost sister, or the answer to a question), a helper and an antagonist. Characters in a quest narrative can be seen as different sorts of 'actant', that is, as fulfilling these various basic roles.

Many dramatic texts are themselves quest narratives. (Think of a number of Hollywood action adventures, for instance.) An 'actantial analysis' of a dramatic script regards characters purely in their mutual relation to the quest – though this and the object of the quest may change.

So, for instance, an actantial analysis of *A Doll's House* might begin by noticing the following. First, we can regard Nora as the subject of the quest, a miraculous change in her husband's attitude as its object, and Krogstad as an antagonist. But, as the play develops, Krogstad not only suffers a change of heart and destroys the evidence of Nora's guilt but his antagonism itself can also be read as a force helping Nora along on her newly-to-be-discovered quest – that of self-determination.

The play can be analysed in terms both of psychological motivation and of quest narrative. And it is best understood in both these ways, in relation to one another. To *reduce* the play to psychology misses its **rhetorical** effect – the way in which it works persuasively on its audience. Either the audience experiences the change of quest along with Nora – or it watches her realizing that a new quest awaits her. We are, arguably, all subjects of one quest or another.

There are, of course, other narratives than quest narratives, in which characters are closely tied to the plot: Aristotelian tragedy, for instance, which we discuss elsewhere.

## *Formal function*

This can be crucial not only to particular plays but also to whole systems of theatre. The most celebrated is that of classical Athens, where the Chorus mediates between the main actors and the audience. They watch as if on behalf of the audience and comment between the episodes on the action, evaluating what has happened, predicting what might happen next. Often they are divided into two semi-choruses who debate with one another. The Greek chorus often has a group identity, such as old men. It speaks from a recognizable position.

The Greek chorus is thought to derive from religious practice. The tragedies were written for an annual event which was part religious festival, part civic competition. But the festivals and the tragedies written for them were most significantly occasions of communal reflection, when both valued myths and ideas about the new city state were publicly thought through. The chorus is a fundamental part of this public dialogue.

In *The Fire Raisers* (1958), Max Frisch makes fun of the way modern
bourgeois people think about their society and their place in it. Between the
scenes, a chorus of Firemen come on stage and enact what is a pastiche (see
Figure 2.6) of the Greek chorus.

# Character articulation

In this section we look at the *articulation* of dramatic characters. When we
articulate an idea, we give it a particular shape in order to put it across to
our hearers. Similarly we are concerned here with particular shapes with
regard to characters, and what these shapes do in relation to the audience.
We shall be looking at three sorts of character articulation: *external* (how
characters as whole things are articulated before an audience); *internal*
(what shapes, or internal articulations, there may be in any given character);
and *logical* (the shape of the *selection* of characters put before an audience,
the *dramatis personae*).

Let us start with an external articulation.

## Positioning

You will probably be familiar with the regular and useful distinction between
*sympathy*, 'feeling for' a character, and *empathy*, 'feeling with'. The latter is
often held to be the best form of relationship to be had with a character. But
such a claim ignores the vast variety of ways in which plays can work quite
genuinely – and as great pieces of art, entertainment or politics – without
an ounce of it. Famously, Brecht wanted his audiences to keep a *critical
distance* from his characters. Similarly, most comedy relies on – invites – the
audience to maintain an *objective* rather than subjective relationship with
the persons.

'Subjective' and 'objective' may need some explanation. Put simply, subject
means 'self '. Object means 'other'. If I take a subjective view, it is my own:
maybe I think only of my own interests, or rely only on my own knowledge.
If I have a subjective relationship with a fictional character, I imagine myself
in their situation. But, if I take an objective view, I try to treat my own
immediate perceptions as being of no more value than those of others, and
gather in evidence and try to come to a conclusion that all other reasonable
people would agree with. If I have an objective relationship with a fictional
character, I look at them from the outside, look at them in their own situation.

So 'subjective' and 'objective' are each used in two interconnected ways.
They refer both to the *attitude of* the viewer and to the *attitude to* the thing
viewed.

If I make a subjective response to a real person, I am being very closely
engaged with them. But: I may mistake them for myself, or only think of
them in terms of my own interests, or fail to see their own choices given their

situation. If I make an objective response to a real person, I am watching them very closely, understanding what they are and where they are. But: I may then 'objectify' them, treat them merely as an object. Theatre makes play with subjective and objective responses to characters – to *fictional* persons. And theatre makers in modern times have argued much about which is the best attitude for theatre to invite from the audience.

Clearly, stereotypes are objectified characters; types are characters to be viewed objectively; sympathy is more objective than empathy. Our job must now be to describe *how* empathy, sympathy or objectivity is scripted to happen, how the dramatic text positions the various characters before the audience.

Let us not forget that in the midst of this is a very basic sort of positioning – the sheer fact that we are looking at a figure on the stage who by convention sees and knows less than we do. This is the situation of *dramatic irony*. Usually a matter of dialogue and plot – words said to one character and not another, something that happens without a character's knowledge – we can also usefully think of a very physical example: 'Look out behind you!'

## Registers of performance

At Manchester University George Taylor did a very useful exercise with students which we can link with what we said above. The difference is that we are here concerned first with the actor, not the audience. Using practical examples, he asks how we can describe the various relationships between an actor and the role they play. Clearly, the way the actor acts significantly affects the way the character is positioned before the audience. Our own term for this set of relationships – between actor and role, and between stage and auditorium – is *register of performance*.

Different sorts of dramatic script invite or assume different registers of performance. And what is invited or assumed is a matter not only of the type of play (say, farce or tragedy), but also the prevailing theatrical conventions (see p. 10). Doing George Taylor's exercise might generate the following series:

Presentation
Narration
Demonstration
Representation
Imitation
Impersonation
Identification
Realization
Possession

If I *impersonate* a police officer, I fool you into believing that I am one. I can *present* Boadicea if I dress up in robes, helmet and shield and stand in a tableau. Maybe as performer I also tell her story, *narrate* her from the tableau. You see the picture and hear the words.

Nowadays, the *identification* of performer with role is perhaps dominant. It is commonly supposed to constitute 'proper' acting. But, as we said at the start of this chapter, this assumption is very local to our time and culture. It emerges most strongly at the moment of Naturalism, becomes encoded in the Stanislavskian system, and via the 'Method', as developed by Lee Strasberg and others in New York, feeds into cinema and then television (see Shepherd and Womack 1996). We might consider that television, in presenting and framing actual slices of life alongside fictional texts, has been a key factor in promoting this sense of what is 'good' or 'proper' acting.

If the rule of identification emerges strongly in the late nineteenth century within Naturalism, then this can be related to the fact that Naturalism as a *movement* – it had declared aims – insisted that art should *accurately reflect* life. This insistence on an objectivity that was 'scientific' can itself be related to a project of laying bare the brute facts of modern life under capitalism – in particular, the double standards pertaining to women, the facts of poverty and the hypocrisies of organized religion. It was this emerging movement which Ibsen was reaching towards in *A Doll's House*.

Yet cultural workers like Brecht in Germany from the 1930s insisted that Naturalism could only show *surface appearances*. What mattered for Brecht were the larger structures of society and history in which individuals and collectives choose between one action and another. The audience should be encouraged to concentrate on these structures and their own relationship to them, rather than becoming bound up with the fate of one individual. They should become more objective. To become embroiled in the minute details of a personality is like not seeing the wood for the trees. And it invites a fatalistic attitude, the sense that things cannot change, that environment entirely shapes and limits ('determines') the individual. According to his analysis, the best way of gaining a clear understanding of social life and individual behaviours and responsibilities – which must include our ability to *change* things – is to *typify* situations and persons, to show them in their general aspect, and for performers and audience alike to stand 'outside' the staged situation. The actor *demonstrates* the character. This, said Brecht, was now a more *realistic* form of theatre.

Theatre makers like Grotowski and Artaud at different times in the twentieth century invited performers to be totally *possessed* by their role. The performer became something like a religious celebrant, sacrificing themselves to the act of acting. Often the confessional or self-sacrificial activity of the performer was much more important than any detail of the fictional person as such.

One of the most immediate and powerful ways of being possessed by a role is to act in mask. And this of course includes the comic mask. The performers of the Italian *commedia dell'arte* (see Rudlin 1994) played characters based on fundamental drives; the mask helped them enter fully into those drives.

It might be difficult for many Western spectators to feel empathy with Grotowski's quasi-tortured religious celebrant. But do we not also expect of Hollywood stars like Leonardo diCaprio that they also sacrifice themselves to their role, become obsessed by the part? We probably do. So does Hollywood's version of Stanislavski's system in its 'Method' acting offer empathy? Or an awesome spectacle?

Very commonly, now, we hear five notions put in combination as the recipe for good acting: '*rounded character*' – taken to mean both *plausibility* and *psychological complexity – identification*, and *empathy*. Probably the most respected commendation of empathy comes from Aristotle, who described how Greek tragedy worked (see also p. 34, below). The audience must empathize with Sophocles' Oedipus, for instance, in order for them to feel and then purge the emotions of pity and fear at the end. But what register of performance do we imagine held sway in Athens in the fifth century BCE? How like today's dominant recipe was it? Imagine Leonardo diCaprio in platform boots, masked, declaiming verse to an audience of thousands in the outdoors. Imagine a chorus, singing and dancing in highly rhythmic fashion, **mediating** the character and the plot to the audience between each short episode. Accidentally killing your father and then marrying and having sex with your mother is a terrible ethical bind, but Sophocles does not write this situation with much psychological complexity. The proposition is terrible enough to draw us in – and Oedipus is a figure deserving of our respect. This and the drive of the plot are what construct empathy. And what can 'roundedness' mean in these circumstances? That we know what sort of child Oedipus was?

As we write, a theatre critic is complaining on radio that, in his most recent movie, a famous film actor loses himself so much in the role that he disappears. So identification clearly has its problems if the actor forgets to *project* something to the audience. For this critic, *realization* (see the list above, p. 31) fails to communicate.

'Character' only exists in the context of the variable and specifiable relationship that we have called register of performance. Dramatic texts are written in the expectation of performance, and performance modes differ from culture to culture, time to time. And recall that, while each of these various registers may turn up in a variety of historical or cultural contexts, we shall want to begin to understand how they operate – and what significance they have – in each of those *particular* contexts. Brecht learnt some tricks from the Renaissance stage: but emblematic, demonstrative playing means something different in a Marxist context from a Renaissance **humanist** one.

Let us now move to more 'internal' questions of character articulation.

## Dynamics

It is common to speak of 'character development', though rather ambiguously. Some people mean that the character changes (matures or learns), others that character detail becomes progressively apparent to us – rather like the way a photographic print develops. We prefer to discuss this second sense under the heading of 'delivery' (see p. 37, below).

Character dynamics are clearly very much tied up with the plot. Characters change because of what happens in the action. And character dynamics work differently on the audience according to what sort of positioning the character has in relation to the audience. The most familiar case is surely that of the **protagonist** in Aristotle's description of Greek tragedy just raised on p. 33. Here, plot and character are strongly interdependent, and the audience tracks each closely through the contract of empathy. The character rises, suffers a change of fortune, falls and finally meets a catastrophe. Drawn into this dynamic, the audience are positioned to share in the *anagnorisis* – the character's recognition of their fault, or *hamartia*. Augusto Boal (1979: 25–47) gives a very concise summary of Aristotle's tragic scheme – though it is important to be aware that he is criticizing it at the same time (see p. 88).

An unpublished play performed by the Communist Unity Theatre in London in 1937 plays with the conventional relationship between plot and character dynamic. Towards the end of Herbert Hodge's *Cannibal Carnival*, Joe the Policeman suddenly – and for no reason set up by the plot – 'comes over all class conscious' and joins the oppressed against the oppressors. A question is being asked about just what sort of narrative in the real world – what sort of politics – would make real policemen and others like them change sides.

There are two sorts of change a character might undergo. They might change in *themselves* – become more humble, wise or generous. Or they might change *their situation* – become married, dead or prosperous.

In *A Doll's House*, Nora develops from being naïve and childish into a mature woman who can clearly see that she has been living a lie. She becomes committed to her own self-discovery. Her situation changes from a security which was also, however, a trap, to a liberty which is also, however, a step into the dangerous unknown. She has lost her children.

## Continuity and discontinuity

People develop in life – they learn as they get older, for instance – but they remain the same person. The majority of stage persons are similarly *continuous* characters. But others are *discontinuous*.

As models of human potential for adaptability, Brecht's characters are intended to be taken by the audience a scene at a time. We should not look for a character 'through-line' of the sort Stanislavski recommended to his actors, but look at the character afresh in each scene. Indeed, Brecht is suggesting that we ourselves are discontinuous, that we can reinvent ourselves if we want to. He makes a somewhat crazy parable out of this idea in *Man Equals Man* (1926).

Some characters are split on stage between two actors. Noël Greig has Sam in *Poppies* (1983) witness himself as a much younger man. And in

*The Good Person of Setzuan* Brecht famously has one actress play two roles, the generous prostitute Shen Te and her hard-nosed male cousin Shui Ta – whom she has invented. While Shen Te invents her cousin within the fiction, we are invited to watch as if they were two people. In this 'split character' Brecht examines the rigid gender system he sees in cahoots with the capitalism he criticizes. To survive as 'feminine', Shen Te needs the 'masculine' aggression of Shui Ta.

Some critics complained that Nora's psychological development in *A Doll's House* was implausible. The development we noted on p. 9 was too sharp for them. But, just as we have seen that Ibsen sets up Krogstad as a stage villain only then to reveal complexity, so Nora at the start seems to have been set up deliberately as a false signal. As Marker and Marker (1989) show, Nora in the opening moments is drawn as a stage type very popular in 1879 – the delightfully innocent, young, happy, carefree yet devoted housewife. She is an ideal type from the romantic drama that many in Ibsen's first audience would have admired – and they would have expected her to end the play yet more happily married. The actress who played her, Betty Hennings, was famous for playing such parts.

Naturalism – the movement which Ibsen was finding his way towards, helping to establish, in this play – began primarily as a movement concerned with the relationship between individuals and their environment: the social, historical and biological constraints put upon their self-realization as fully human individuals. It was concerned with the contemporary, with the here and now. Often it was pessimistic, suggesting that we are all somehow trapped (see p. 32). But it was primarily a *critical* movement. It challenged bourgeois convention. It suggested that it was time to learn new roles in life, to stop living according to old rules and assumptions – because these were damaging to us.

We saw in the last subsection that Naturalism aimed to lay bare the true facts of contemporary life. It wanted to unmask hypocrisy. It took an *ironic* attitude – it assumed that there is a truth to be found behind appearances.

Ibsen's play has a deeply ironic structure. Not only does Nora discover that she herself has been playing a role which stifles the 'true' one she might find in life: the audience also discover that the pleasant fictions on their stage mask the reality surrounding them – and that the theatre is a place where they have tried to sustain such fictions about their own lives. Just as the play suddenly splits from being an apparently well-made play into something much less comfortable, so Nora *as a presentation to the audience* splits from stage type to ethical and psychological complexity.

Of course, Nora's naïveté at the start is part of this psychological complexity. But, for the play to work as we suggest it was intended to, the audience must only realize this *after* they have at first taken Nora in as a simple character. Ibsen gives the actress a hugely challenging yet very exciting task – to play Nora *both* as continuous character *and* as discontinuous character. She is being invited to juggle two registers of performance with great skill (see Cima 1993).

# Character conception as authentication
# or point of interest

The critic who complained that Nora's development was implausible may
himself have been in tune with the emerging conventions of Naturalism. But,
even while the conventions of close psychological identification between
actress and role were not yet established, the majority in that first audience
could have accepted what we might now find artificial or stagey acting as a
vehicle for communicating the truth of a psychology. *All theatrical watching
is conventional*: we accept the signs made by the theatre as referring to
something in real life, or to something in a fiction which we can somehow
relate to real life. Through the lens of late-romantic acting styles, then, that
audience will have expected to see 'truths' about their lives, or life in general.

The actor's words and gestures do not need to be indistinguishable from
those of real life in order for an audience to take and accept them as signs
which are 'true' – which gesture persuasively towards real life. In other words,
any number of acting styles, or registers of performance, can *authenticate*
the performance, act as a guarantee that the stage is worth watching, that
something meaningful is going on.

In the German city of Weimar in 1800, at the theatre of Goethe and
Schiller, what helped authenticate the performance, to make it 'real' in
relation to life and human value, was a *gracefulness* of bearing, the use of
only the right hand for gestures, and the use of only particular gestures with
definite meanings (see p. 120).

Brecht insisted that a truly realistic drama must delve beneath and beyond
the obvious 'given' of a particular situation, or the details of a particular life.
Thus it is the *distance* between performer and role which helps authenticate
the Brechtian stage.

The notion of '*character effect*' might help us here. It simply refers
to the constructed *illusion* of a whole personality – complete with inner
consciousness, past history, spleen, kidneys and grandmother – which certain
dramatic texts strive for, and perhaps most do effect to some degree. We can
usefully ask the question, what actually produces this illusion, how is it
achieved? Alan Sinfield (1992) has suggested, for instance, that the character
Hamlet appears 'rounded' because there is an *excess of meaning* related to
him. It is not so much either that we know everything about him, or that
we know little and so become curious about him as if he were real. Rather,
Sinfield suggests, it is because we know more than we need to – as we do
about people close to us in real life.

We have established that Naturalism, the movement Ibsen helped install in
the theatre, was typically concerned with the split between life as it appears
and how it actually is. At the level of character there is the split between the
role the character plays in their life, and the underlying reasons – what it is
that motivates the playing of that particular life-role. The audience are not
invited to relish the task of finding out the complex truth of the character,
of filling or rounding out psychological being, of solving the 'riddle' of

character. It is the struggle to find a meaningful role to play in life which is the actively interesting part. The crisis of role, not its 'roundedness', is the fundamental *point of interest*.

So, at the beginning, the complex characters of Naturalism were to some extent split or discontinuous characters. The complexity of characterization was at one and the same time a point of interest (because of the crisis of life-role) and an emerging means of authenticating the theatrical event.

What has happened since is that the point of interest has subsided, while psychological complexity as character effect has become the dominant mode of authentication.

'Serious' dramatic texts thereafter have increasingly come to offer the players clues about character which they must interpret and, increasingly, come to their *own* sense of. Naturalism as it developed became a drama about very particular individuals: the actor's interpretation of the role became a key factor in the meanings playtexts made for an audience. It is this work that was addressed by Stanislavski's 'system', the set of exercises he developed for actors at the Moscow Art Theatre early in the twentieth century.

So we are now in a position to see that the 'obvious' recipe of rounded character, psychological complexity, identification and empathy is only quite local to our own circumstances, and developed in circumstances that have now passed us by. And, as some still newer, some rediscovered and always various ways of playing are developed with theatre audiences of today, we see that recipe gradually falling into residue.

# Delivery

Recall from p. 33 that by *character delivery* we mean the way that a character is progressively revealed to us. We shall look at two things – how the character is revealed to the audience in performance; and how they are delivered on the page in the playscript. Let us start with the first, delivery in the theatrical text.

In some plays the audience get to know the character straight away. In others the character unfolds to them as the play progresses. This is what we mean by *character delivery*.

Let us use the example of the British TV detective series *Lewis*. Character here is conceived psychologically. Fairly complex portraits are made of people we might recognize, and they typically doubt themselves, tell themselves or others half-truths or half-lies, and seem to be disturbed by a shadowy personal history. As an audience we can be interested in them 'as people', as well-drawn and detailed portraits of folk just like us. But is this really what is offered as our main point of interest?

In terms of *plot* what holds and indeed drives our interest along is the puzzle of evidence about the crime, and its gradual unravelling for us and for the detectives. Included in this is the ironic distance between our own knowledge or guesses and those of Lewis. And it is here in particular that the *delivery* of character becomes important. What this series did so well, and what is a staple of its genre, is its *enigmatic* delivery of character. We see a character make a statement on screen. She is perhaps the lover of the murdered man. As she speaks, we not only listen to her words but we also watch her eyes mist over, hear the catch in her voice. We are aware that we are in the presence of 'subtext' – that we glimpse the real role beneath the publicly lived one – yet we cannot just now ascertain what the reality is. There is a secret to be discovered. And we are to encounter several such characters, several potential suspects, in the course of the programme.

A psychological 'conception' of character helps authenticate this detective fiction for its medium, for television – which, as we suggested above, mostly cannot tolerate 'implausibility' of personation except in comedy. What is principally delivered is a deliciously complex web of clues, and much of our enjoyment is gained from tracking those clues to some sort of conclusion. But part of our enjoyment, too, is precisely the game of 'fathoming out' those who are suspects or whom we have come to suspect are later going to be revealed as suspects. The split between reality and lived role becomes in this case part of the apparatus of intrigue and irony in the drama. We are not principally interested in the relationship between people and their environment, or indeed in the complex working of a particular psychology, but in the repeated thrill of suspicion and discovery. Irony is not confined to the plot. Suspense operates both at the level of the plot *and* at the level of character delivery.

Let us now turn to the way in which the dramatic text delivers character to the actor.

Of course, any actress worth her salt will enter fully into the life of the character she plays, will make it fully 'rounded', will work hard to understand her motivation at various points in the play, particularly in relation to her more general motivations, her conscious and unconscious life aims. And, of course, what can be gleaned or imagined about her life offstage – including before the start of the action – is important grist to this mill. She will bring all of this information to bear on every moment in the play's action.

But everything that is 'obvious' in the last paragraph we now know to be obvious only for the plays of later Naturalism and its residue. The actress playing Nora will miss half her part if she reads the play through that set of spectacles.

Shakespeare and other actors of his day – around 1600 – got their parts all right. They received the role they were to play. But a 'part' was precisely that – a roll of paper (a 'role') – on which just the lines they were to speak and their cues (the line immediately preceding theirs) were written. There was no such thing as the book of the play to refer to – and nobody was going to copy out the whole play a dozen times, just for the sake of a production. Why? The reason is because both character types and certain sorts of speeches followed fairly predictable patterns – and because actors specialized in particular sorts of role. Parts might well be written specifically for them. In addition, consider that verse writing very efficiently scripts breath, body and emotion (see p. 77). As we established in Chapter 1, the Renaissance stage worked emblematically as much as it did psychologically. A piece of verse might suggest an emotional state, establish the character's expressivity; but the situation in which the speech was to be delivered was always very clearly drawn. Indeed, the verse itself often helps make the emblem (see p. 77). It is speech and emblem together which make the clearest sense, deliver the most potent 'truth' – not the character's 'through-line'. We pointed to an obvious Renaissance stage emblem – Desdemona kneeling – in Chapter 1. But we should be ready to see every scene, and every part of a scene (see pp. 108–9), in a Renaissance play as a fresh emblem, a fresh stage picture.

Our final thoughts on character articulation now turn to the selection of characters.

## The *dramatis personae*

The persons in a classical Athenian tragedy – apart from the odd messenger who brings bad news – are grand people: princes, queens, military heroes. Aristotle later assumed that only people of rank would attract empathy – while superheroes and gods would not, because they are too unlike us.

Shakespeare's stage, what used to be called the 'Golden Age' of English drama, has characters of a much wider social range; though those of lower class tend to be the comic characters. It is often suggested that Renaissance dramatists were thinking, consciously or not, about the whole social fabric because society was changing so rapidly. It is also sometimes suggested that this was a time of increased democratic feeling.

In the prologue of Nicholas Rowe's *The Fair Penitent* (1703), the actress speaking the prologue declares that this is no tragedy of princes, but of ordinary middling sort of folk. Middling folk now wanted to see themselves on stage in serious situations.

Miller's *Death of a Salesman* (1949) has as its protagonist a lower-middle-class shoe salesman.

What classes of people are represented in the drama, and what sort of roles they play, tell us much about the culture in which a theatre operates, and the role it plays within it. That it was an actress delivering Rowe's prologue is, of course, significant in itself. Women were not allowed on the professional stage in England until the Restoration in 1660. Most of the major characters in plays written today are probably still male.

## Further aspects of dramatic character

There are three further aspects of dramatic character for us to consider, following on from p. 23.

# Discursive function

One possible basis of character conception we suggested on p. 27 was 'discursive'. The character speaks a particular discourse, a way of talking about the world which is structured in a particular way (see p. 55). Thus, for instance, Dr Rank in *A Doll's House* turns out not to be the *raisonneur* we expected. He is rather a resigned sort of chap – ready to die, a bit sad with life, and believing that his illness is the result of his father's dissolute life.

Now, this discourse of being resigned to the fact that your life is shaped/ **determined** from the outset is not just important to Dr Rank personally. It is a proposition that Ibsen clearly wants us to think about and consider. So, while Rank does not state this as a world-view as a *raisonneur* might, his character nevertheless contributes to what the play itself seems to be 'saying to' or 'discussing with' us. In the same play, Helmer suggests to Nora that a criminal parent will corrupt their children just by being with them. Nora believes him and abandons her children. This sort of question was on many lips in 1879. So the discourses of characters can contribute to the discourse of the play as a whole.

But this sort of contribution is made by more than what the characters say and do. Their character dynamic will be significant – what happens to particular sorts of person, and why. And by 'particular sort' we need not mean 'sort' in real life. Our mapping exercise on p. 23 helped us organize the *dramatis personae* according to their *value* in the play's scheme. Part of the play's discourse – its structured way of speaking about the world – is what it shows happening to particular sorts of value.

# Aesthetic function

Characters can deliver sheer pleasure – because of the way they speak or the way they behave; because they are such outlandish, or typical, characters; or because they are so wonderfully subtly or deliciously crudely drawn. Alongside all the other five functions we consider, and connecting with them in ways we can play with in our commentaries, is this question of the direct pleasure witnessing a stage character brings: what we shall call the *aesthetic aspect* of character.

# Vehicle

In some sorts of theatre, the character is principally there as a vehicle for the performer's special skills. This is the case with various sorts of clown, like *Arlecchino* (Harlequin) in the many scenarios of the *commedia dell'arte* (Rudlin 1994). We might say that, among other things, the character here is a *vehicle* for the performer. Some of the Italian Dario Fo's characters written for his own brand of political clowning were derived from the *commedia*.

The part is a vehicle for the display of his own comic skills, though Fo regards those skills as a vehicle in turn for progressive political satire.

# Character at work

We have come a long way since the opening of this chapter. Let us end it by looking at a few examples of character at work, to review what we have learnt.

Let us return once more to Krogstad as a stage villain who turns out not to be one. We have said that he feels wronged by society. But Nora herself wrongs him. In the first act, she is very pompous about her husband's new job as bank manager. She promises Mrs Linde that she will get her a job there. She crows about this to Krogstad, whom she treats with absolute disdain. When she learns that Krogstad has been a clerk at the bank and was recently fired by Helmer she has to back-track and insist that she meant him no harm. Ibsen here ties a nice knot for Nora and audience alike. For Krogstad is indeed a threat to Nora, because he alone knows her secret. He is, for the time being, the villain of the piece. But part and parcel of his 'villainy' is his class status. Nora is a snob, and the audience are thrown into this collision of the stage type they can comfortably hate and Nora's embarrassing echo of their own habitual class prejudice. People are not what they at first appear.

The medieval **morality play** *Everyman* (*c*.1498) concerns the fate of a character called Everyman. He stands for all people – or, rather, men. God sends Death to stop him on his complacent way and to warn him to prepare for the end of his life, for the judgement to come. He resists, and tries to find a way of delaying. He asks various characters – like Friendship, Kindred and Goods – to help. But eventually, finding his quest for delay an impossibility, he sets out on a new quest to make atonement for his sins in life. His helpers now are such as Knowledge, Confession and Good Deeds; so, in the end, he dies well. Morality play characters like Greed, Sloth, Patience and Confession have since been called 'personified abstractions' – ideas and values important to us are made into whole characters on the medieval morality stage.

The dramatic writing that was powerfully emergent in the Renaissance period in England gave the effect of an inner personality. It portrayed an individuality which is at least as important as, and comes before, one's social position; and it portrayed individual *expressivity*. The emergence of this sort of writing is one important element of a cultural practice which is itself part of a massive transformation of social and economic conditions. While there are arguments as to the relationships between them, these changes can be specified as the emergence of capitalism within and against feudalism; the rise of Protestantism; humanism; and sceptical reasoning.

Yet alongside this emergent 'psychological' writing in Renaissance plays is the sort of 'emblematic' writing we have identified. The logic of the 'personified abstraction' – a clear and definite basis to the conception of the character – remains as an active residue from the past. So, in Renaissance plays, two different ways of writing character occur side by side, and we appear to be invited to 'add them together' to get the complete picture. The same character is frequently composed of both psychological and emblematic aspects. To read a Renaissance play as if it were Naturalism or a TV soap is, quite clearly, to misread it, to miss its own **rhetorical** procedures, the way it works persuasively on us.

*But personified abstractions are there on the TV screen, too.* In a much less declared way, contemporary **dramaturgy** almost always uses particular characters, if not to stand for, then at least to *conduct* particular qualities – to enact them in particular situations. The 'type' is more than a sort of clearly outlined, cartooned representative of a recognizable social group. It is not simply a case of making the picture of the individual character clearer or easier to handle. The abstraction, the deliberate bracketing off or downplaying of psychological complexity or personal history, allows questions to be asked about typical *beliefs and actions*. Soaps and detective dramas are good cases in point. This does not, we would contend, make them 'bad' dramas. If it did, it would make much of Aeschylus, Sophocles and Euripides bad, too.

All characters are in some way or another 'models' of human behaviour. This chapter has set out a number of ways in which we can think and write about what sort of models there are, and how that modelling works.

# 3

# Dialogue

## The workings of dialogue

### Theatrical communication

Let us start by stating the obvious: what is said on stage is designed to be heard by the audience. When one character speaks to another, he or she sends a message – about themselves or their desires or what happened last week – to the other character, who receives this message. But this onstage communication itself, involving both sender and receiver, can be thought of as another message, one being sent from the stage to the audience – again about character, action and circumstance, but always a slightly different message from that between character and character.

In theatre, then, there are always two lines of communication. First there is communication between characters. Second, there is communication between the stage and the audience. Our own preference is to speak of this second message being sent from the *stage*; others, like Mick Short (1989), speak of it being sent by the *author*. Both are reasonable ways of putting it.

Stating the obvious can help us think about varieties of theatre and varieties of character. In stage Naturalism and almost all TV dramas and films, the audience 'overhear' what passes between characters. But, in medieval drama and still in the Renaissance, in Brecht's theatre and much TV situation comedy, the fact that a message is being sent to the audience is not hidden but rather declared, either implicitly (in the attitude of the performer: see p. 31) or explicitly, by a character speaking directly to the audience or camera.

Let us think briefly about the character who stands and speaks alone (*solus*) on stage. In a soliloquy such as Hamlet's famous 'To be, or not to be' (3.1.55 ff.), we can imagine that we are overhearing. Maybe he is talking to himself – or maybe the convention is being assumed that we are hearing his thoughts. But our best bet is to assume that, in Shakespeare's time, speaking *solus* always includes the convention that the character is speaking directly to the audience. Hamlet – and the stage he is on – is discussing the purpose of existence directly with us, as well as with himself.

In the famous opening speech of Shakespeare's *Richard 3* (1592/3), Richard stands alone and tells the audience directly about three things. First, he sets up the situation, that of peace after war. Then he describes himself, as being unfit for such tranquil times. Third, he tells us what he is going to do, which is trick his way to power. Richard here acts as Narrator (or Presenter, Chorus) to his own play. Many plays have such special characters dedicated to announcing the theatrical presentation. But this speech – especially its middle section, which is based on the self-presentations of the medieval **Vice** – is fun because it tells us more about Richard than he plans to tell us himself. Here, after all, is a man who *revels* in his wickedness (see Clemen 1986).

Narrators, asides (when a character turns away from a conversation to comment on it or their real purpose in it), self-presentations, soliloquies and choric songs remain an important part of the dramatic repertoire today. And always implicit, though often explicit, in all dialogue, is that second line of communication we have noted between stage and auditorium. We shall be talking a lot more about these two lines of communication when we consider some much more recent work (see pp. 172–3).

# Functions of dialogue

We are concerned in this chapter with dialogue as something spoken on the stage. What does it deliver to the audience? Looking back now to Chapter 1, Figure 1.1, we can start with the following:

- *conversational exchange between characters* (see p. 58, below);
- *information as to time and place*;
- *information about action* (what has happened elsewhere: see p. 97);
- *actual enactments* (like accusations, confessions: see p. 67);
- *information about characters* (how they speak and what about; what is said of others).

This makes a useful checklist when reading stage dialogue. We can now stand back a little and see just what it is designed to deliver to the audience at any one time.

The weighting of these various functions will differ throughout the play. Most begin with some sort of *exposition*. While information about time and place will be scattered throughout, an audience is typically told about the here and now at the beginning. Exposition may be declared – say, a Narrator gives it – or 'woven in' to the dialogue. If the play begins when the action it is concerned with has already begun (say, the murder has already been committed, or the feud between the families has lasted three generations already), the exposition may refer in detail to past events. Plays such as this are said to begin *in medias res* (Latin: 'in the middle of things'). When delivered by a character, exposition is both information about the situation and previous action, and implicit information about the character. Most exposition, then, also delivers the character's 'perspective' (see p. 101). Consider, for instance, Nora's conversation with Mrs Linde in Act 1 of *A Doll's House*.

Information about characters is embedded in dialogue in a number of ways. As well as what others say of them, we have each character's own expressivity – the sort of tactics they use in conversational exchanges (see p. 58, below); what they say about themselves (though we need to distinguish between what *they* say they are and what *we* make of this given the circumstance of its saying); their typical mode of expression, throughout or in various circumstances (are they rational, passionate, devious, tender?); their declared or implied beliefs.

## Idiolect and sociolect

All of us speak in a particular way. We have a recognizable style of speech. Perhaps we use irony a lot. Do we tend to insinuate things? Are we crisp and to the point, or loquacious? Do we use simple words and sentences, or obscure words and tangled **syntax**? A person's particular way of speaking is called their *idiolect*. Dialogue often establishes stage character through idiolect. Think of Wilde's Lady Bracknell in *The Importance of Being Earnest* (1895).

Yet social groups also share a common way of speaking. This goes beyond accent. In Britain, the way in which people from Liverpool present themselves and interact with others, the way they put things, is recognizably different from the way people from Tunbridge Wells do these same things. The same goes for agricultural workers versus City of London office workers. A shared style of speech is called a *sociolect*. In plays, sociolect quickly establishes the character's social origin or status.

Given that sociolect is crucial in the creation and perpetuation of stereotypes its function is of interest to dramatists who want to challenge stereotyping. For example in Kwame Kwei-Armah's *Seize the Day* (2009), done in the Not Black and White season at the Tricycle Theatre, the young Black male Lavelle moves between modes of speech. He is a mugger who was hit by Jeremy, a TV celebrity. A condition of his probation is to return to Jeremy's house to meet him. Lavelle says he will not apologize. Jeremy asks why he is there. Lavelle: 'Cos you coerced me, innit? What's a mans to do? Go jailhouse or spend a few months with a some dry do-gooder? Not hard when they put it that way, is it?' Jeremy responds: 'You have a very interesting vocabulary, Lavelle. That kinda … I don't understand street black stuff and then, nice words …' The 'nice' word, the unexpected word, is 'coerce'. Lavelle says: 'My mum never allowed me to speak of *black* in the negative. So she taught me other words. (*Deliberately.*) Innit?' Lavelle is also capable of talking like Jeremy. We are told he left school with very high grades. Jeremy, also Black, calls Lavelle a 'minstrel' because when it suits him he will change his speech mode and 'play the nigger' (pp. 128–9). The scene demonstrates how the management of idiolect and sociolect connects into issues around racial identity, class difference and survival.

# Dynamics

In this subsection we are concerned with the push-and-pull of dialogue – both between characters and between the stage and the auditorium.

## *The dynamics of exchange*

Even with simple characters we are drawn into the cut and thrust of an argument, or the verbal embraces of young love, or the stunned response to bad news. Regardless of characters or the details of the fiction, let us say that *dialogue demands its own empathy* – we easily imagine ourselves in such a situation; these exchanges are ones that could be ours; it might be our own story. Such exchanges most certainly will have happened in our own *real* story.

Drama plugs into our most basic desires, fears and wants. Just as the clown slipping on the banana skin makes our stomach turn, so the threat from the outsider makes us look over our own shoulder. All of us feel threatened in some way, and theatre stimulates that fear and many other basic feelings. We easily – automatically – imagine ourselves as part of the situation shaped by the dialogue. As we wrote on p. 31, 'Look out behind you!'

So while dialogue constructs character and action, and we can become good at describing this, we also need to show how local bits of dialogue involve the audience in the cut and thrust of position-taking, challenge, triumph, defeat; the securities of meeting and embrace; the joys of recovering lost ones; the thrill of verbal abuse and profanity; the feelings of isolation but also relief when confessing guilt. Then we are going much further in describing how the play as a whole works on the audience.

This aspect of the dialogue can best be explored by making diagrams (we have sketched ours in Figure 3.1): this is especially handy for directors. Is it a stand-off between two forces of equal strength? A meeting of minds? Or maybe it is an **apostrophe**, in which the speaker reaches beyond the immediate situation, to address someone or something not present – like a god, nature or a dead hero?

It may be that a particular sort of exchange occurs several times throughout a play or scene. If so, then perhaps an opposition between specific characters, or some other sort of relatedness like trust, love or suspicion, is being gone over again and again. Or perhaps the dynamic between them changes over time. Either will be significant. And some plays are *full* of, say, questionings, or clashes, or people talking past one another. If so, we need to spot this and

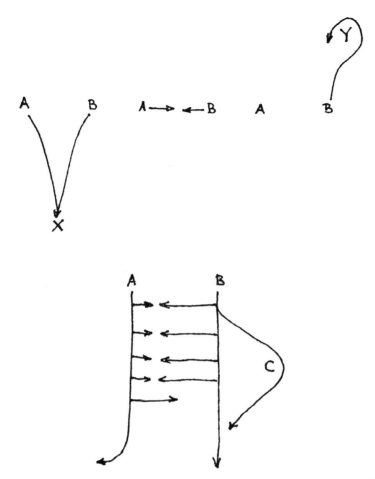

**FIGURE 3.1** *Sketching dynamics of exchange – some examples. In the complex exchange, B dominates the conversation by drawing C into agreement, and by questioning, commanding or insisting on things to A. Eventually, A fires off a parting sally and quits.*

comment. The section below (see p. 58) on conversational exchange will help in this work.

The dynamics of exchange can sometimes be formalized. An example is *stichomythia* (Greek, 'stitch rhyme'), in which two opposing interlocutors repeatedly turn what their opponent has said around to make it the pretext for a fresh attack. The argument feels as if it will be never-ending. They are implacably – and creatively – opposed. A famous example is the argument between Antigone and Creon in Sophocles' *Antigone*:

ANTIGONE:   Ah the good fortune of kings.
               Licensed to say and do whatever they please!

CREON:        You are alone here in that opinion.
ANTIGONE:   No, they are with me. But they keep their tongues in leash.
CREON:        Maybe. But you are guilty and they are not.
ANTIGONE:   There is no guilt in reverence for the dead.
                  [etc. etc.]

(scene II, p. 270)

*Stichomythia* quickly develops the opposing sides of the argument. It concentrates the argument. And, especially when done in emulation of Greek examples such as this, it is a point where the dramatic text declares its own artifice, the fact that it is composed.

## Structural dynamics

On p. 44 above we noted that dialogue delivers *exposition* – it provides information to the audience. A great deal of drama uses suspense to move an audience and to maintain its attention. In the TV courtroom drama, we know that the truth is there to be found. If the world is just, then the characters we like *must* end up innocent. If dramatic irony works on us by giving us more information than any one person in the fictional world, then suspense works in the opposite direction. *Someone* knows the truth, but that is not us just now. Then the revelation comes and we feel release. Both withheld exposition and anticipated action (she says she will be revenged on him: we wait to see how, when and if she will succeed) create suspense, and both are the creations of the dialogue. This management of the dialogue with regard to the audience's knowledge is an important part of the play's overall design. It works through a movement between non-delivery and delivery of plot information. This activity of holding back and releasing information is part of the dialogue's *structural dynamic*.

Another aspect of the structural dynamic of dialogue is the way it scripts the sheer *verbal energy* of the stage. We can let a word drift from our mouths or force it out. The 'Get' in 'Get off my foot' has a different 'attack' if I say the sentence with patience or in anger. Similarly, we can inspect how the energy of dialogue at the start of a scene affects the scene's 'attack'. Is the dialogue urgent or composed? How does this scene hit us, or invite us in? And what is its 'cadence'? Just as a sentence has its rise-and-fall pattern or even tone, so a scene has its own cadence too. The cadence comes from the shape of the dialogue's energy as much as that of the action. And then, is this scene which is full of violent language followed by one of whispers or gentle laughter?

Contemporary plays have developed detailed mechanisms for controlling dialogue energy. The most regular device is overlapping lines: 'I had a small flat in the West End, which I would rent out you know,/ so I said, "Look you're gonna move somewhere else …"' '/Oh God that was a terrible place … that was the most scariest place I've ever lived' (Bhuchar's *My Name Is…* p.10) The slash indicates the point of overlap. Such overlapping uses an audience's familiarity with the structure of dialogue in order to produce new rhythms and intensifications. That familiarity, and its expectations, are also managed by formal devices that slow down or break the patterns of exchange. McDowall indicates how such devices can be scripted: his prefatory note to *Pomona* lists, besides the regular slash, a dash indicating 'an interruption of speech or train of thought' and an ellipsis indicating either a trailing off ... or a transition'.

One of the most regularly scripted dialogue-management devices is the 'beat'. In the example below sixteen-year-old Jennifer asks Hench about his and his younger brother's education:

HENCH:          Boring, innit.
*Beat.*             *Jennifer looks depressed for a second.*
JENNIFER:       I have to redo Year 11.
*Beat.*

                    Where does Bobbie go?
*Beat.*
HENCH:          He's meant to go to a unit. (Jordan p. 50)

The 'beat' could be taken to indicate the persistence of the overall rhythm of exchange which then makes noticeable the momentary non-response. Into that non-response we then read such things as personal or interpersonal difficulty. It can of course also be used when one person is speaking alone, but still works to draw attention to something that should be said but hasn't, or something unarticulated that hangs in the air.

## The management of silence

As an intervention in the flow of verbal text the 'beat' is one of a set of devices for organizing what characters don't say, for managing silence. While 'beat' is favoured in modern playtexts, historically the most well used device is the *pause*. Pauses and silences have been scripted into plays since at least the early nineteenth century. They have various uses which range from triggering a new phase in the narrative to revelation of a character's inner preoccupations. Early melodramas were occasionally punctuated by a 'pause of mutual apprehension' as each character realizes something about the identity of the other. In Pinter's plays the pause is often ominous, precisely because it is not possible to tell what is being thought or what is coming next. When you encounter a scripted pause it's always worth asking what the pause is there for, what work it's doing.

We also need to be alert to its length. Plays now tend to offer detailed instructions as to the varieties of length of silence they require. In Simon Stephens' *One Minute* (2003) Anne, whose daughter has been abducted, asks the policeman Gary: 'What am I going to do?' Gary: – Anne: 'What am I going to do Gary?' (p. 56) The dash for Gary indicates, as Stephens' note says, 'an inability to speak or complete a word or sentence'. It is part of a whole system of silence management which ranges from trailing off (marked as ellipsis) through 'beat', 'pause', 'long pause', 'very long pause', 'silence'. Stephens also indicates the length he requires for blackouts. *One Minute* begins with a ten-second blackout. But such pauses and silences are far from being devoid of sound. Stephens suggests that silences 'could be punctuated. Perhaps brief, intrusive warning beeps. The kind of sound that fax machines make when they run out of paper' (p. 4). The noise punctuation calls attention, much as does the beat, to the fact that it is specifically words that are missing, that something cannot be said. The first dialogue between Anne and Gary ends with this speech by Anne: 'Don't go. *Silence*. My husband can barely speak. I want him to. *Pause*. Every day she changes. Grows. *Pause*. The idea that she is in pain. Or, or, or, or crying even. *Pause*.' (p. 10) The sense of Anne's distress is constructed out of a series of punctuations in the flow of words. It begins with silence, which marks a change of gear from the preceding conversation. Out of that silence come very brief sentences, broken apart by pauses. The pathos of Anne's final line is constructed by simple repetition 'or, or, or' as even the brief sentences break down and fade off into silence. The eloquence of this is not done by words alone but by the managed interplay between words and non-words.

Thus while some devices control energy by raising sound level, as two people cut across one another or speak simultaneously, other devices do so by reducing it. Through these devices it is not just energy which is generated but also a sense of a character's preoccupations. The audience is brought closer to characters through experiencing disruption to their expectations about dialogue's structural dynamic and through learning to read a detailed system of silences.

By contrast Brecht invites his audience to look with detachment at some energetic dialogue. In scene 13 of Brecht's *The Life of Galileo* (1943a), Galileo's friends wait in suspense to learn whether the Inquisition will get him to recant his heterodox views on the motion of the earth. While their talk is urgent and excited, Brecht makes this a scene which shows suspense rather than making us feel it, by the technique used throughout this play, and regularly by him elsewhere, of using scene titles. A placard on stage has already told us that the scene will show that Galileo recants. Brecht deliberately removes the suspense. His scene title blunts the 'attack' of the scene. He wants us to concentrate on some other things instead. Here are people making a drama out of Galileo, treating him as a hero and the object of suspense. And downstage is the figure of Galileo's daughter, praying. Yes, indeed, we see that Galileo has driven Virginia into religious superstition. But she is also part of the general *gestus* of the scene (see p. 121): that is to say, Virginia is not the only person in the scene who believes in miracles.

# More functions of dialogue

## Textual register and expressivity

On p. 45 above we identified the expressivity of characters as one aspect of dramatic dialogue: characters speak about themselves, express emotion and reveal aspects of their character through the ways they relate to people. *Textual expressivity* is another aspect. We can think of this in terms of the play's register from time to time or throughout. Consider part of the closing moments of *King Lear*:

KENT:       Is this the promis'd end?
EDGAR:      Or image of that horror?
ALBANY:     Fall and cease! (5.3.263–4)

While not a declared chorus, the characters are speaking *as if* a chorus. The three half-lines melt into one another across the different speakers; all speak of the same thing. The three men are here an onstage audience to the terrible events that we, at our safer distance, have also witnessed. As people within the fiction they are responding to events that have 'really' happened. But the lines are also a piece of self-presentation by the play. In the playhouse we respond to the composed, formal nature of this dialogue.

Consider that verse in itself puts a play into a different register of expression. While all dialogue is composed, much prose dialogue is designed to hide this fact. It is *pseudo-colloquial*, pretend everyday speech. But verse is language which draws attention to itself as a composition. It frequently confers a sense of dignity and seriousness on the play. Hence the regular distinction made between *verse for tragedy* and *prose for comedy* in Renaissance playtexts.

All the same, verse can be used for comic effect – like the 'old-fashioned' verse Shakespeare has the mechanicals and the players use in *A Midsummer Night's Dream* (1594) and *Hamlet* (1601) respectively, or the tightly rhyming, sparky verse which gives Bartlett's translation of Molière's *The Misanthrope* (1666) such a comic lift. We look a little more closely at how Shakespearean stage poetry works below (see p. 77).

## Modern uses of verse and formal language

In the modern period verse has been put to several new uses. In *Job Rocking* (1987), for example, different sorts of verse create what Benjamin Zephaniah calls a 'theatre of rhythm' (Zephaniah p. 144). In a more recent play, *King Charles III* (2014), Mike Bartlett explores how verse can produce a modern version of a Shakespeare history play. Here verse is less important for its musical quality, its communication through rhythms, and functions instead to create a sense of large-scale public events. Charles defies his ministers and produces political crisis: 'Whatever many like to think, there is/ A wise and ancient bond between the Crown/ And population of this pleasant isle.' The 'ancient' idea is enacted in the verse and its register. At the same time the play maintains a quality of 'quotedness', sounding like something we may have heard before (as we might, if we watch Shakespeare). *Charles III* is not so much a history play but a fantasy about a possible history, a fantasy which, through the verse, always comes with a wry self-awareness, as when Charles's wife congratulates his younger son: 'I've never heard you speak in such a way/ With passion, strength and rhythm too' (pp. 57–8, 88). The verse promotes scepticism rather than solemnity about public figures.

Against the public function of verse in *Charles III* may be contrasted a different function drawing from a very different tradition. In Emteaz Hussain's *Blood* (2015) Caneze tries to rap like her boyfriend Sully, as a way of dealing with her problems. While he beat-boxes in the background she develops her rap, first trying to block out his noise and then finally harmonizing with it. She returns to this rap in the penultimate scene. By now she has been abused by the man that her family forced upon her and has returned to Sully. After an argument, alone on stage, she does her rap again, this time ending by cutting herself. When Sully returns she reads him the letter that confronts her family, and he responds with the line, delivered freestyle, 'blood is thicker than water'. She and he then alternate: 'love is thicker than blood/blood can't exist without water/water can exist without blood' (pp. 64–8). Coming towards the end of a play where the characters slip between prose and various sorts of verse, including rap, the shared rhythmic lines here are the vehicle which consolidates and celebrates their partnership. Clearly while Bartlett's verse evokes and derives from the literary tradition of Shakespeare the rapping in *Blood* draws on a subcultural tradition. But verse and formal language are useful tools for articulating a diversity that goes deeper than the imitation of subcultural expressivity.

Take Yael Farber's *Molora* (2008) about the process of Truth and Reconciliation in post-apartheid South Africa. The play is a version of the classical Greek story of Clytemnestra and her daughter Electra in which Electra takes revenge for Clytemnestra's killing of her father. Farber incorporates text from the dramatists who told this story: Aeschylus, Euripides and Sophocles. But she opens the play with a very different ancient tradition. Instead of the Greek chorus she uses the choral singing of the rural Xhosa people. The Chorus is then used throughout: to play small roles and to interact vocally and physically with and around the principals. When Orestes enters the action a Xhosa initiation song is sung, then he dances with the Chorus, and then they ululate as he continues on his way. There is a sense that the Greek tragic story, the vehicle for exploring truth and reconciliation, grows out of something both different and more ancient, where the Xhosa women pre-exist, and continue beyond, that story. It's a staging of difference within shared purpose, history within a larger process.

One of the most exciting, and pleasurable, explorations of both poetry and formal language is Kaite O'Reilly's *peeling* (2002). The play consists of the conversation between three members of the chorus of a classical play that we never see. Wearing enormous costumes they chat offstage between those moments when they have to be on duty as part of a performance that we understand to be going on alongside them. What links these three performers, and informs much of their conversation, is the fact that they are all in various ways disabled. This situation becomes a vehicle for exploring, first off, the interplay of different sorts of language. The play they are performing is a version of *The Trojan Women*; Alfa is deaf and uses British Sign Language; all three do Audio Description of what is being gestured and said between them; and all three gossip. *peeling* opens with *Trojan Women*, containing such lines as: 'Our children will stand, clinging to the gates, crying through their tears'. A lighting change places us offstage: 'So where were you? I turn round in the tableaux and there's an empty bloody dress beside me...!' 'I got stuck, having a fag in the loo.' Alfa apologizes, saying sorry in BSL, while Coral, in AD, says: 'Alfa signs "sorry" – her right hand drawing concentric circles over her left breast.' (There is a distinction between speaking AD and speaking as 'self'.) From here they wonder what relevance their huge costumes have to *The Trojan Women*. 'It's probably meant to be ironic.' 'That's what they always say when they bung together classic texts with contemporary stuff.' Beaty, reading from the programme, says: 'Apparently, according to the director's notes, we've all been deconstructed.' Alfa replies: 'I thought I was being a metaphor.' 'For what?' 'I don't know. I didn't think to ask what the motivation of my metaphor was.' (pp. 9–10)

Not only are there different languages there are different discourses: the language quoted from the programme note sounds different from the gossip. It feels more remote from daily life than BSL. The women show a fluent and witty ability to move across languages and discourses. Slipping seamlessly between BSL, AD and 'normal' speech, they are also in ironic command of dominant culture's discourses on art – poking fun at the pretentious use of 'deconstruction', 'metaphor' and 'motivation'. Their carnival-like banter (think of the fag on the loo) empties the discourse of its conventional authority. Meanwhile, both the banter and the play's genuinely metaphorical structural device speak to marginalization. Disability is the condition of being placed 'off-stage' by a society that fails adequately to accommodate one's 'impairment' – or plain difference, as many deaf people insist. O'Reilly puts both this critique from the wings and the fully competent, powerful and confident bodies of socially disabled people front-stage. In a very short space of time the play establishes a brilliant shimmer of linguistic dexterity, and, most importantly, stages the social definition of disability.

The linguistic play sets in motion ideas about how language carries cultural and social value. In setting formal languages alongside one another, for example classical verse and BSL, it asks what formality of utterance does, how it functions. So too in setting registers alongside one another within conversation, for example AD and gossip, it explores how registers are used interpersonally. Having access to language gives power: AD may be used to misdescribe in order to provoke a character. At the end of Act 2, while Beaty slowly recites a list of different sorts of bread Alfa signs a story of a disabled woman who survived the death camps. O'Reilly insists that this speech may never at this point be done in English. Audience members who do not know the visual language Alfa uses do not have access to the speech, experiencing at this point their own lack of ability. And although Beaty is speaking English nobody has access to how this list of breads functions psychically for her.

Within this exploration of language and difference the play shows how the most formal language, that of the classical tragedy, enables access and produces empathy. When Andromache in the tragedy has her baby killed, Alfa and Beaty watch, absorbed in the fictional action, both speaking Andromache's words and commenting, distressed and angered. Coral in AD describes their reaction and hers, meanwhile in her 'own' voice trying to ask whether in performance the other two ever watch the audience watching the show. Thus as audience we watch two women drawn into the mechanisms of classical tragedy while the stage we watch looks back at us, asking how we watch.

This is more than an exploration of language and power. When Coral speaks AD and then speaks in her own voice, when Alfa uses words and then signs what cannot be said in words, we are uncertain as to what is anybody's 'own' voice. With their commentary on themselves and their linguistic play the women are difficult to pin down. This is the context for the question to us about how we watch. Early in this highly self-reflexive play a disabled performer says she assumes her function is to be 'a metaphor'. O'Reilly's exploration of languages is a mechanism for questioning what we, as audience, assume disability to be.

## Formal framings: prologue and epilogue

Plays of the Restoration in particular are marked by speeches to be made outside of the play's action, but most certainly as an important part of the stage presentation. Spoken by a performer out of role, yet inevitably also associated with the role they do have, these prologues and epilogues might well refer to the content of the play. But their main functions are to: speak on behalf of or in celebration of the author; defend stage practice against its detractors; seriously or impishly criticize other playwrights; establish an often witty relationship with the audience; and add to the speaker's charm and authority as a professional. We are mistaken if we ignore these as part of the play.

## Theme

Read an introduction to any Shakespeare play and you will find that there are themes of nature, or kingship, or Christian redemption, or some such else. A common exercise to be given in class or examination is to set off in search of theme and imagery, to see how one supports the other (for example, animal imagery may contribute to a theme of human nature). While all plays have their themes, it is verse which tends to support imagery (metaphors and similes) and allusions (to fable or classical learning); these in turn set up one or several *frames of reference* for understanding the action and characters. They declare what the play is about.

It can be the case, of course, that a playwright is showing off a bit, or attempting to heighten the tone of the play by introducing such explicit thematic material. But, in the best plays, imagery and allusion are not bolted on as if to illustrate the theme. Rather, for the playwright they have become the terms in which the subject matter, the story, *needs* to be handled and imagined.

And neither is theme confined to dialogue. It is also constructed by the characters and their action. 'Spotting' a theme by spotting imagery and allusion is only the beginning of really getting down to thematics. A list of quotations is not enough. With which character is the image connected? In what way? In what circumstances is it uttered? What relationships can we map between such characters, and what does this do to **articulate** theme? What do the plot and its resolution – if any – do to the shape of the theme? How do the various themes in the play relate to one another? Diagrams will help.

## Ideology and discourse

In the table of modes of character conception in Chapter 2 (see Figure 2.6), we used the terms 'ideology' and 'discourse'. They are related, but subtly and usefully different. For our purposes here, let us take 'ideology' to mean a fixed belief. Perhaps I believe in the Christian god, or capitalism, or hanging for murderers. It can then be said, with no offence to believers, that I have a distinctive religious, political, economic or judicial *ideology*.

But, in a more diffuse way, I may habitually talk in terms of things these days having gone downhill; or as if I truly expected that the goodness of heart of special people would always magically save the day. In these cases I would be speaking either pessimistic or romantic *discourse*. A discourse is a structured way of speaking about the world. Ideology and discourse interlink, of course. A feminist believes in the rights and value of women, and that men have frustrated these – this is her ideology. But she also uses feminist discourse – a structure of arguments, assumptions and analysis – to think about and argue for that cause. Characters may speak from an ideological position; they may also set up a particular discourse for the audience to interact with.

When Edmund in *King Lear* (1605/6) says, 'Now, gods, stand up for bastards' (1.2.22) he is speaking a discourse of self-determination. He introduces into the play – and acts upon – the spoken assumption that people can make themselves into what they want to be. Power and wealth come from what you do in your life, not from your status at birth. When he speaks this line, he has just performed a nasty yet *amusing* trick on his superstitious father. Opposing Edmund's discourse, Shakespeare sets the discourse of loyalty spoken and performed by Kent and Cordelia. Both of them speak and act from the assumption that there is a bond of mutual respect between ruler and ruled, father and daughter. But all this does is to provoke Lear into sending them into exile. Meanwhile, Edmund quickly turns out to be very cruelly selfish. Both discourses, then, have their downside. Many commentaries on the play note that it is written at a time of great and rapid change in the basic social and economic fabric of England. The feudal system, with its discourse of mutual bondedness, was being displaced by capitalism, with its discourse of self-determination. The play seems to show the old system in hopeless decay, and the one supplanting it as potentially very dangerous. This clash of discourses happens within a framework of more general discourses scattered throughout the play about human needs and desires, power and government, the nature of humanity, popular knowledge and redemption through faith.

So 'discourse' might prove to be a better word for us to use than 'theme'. All of us speak our own set of discourses. Each character will speak theirs. In many plays, character discourse is being offered to the audience to interact with – one of the key functions of such a character in the play is to carry and perform this discourse. Imagery and allusion intensify discourse, make it more recognizable as the thing we call 'theme'.

A play like *Lear* (there are many) sets up a system of discourses that interact with one another. The action sets them in play with one another. Many dramas do this, of course, and it is particularly useful in those that deal with social diversity. We have already noted the exploration of sociolect in *Seize the Day* (pp. 45–6). In another scene Jeremy, a candidate to be the first Black Mayor of London, is instructed by Howard (also Black) in writing his election material: 'As "black men" we have a problem and we have to deal with it. Write that down.' Howard advises that Jeremy gain the trust of the electorate by coming down hard on his 'own people'. Jeremy asks 'what do they, your own community, think about it?' 'What, black people? Fuck black people, my friend. They do what the man tells them to do.' Jeremy follows Howard's advice but when the text is published he is confronted by the youth Lavelle: 'Don't you understand, when you talk about us like this time and time again, you turn us into shit. You lot do it all the time.' (pp. 134–5, 143) Showing how the discourse is cynically constructed and then identified as specific to a particular careerist group, the play presents a clear object-lesson.

More testing for an audience are those moments when they are exposed to a discourse which is antipathetic to their world-view but which is not framed or safely balanced. The character Danny, an ex-soldier, in Stephens' *Motortown* (2006) rages at the corpse of the woman he has just killed: 'Yer see them, don't yer? Fucking leave university and get a fucking house together and spend all day in their shitehawk little jobs hoping that one day they're gonna make it as a fucking big shot. But they're not. They never will. They're shrivelled up Home Counties kids and they march against the war and think they're being radical. They're lying.' (p. 188) An ex-soldier, back from Iraq, may commonly be supposed to be damaged in some way and potentially violent. Danny does the violence but combines it with a not-often reported articulateness. His discourse makes him a challenging figure to watch at this point. For in the sorts of theatre which show such plays as *Motortown* the audience tend, in the main, themselves to be educated anti-war liberals with jobs. There is more on discourse, in the context of apparent truth-speaking, on p. 179.

Lastly here, we have said that discourses, foregrounded as 'theme', often set up *frames of reference* for understanding the play. Some plays contain any competing discourses within them in a single discourse which acts as a sort of 'outer frame' – the audience is invited to regard it as superior to the others. We could call this the play's *discursive frame*. The discursive frame of all Brecht's plays after around 1930 is Marxism. Within it, he sets up discourses of ethical behaviour, imperialism, gender relations, human nature and so on.

## Sententiae

Often we may feel that a character is the author's mouthpiece, that by this means the author is 'laying down the law'. A more polite way of saying this is that the author is being *sententious*. Many Renaissance plays have characters deliver lines like Delio's '*Integrity of life is fame's best friend, / Which nobly, beyond death, shall crown the end*' (5.5.120–1), which conclude Webster's *The Duchess of Malfi* (1614). Since it comes at the end, is spoken by a morally worthy character, and is set out as a unit of verse, we can take it as a message coming (somewhat) directly from author to audience. Proverbial statements such as this are called *sententiae* (sing. *-tia*). When, in the same play, the tyrannical Ferdinand thanks Bosola for his plain speaking with the *sententia*, '*That friend a great man's ruin strongly checks, / Who rails into his belief all his defects*' (3.1.92–3), he is speaking good sense but with utter insincerity. The lines thus come to have an ironic relationship to Ferdinand himself.

We can think of *sententiae* as bits of discourse specially foregrounded by a play. In some plays we may find characters delivering *sententiae* that establish their discursive position rather than that of the author; or sententious characters (this is their idiolect) who do not speak so formally.

## Signature

Many playwrights have their distinctive style. Not only the language which their characters speak, but also such features as the patterning of speeches, the pace of action, the relationship between action and event (see p. 79) are recognizably theirs. Wilde's epigrammatic and ironic style, and Orton's later emulation of it, declare the presence of the author behind the text. It is as if the play were being 'signed' by the author. When we sign a letter we are saying, 'This is my message to you.' A distinctive style which declares authorship is called *signature*. Pinter's pauses were part of his.

## Pleasure

Let us not forget that composed language not only persuades, it also gives pleasure. We go to the theatre to witness art as much as fiction. Our commentaries need to attend to the direct pleasures written into stage speech as much as to its dramatic content.

Pleasure is not confined to effects of beauty. Language can be surprising, acrobatic, wonderfully various as well as magnificently measured.

Of course, the relative beauty of speaking will be part of the system of idiolects at work within a play. Maybe the 'good' or 'high' characters speak well and the 'bad' or 'low' badly – though villains often get the best lines!

# The workings of conversation

What goes on in a conversation? Linguists have for some time studied the ways in which people interact through talk in everyday life. The insights and methods of analysis developed in this branch of study, Sociolinguistics, can help us in ours. So we are here concerned with the *interpersonal* functions of stage dialogue – what passes between character and character. If, later on, you want to pursue these ideas in more detail, a good place to start is with Short (1989), from whom a number of topics have been borrowed here. Burton (1980) was the first booklength study; Part One is especially useful, containing studies of a play each by Pinter and Ionesco.

Let us imagine a conversation between two people. They take turns. A says something, B responds:

(1) A: Lovely weather we're having.
(2) B: It's gorgeous. Have you come far?
(3) A: Took about twenty minutes walking. The bus takes longer. It goes all round the houses. Imagine trudging all round the estates in a bus in this heat, full of screaming kids with their buckets and spades. No, I'd rather walk, me. I've always been a walker, really.
(4) B: The sea's so calm, isn't it?
(5) A: You a walker?
(6) B: If I want exercise, I prefer to swim.
(7) A: Get yourself some stout boots, old girl. Otherwise you'll get blisters.
(8) B: I'm going for an ice-cream.

What comments can we make?

# Turn-taking

Participants in a conversation take turns. What they say invites a response. In the first exchange (1, 2) A's opening gambit is to make a statement.

B affirms by making a similar one, and then invites A to respond to a question. If the conversation continued like this, we would have a succession of cues and responses:

A: cue
B: response – cue
A: response – cue
B: response – cue
 … and so on

Looking at (6), we see that response and cue need not be separated out for the conversation still to run smoothly. B has responded to A's question by inviting comment on another form of exercise: the cue for a further response has been made.

The conversation ends when the chain of cue and response is broken. Here, at (8), B breaks off the conversation by declaring her departure.

# Types of turn

There are three obvious types of conversational cue: statements, questions and commands. Each can be responded to differently. Here are some suggestions:

statement   affirm
            deny
question    answer
            refuse to answer
            ask for qualification
command     obey
            question
            refuse

Remember that a response can itself constitute the next cue. You ask how big I am and I ask for qualification of your question: 'Do you mean how heavy or how tall?' Or you tell me to pick up your bag and I say, 'I daren't, because of my back.' Clearly, the preponderance of a particular type of cue in a conversation from one party or another can be significant, especially if it changes over time. I begin my job interview answering the questions fired at me, each answer merely cueing my interviewer's next question; then I negotiate room to make some statements of my own; having gained confidence, I ask a few questions myself. If I am not terribly impressed by what I am hearing, perhaps I demand to know what their policy is with regard to equal opportunities (and see Pfister 1988: 148–54).

We shall return to questions, commands and statements below, on p. 66.

In passing, let us note that drama improvisation games depend very much on the easy flow of cues and responses back and forth between the participants. Failing to provide cues to your partner 'blocks' the game.

## Topic control, initiation of exchanges and lexical control

All the same, one of the factors that makes improvised, real-life or scripted dialogue interesting is its departure from regularity. Unexpected or unwarranted responses are made to cues, and those responses become the cue for the conversation to take a different direction.

B's casual question at (2), which merely contributes to an exchange of pleasantries, is met at (3) with what threatens to be a life history from A. B tries to divert from this by talking about the sea and swimming at (4) and (6). But A persists with talk about walking, to the extent that (7) is no response at all to (6), but rather a continuation of A's own (5).

A has tried to hog the conversation, to lead it in a particular direction. B responds by trying to return the conversation to an exchange of pleasantries – or, perhaps, to take control of it herself, 'digging in' around the topic of swimming. A major feature of this short conversation is a struggle over *topic control*.

Note also that B attempts to begin the conversation afresh at (4) with the switch from walking and the estate to the sea. She does this in some desperation. But other speakers may habitually initiate exchanges because they are, for instance, in positions of authority (the interviewer) or are very sociable or supportive people. B takes A's (1) for just such an opening. Both the character habits and the local details of *initiation of exchange* are useful things to spot.

Suppose that A had been bossy in a different way, not by insisting on the topic of conversation, but rather by doing this:

(4)  B: The sea's so calm, isn't it?
(5')  A: Placid.
(6')  B: I think I may take a swim.
(7')  A: Go for a swim.
(8)  B: I'm going for an ice-cream.

A's (5') is not so much an affirmation of (4) as a correction to it – confirmed by the further 'correction' of 'take' to 'go for' at (7'). A is trying to insist on how things should be expressed, what the proper words and phrases are. A is attempting to take *lexical control* (see Short 1989: 156–67).

# Length of turn

A takes control first by talking at length at (3). Even if there were no struggle over topic control, the long turn might well signal a desire to dominate the conversation. Imbalance of *length of turn* is one indication of power difference in a conversation.

But we cannot make it a rule that long turns mean domination. Consider, for instance, a confession to a priest. Have you sinned? A long answer signals the worthiest surrender to mercy or justice. Here, speaking at length is a way of surrendering.

Similarly, while it has been suggested that short turns of equal length – like (1) and (2) above – signal an easy familiarity between the speakers, we might also imagine such a rhythm at work in a fierce argument or, say, the questioning of a truculent offender by a police officer. *Stichomythia* (see p. 47, above) is a battle of wits conducted through short exchanges.

So, too, long and equal turns might signal deep intimacy, but they might also result from two people trying to speak their own monologue.

Length of turn, then, is a significant factor in the dynamics of conversation, but there are no absolute rules for its interpretation. We can make useful observations about length of turn in conversations we meet in dramatic dialogue if we attend to

- *relational factors*: Has the length of turn changed in the course of this conversation? Is this bit of dialogue different from the last or next? Why?
- *combinatory factors*: What other markers are there for intimacy, power difference, etc. (examples might be tone of address, topic control)?

Length of turn, if we attend to relational and combinatory factors, is one piece of data we can use in our commentary on dramatic dialogue. It is one important characteristic of the conversation being staged. But note that it also contributes to the feel of the stage, its 'temperature' or energy, the rhythm of a scene. This is as much a proper part of our commentary as is attention to what is going on between the characters. Consider how length of turn gives a different feel to a Pinter play as compared to one by Ayckbourn.

# Terms of address

Our two conversationalists do not refer to one another by name. Perhaps they are a little familiar with one another, perhaps they have only just met. We cannot tell from the conversation itself. But there is one act of naming, and that does tell us something. At (7) A calls B 'old girl'. This is a very familiar and potentially deprecatory term of address. We can tell that A and B do not know one another well, from A's question (5), 'You a walker?'

Clearly, then, A is being presumptuous or insensitive or both. Perhaps this, as much as the one-sidedness of the conversation, makes B break it off.

The adult in the Catholic confessional is addressed as 'My child' and responds with 'Father'. Butler and aristocrat refer to one another as 'Your Lordship', or 'Lady Margaret', and 'Jeeves' respectively. The policewoman who has stopped me for speeding calls me by my first name, and I call her 'Officer'. The male interviewee for the job is addressed as 'Mister O'Toole' but addresses none of the interviewers by name, out of deference. One of the panel calls the female interviewee 'Ms O'Toole' with such a deliberate emphasis that it signals hostility.

So an important marker for the type of relationship between characters – and for the breaking of the rules of decorum such relationships entail – is the system of terms of address the speakers employ (Short 1989: 154–6). Are surnames or forenames used, and by whom? Are there terms of endearment or of insult? Do such usages change in the course of the scene or play? Are the usages scripted so as to appear appropriate to the circumstances, or not?

An obvious point of reference for us is the names Torvald and Nora use in *A Doll's House*. In Act 1 they call one another by these forenames, but Torvald also calls her 'squirrel' and 'songbird'. She uses no such diminutive in return, though she refers to herself in the same terms. In Act 3, Torvald still refers to her as his 'songbird' but without her compliance: she has 'changed' (p. 96), and no longer surrenders to Helmer's attempts to dominate and contain her.

So we have in this play a pattern, an 'economy', of naming: there are significant differences between characters and from one time to the next. A good account of this **economy** of naming would tackle the irony Nora is scripted to employ in Act 1 when she refers to 'we larks and squirrels' (p. 26). She is proud of her secret, and her use of the plural challenges Helmer's power to condescend. A good account would also note Helmer's extension of this patronizing familiarity into criticism and correction of Nora's behaviour: he calls her (in translation) 'squanderbird'.

We have just used the phrase 'patronising familiarity'. But not everyone would agree with us. While we would rather not chat with them ourselves, there are no doubt still some folk around who would find Helmer's naming of his wife sweet, loving and perfectly normal. Certainly there were such people at the play's first performances, as contemporary reviews attest (see Marker and Marker 1989: 46ff.). Ibsen seems to offer his first audiences a conventional picture of domestic bliss, which they come to find sickening as the play progresses and as they look back at its beginning. They seem to be prompted to change in tandem with Nora.

The prevailing social conventions, both those in the theatre and those supposed in the fiction, are important factors in our interpretation of these patterns of naming. When in 1956 John Osborne has Jimmy in *Look Back in Anger* say to Alison, 'Bears and squirrels *are* marvellous' (p. 34), he seems certain to be prompting us to squirm. And any *aficionados* of the theatre in his audience would surely instantly think of doll's houses.

In modern English we refer to the second person as 'you', whether one or many, familiar or stranger. In French, the singular and plural forms *tu* and *vous* respectively have fallen into a usage which signifies degrees of familiarity. In the singular, *tu* is used with lovers, friends, family and pets, while *vous* is used in both singular and plural with strangers and others deserving respect. It is usually insulting, then, to address your teacher as *tu* or your husband as *vous*. Several languages have a similar 't/v' rule. Consider the German *du* and *Sie*. English *used* to, in the distinction between 'thee/thou' and 'you' – and this is significant for Renaissance and earlier texts. In fact, English *still* does have such a distinction in its 'non-standard' regional dialects.

In reviewing *terms of address*, we have looked at *naming systems* (forename, surname, title); *pronoun systems* ('you'/'thou', but consider also 'Come here, you' instead of 'Come here, Miss Persaud', and the patronizing 'does she want a choccie, then?' spoken directly to her); and *given names* (pet names, familiars like 'old girl', insults like 'fat bastard').

## Conversational maxims

We noted above that an easy flow of conversation depends upon the orderly alternation of cue and response. We also noted that some responses are less appropriate than others, as when, for example, B goes off at a long tangent at (3) and fails to respond pertinently to A's 'swimming' gambit with his advice on boots at (7).

The philosopher H. P. Grice has suggested that conversation is a co-operative activity which assumes certain rules or maxims (see Short 1989: 150–4). The co-operative principle is maintained so long as our utterances obey the maxims of:

- *quantity* give the right amount of information (neither too much nor too little)
- *quality* try to be truthful
- *relation* say something pertinent (don't go off at a tangent)
- *manner* don't be long-winded and be clear (avoid prolixity, ambiguity and obscurity)

Some suggest additions to this list. One we might find useful is:

- *respect* give your interlocutor their due (give them the respect they deserve)

Dialogue is often interesting, informative and key to the action when one or more of these maxims is broken. There are four ways this can happen:

- *quietly violate* a maxim e.g. deceive
- *opt out* of the co-operative principle e.g. claim a right to silence

- *avoid a clash* by breaking one maxim e.g. tell a lie to be kind
- *brazenly flout* a maxim e.g. when the customs officer asks if you have anything to declare, reply 'Nothing but my genius'

At (3) A breaks the maxims of quantity and relation, quite possibly through quiet (unintentional?) violation. Perhaps at (7) the maxim of relation is brazenly flouted. That would depend on how the line was played. Our maxim of respect is also broken at (7).

While A hogs the conversation at (3), the maxim of manner is not broken in a strict sense, since the expressions used are not long-winded in themselves. (A does not say 'their gleaming buckets of red and blue, spades of vomit yellow'.) But perhaps the *curtness* of 'Placid' at (5′) ought to count as breaking that maxim? And does it maybe also break the maxim of respect?

Once again, we should avoid thinking that there are hard and fast rules. Grice has provided us with a very useful – and *flexible* – framework which can help us spot, analyse and comment on significant exchanges in a scripted conversation.

## Conversational and conventional implicature

The idea of 'subtext' is a familiar one to most students of drama. A character says one thing but we know they mean or are thinking another. Perhaps a stage direction has told us this directly; perhaps they are contradicting something said before or after; perhaps they are contradicting or simply not saying what we have come to understand to be their true motives from a whole assembly of such information. The idea is most familiar in the context of Stanislavski's prescription that the actor find the character's 'through line' and a psychological 'inner truth'.

The notion of *implicature* in linguistics takes us into similar, but slightly wider, territory. 'Implicature' is a bit like 'implication', and, to be frank, for our own immediate purposes we can treat the words as meaning the same thing.

When B above at (8) says she is going for an ice-cream, she is perhaps quietly violating the maxim of quality in order not to break that of respect. Or maybe she breaks it simply to make an easy exit. What seems to lie behind her words is something like the *conversational implicature* that A is a jerk and that she has had enough of the running monologue. She does not say it directly, but makes the clear implication. Remember that audiences often know more than the characters. A conversational implicature may sometimes be scripted to be clear to the audience, but not to the character being addressed. If this were a sketch for performance, fun could be had just as well by having A remain oblivious to the implicature, or by spotting it and ... well, responding or not?

When A at (3) above paints the picture of the bus and the estate, the conversational implicature is that s/he is above the ordinary. The character does not directly make this claim, but it is made all the same. But the speech also comes near to the *conventional implicature* that *all* housing estates and *all* public transport facilities are unpleasant. A implies that everyone in their right mind despises such places. Conventional implicatures are often marked by the use of connectors like 'indeed' or 'so' or 'in truth'. A might say something like, 'Indeed, it is a very shabby route through the estate.' Conventional implicatures mark out the speaker as part of or an aspirant to a particular social group; they declare that they share the appropriate standards.

Short (1989: 150) shows how Wilde scripts conventional implicatures for Lady Bracknell. He also shows how, in *A Man for All Seasons* (1960), Bolt scripts the character Rich's discomfort when under interrogation. For instance, when Norfolk asks, 'When did Thomas give you this thing?', Rich replies, 'I don't exactly remember.' The 'exactly' breaks the maxim of manner, but quite unintentionally on the part of the speaker (p. 154). Bolt will not have looked up unintentional implicature in a textbook in order to script this discomfort; but the notion of it helps us understand how his scripted language is working – both in the conversation and between the stage and the auditorium.

## Scripted conversations

Through the ruse of a short scripted conversation, we have here explored some of the interpersonal aspects of social (real-life) conversation identified by social linguists. Now, clearly it would be a dull playwright – and a confused one – who sat down to script dialogue according to these 'rules'. However the playwright comes at the act of scripting dialogue, though, that dialogue will to a greater or lesser degree share the basic aspects of social language. The rules social linguists have identified come automatically to us in conversation, and just as automatically to the playwright.

Nonetheless, all dramatic dialogue is a *representation* of social conversation. The unwritten rules operate in a more condensed, more efficient way. And sometimes we can spot the playwright exploiting the rules, pushing the dialogue into bigger, clearer shapes to the point that the artifice becomes delightfully clear. For example in the plays of Pinter, Wilde and Orton we can hear the written shapes, feel the punctuation. But this exploitation of the rules can also go in another direction. Throughout her play-writing career Caryl Churchill has explored the mechanics of dialogue. In *Escaped Alone* (2016) the play seems largely to consist of conversation. This conversation sounds recognizable, as the way people speak. But at the same time it is very carefully constructed. Let's take an example:

SALLY:      corner shop
LENA:      don't like the

| | |
|---|---|
| VI: | mini-Tesco |
| LENA: | bit far |
| MRS J: | used to be the fish and chip shop |
| VI: | that other one's gone |
| SALLY: | the old grocer |
| VI: | I'd do a shop for seventeen shillings |
| LENA: | so what's that in |
| MRS J: | fifteen's seventy-five p |
| VI: | but we earned nothing too |
| SALLY: | so who does the shopping if you can't go out? (p. 9) |

Punctuation is withheld, and there is a flexible relationship between the fragmentary lines. Lena's first line doesn't necessarily respond to Sally's, whereas Vi may be commenting on it. From here Vi follows her own line of thought about life in the past. Lena's second line seems to be an explanation of what she doesn't like, and as we later learn from Sally's question (which is directed to Lena, picking up from what she said seven lines earlier) she has problems with walking. Sally's 'old grocer' and Mrs J's 'fifteen's' both seem to be responses to the immediately preceding line. This pursuit of individual lines of thought across several exchanges, where topics may be revived from much earlier, is combined with moments of more immediate cue and response. Analysis of such writing has to be aware of the flow across exchanges rather than viewing lines as autonomous units. The script suppresses the obvious rules of dialogue, using fine artifice in the concealing of artifice.

Churchill's craft may be an extreme case, but nevertheless as students we need to be able to deal with it, and anything like it. So while there's no need to approach analysis of dialogue mechanically a reliable working knowledge of the basic principles set out in this section will:

- give us the tools to write more precisely and subtly about bits or aspects of dialogue we might anyway have recognized as significant;
- keep us attuned so that we can spot more examples still.

And let us remember what dialogue is for. A knowledge of the interpersonal functions and mechanisms of conversation can:

- help us approach the text in order to perform it and
- inform our choices on the rehearsal floor.

# Speech acts

## Speech as action

Let us now pick up on statements, questions and commands which we identified as sorts of conversational cue in the last section (p. 59).

The philosopher J. L. Austin was interested in what utterances do in the world. In his book *How to Do Things with Words* (1962), he developed his idea of *speech acts*. Speech can have a direct effect, in the same way that a punch in the face or a tender kiss can. This idea of 'doing things with words' has proven to be a useful tool for analysing what dialogue does on the stage, too. An extended account of speech acts can be found in Elam (1980: 156–70); our account here is based on this.

Austin starts by distinguishing between two sorts of utterance:

- *constative* utterances stating facts
- *performative* utterances doing something with words e.g. commands, requests, vows, namings

For the time being we can use 'speech act' and 'performative utterance' to mean the same thing.

The first line of *A Doll's House* is a command. Nora tells her maid, 'Hide that Christmas tree away, Helen.' Our first impression of Nora made by this 'performative' is of someone who is in control of her situation: she is exercising power.

The last line in the first brief appearance on stage of an earlier heroine, the Duchess in Webster's *The Duchess of Malfi* (1614), has a similar effect. After some short exchanges with her brother, she gathers up the courtier Silvio:

DUCHESS:     You are for Milan?
SILVIO:        I am.
DUCHESS:     Bring the caroches [coaches]: we'll bring you down to the haven.

                                                                    (1.2.146–7)

Her first entrance establishes the Duchess as a confident and powerful woman who instructs servants and organizes men.

Surely neither of these performatives is there by pure chance. Each of these playwrights is scripting words for a female **protagonist** who, in the course of either play, is to conduct a struggle of self-determination in the face of male prejudice and control. Note that as well as the performatives, we have in each example a hint of what is to come. Nora commands the tree to be *hidden* – she fears something. The Duchess gives the courtier a lift – she is easy and familiar. Not everyone in the play – least of all her brothers – will like this.

While both of these speeches are performative – they get the servants to do things – neither is of great direct significance to the action of the play. But, elsewhere, performative utterances are the very stuff of stage action: they change the situation (see p. 79). Consider the first scene of *King Lear*.

As soon as Lear enters, he makes commands: 'Attend the lords of France and Burgundy' … 'Give me the map there' … 'Know that we have

divided / In three our kingdom' (1.1.33; 36–7). Note especially that
Shakespeare scripts a command ('Know that') where he might have got
the same information across with a constative ('we have divided'). The
line thus has similar force to what might have been scripted as an action in
the present: 'I hereby divide'. (Note that we can now add 'proclamations'
to our list of performative utterances. Add others that occur to you as you
get used to this work.)

Lear does not ask his daughters which of them loves him most, but
commands them: 'Tell me, my daughters' (1.1.47). When he does use a
question, it is followed by a command: 'What says our second daughter? …
Speak' (1.1.66–7). What kings do is command; their function is to rule. But
this flood of commands helps establish Lear as headstrong. It leads up to the
disastrous proclamation: 'Here I disclaim all paternal care' as he banishes
Cordelia from his heart and home (1.1.112). This speech act performs a
key action of the play, as do his 'I do invest you jointly with my power'
to Cornwall and Albany and his 'take thy reward' which banishes Kent
(1.1.129; 172). There is something wrong in this play with the commanding
function of kings. If we recall the idea of the formal stage 'emblem' from
Chapter 1, we can now spot one in this scene quite easily. Lear says to the
dukes: 'This coronet part between you' (1.1.138). We do not do Shakespeare
justice if we say that Lear is using a metaphor and means 'divide up the
kingdom'. He is scripted to refer to '*this* coronet'. There is clearly a solid
object in his hand or held on a cushion by a flunkey, a real crown. What
are the men to do with it? Lear is commanding what is either impossible
or intrinsically and *unnecessarily* destructive. If there is a metaphor here,
it is this deeper one about the consequences of Lear's actions. Attention to
speech acts has helped us find it.

Note that a speech act or performative utterance may contain a
*performative verb* like 'invest' or 'disclaim'. Other examples are 'I pronounce',
'I deny', 'I accuse'. Above, we have made Lear majestically underline one of
these performative verbs by saying, 'I *hereby* divide'. But performatives can
be delivered without specific performative verbs. Commands or questions,
for instance, can be accomplished by simply saying 'Bring me my hat' or
'What is your name?'

Playwright Noël Greig did a rehearsal game in which he asked actors to
find a performative verb to prefix every line they were to speak: '*I command
you*, What is your name?' It is a good way to play with motivation and line
delivery. It's fine in such a game to let the performative verbs open out into
unexpected territory: 'I suggest'; 'I implore'; 'I insinuate with every bone of
my body'.

## Illocutionary force and perlocutionary effect

Would it be useful to think of constative utterances (statements) in dramatic
dialogue as having the function of relaying information to the audience

('Lovely weather we're having') and performative utterances ('Die, you dog!') as having the function of furthering the action? Not quite! First, we should consider that a statement of fact can change the situation. For example, as the melodrama nears its conclusion, the young woman declares: 'I am your lost daughter.' Second, a performative utterance might be delivered in the apparent form of a constative. Lear says: 'Ourself, by monthly course, ... shall our abode / Make with you by due turn' (1.1.131–3). Strictly speaking, he is merely stating a fact about the future. But clearly he is insisting that what he says will be the case. The line is, again, a command.

So it looks as though we have here two 'constative utterances' working like speech acts. The speakers are doing things with their words.

Having made his distinction between constative and performative utterances, Austin collapsed it. (It seems that he was in fact planning to do this all along. The title of his book is deceptively simple; it jokingly pretends to be just like a book on 'How to win friends'. He wanted his own audience to think speech acts through with him. We are doing that now.) As Elam (1980) recounts, Austin's work and that of J. R. Searle developed towards the proposition that we think of *every* utterance – every speech act – as being composed of three subsidiary kinds of act:

- *locutionary act* (uttering something meaningful)
- *illocutionary act* (the act performed in saying something)
- *perlocutionary act* (effects produced on the hearer *by* saying it)

So now we can be more precise. When Lear says: 'Here I disclaim all paternal care' (1.1.112), the illocutionary act is one of disclaiming. But its perlocutionary effect is to banish Cordelia. And when he says: 'Ourself, by monthly course, ... shall our abode / Make with you by due turn' (1.1.131– 3) he performs the *illocutionary act* of commanding his daughters and sons-in-law. But Lear ends up being bounced between them with an ever-decreasing retinue. The *perlocutionary force* of the utterance is weak. We might consider that Shakespeare then scripts for Lear a terrible divide between the illocutionary force of his vows and his calls upon heaven or nature and the perlocutionary effect of these utterances (for a brief clear account of illocution and perlocution see Loxley 2007).

The idea of 'illocutionary force' is a useful one. If we think across to Physics, we can note that forces have direction and amplitude (size). Illocutionary acts can have a different force according to the circumstance. If I tell you to 'Go', for instance, I might be dismissing you from the room, encouraging you to go to the party or advising you to see a counsellor. When the Duchess of Malfi tells her steward Antonio to 'Raise yourself ' (1.2.338), the illocutionary force of those two words is exquisitely ambiguous. They are in the act of gently seducing one another. He has lower-class rank but she, according to convention, has the lower rank in gender. She is both commanding him, and inviting him to stand as her equal. The delicious 'wobble' of that moment does two important things. It expresses a beautiful balance in their relationship; and it suggests that they are performing a dangerous balancing act from which they might fall. In addition, the fact that she has already called him her 'upright treasurer' (1.2.294) makes her command easily taken as a sexual pun. As well as the wobble around status, there is one around chastity and sexual directness. Our attention to illocutionary force has helped us to pinpoint and to describe this small but important moment in the play's design.

## The limits of locution

We have given little emphasis so far to the locutionary act, most usually thought of as the successful utterance of a meaningful sentence. At first sight, this would seem to be a 'given' upon which the more interesting areas of illocution and perlocution rest.

But drama is often concerned with extremes, and it is at some extremes that we find locution under pressure. First let us consider an emotional or spiritual extreme. Shakespeare's King Richard has just dreamt of ghosts in *Richard 3*:

RICHARD:   What do I fear? Myself ? There's none else by.
           Richard loves Richard; that is, I am I.
           Is there a murderer here? No – yes, I am.
           Then fly. What, from myself ? Great reason why – Lest I
           revenge …

                                                          (5.3.182–6)

We might say that Richard here has to struggle towards successful composition: he himself is uncomposed ('beside himself '); he struggles to maintain his world-view; and he struggles to compose the sentences with which he makes sense of the world. While Richard just about manages to put sentences together, we shall find other characters in other plays unable to do that. In Winsome Pinnock's *Talking in Tongues* (1991), Leela's '*speech becomes a garble*' (p. 233) as she tries to express her rage about the racism which oppresses her and the feelings of 'pain and absurdity' (p. 226) surrounding her own violent reaction to it. Yet this collapse of standard locution also rhymes with Sugar's story which opens the play, in which 'talking in tongues' figures as a healing process. In the Bible myth, those who talk in tongues speak an ancient universal language, from a time when humanity was united. Pinnock suggests that 'one of our quests is to find our way back to one another' (p. 266).

For our second extreme of three, let us start with a constative utterance which does not change the situation. Such a statement might at least be said to involve the very basic illocutionary act of making sense. But, if I say, 'The handle on the banana is Belgian today', I may be grammatically correct but will be making very little sense to you. Is the sentence meaningful or not? There is nothing wrong with it as a sentence.

If a character said that line on a stage, we might be persuaded – though uncomfortably – that bananas in their world did have handles, and that these were apt to change nationality. Short (1989: 147) shows how, in the 'Absurdist' *One Way Pendulum* (1959), N. F. Simpson has the characters set up a bizarre world in just this way. The perlocutionary effect on the audience is to persuade them – for the purposes of watching the play – that such a situation exists (see p. 164 on dramatic worlds).

In Act 1 of Beckett's *Waiting for Godot* (1955), Pozzo has the otherwise mute Lucky perform this speech:

> Given the existence as uttered forth in the public words of Puncher and Wattman of a personal God quaquaquaqua with a white beard quaquaquaqua outside time without extension who from the heights of divine apathia divine athambia divine aphasia loves us dearly with some expectations for reason unknown but time will tell …
>
> (p. 43)

This is just one-tenth of it. Though for the most part grammatically correct, it seems that it will go on for ever. While the repeated 'quaquaquaqua' mimics the Latin *qua* one might find in philosophical discourse, it also sounds like a stuttering absent-minded professor, a machine run out of control or a duck. When we get to 'divine', it seems that words are fighting in his mind for the right to substitute one another. Beckett here makes metaphysical discourse (i.e. concerning the nature of existence) sound like nothing more than talking to fill up space.

But, as is clear from the above, a disparity between successful locution and making conventional sense can also deliver pure playfulness, a delight in the way that language constructs sense. It might also lead us into serious consideration of the power of language to construct our view of the world around us. We shall meet with the persuasive power of what at first seem to be mere locutions later, on p. 72.

As a third extreme of locution, let us consider language which is so elegantly composed that it seems to be skating on thin ice. At the opening of *The Duchess of Malfi*, Antonio delivers a speech which describes his idea of the ideal court:

> In seeking to reduce both State and people                    5
> To a fix'd order, their judicious King
> Begins at home. Quits first his royal palace
> Of flatt'ring sycophants, of dissolute,
> And infamous persons, which he secretly terms
> His master's master-piece, the work of Heaven,               10
> Consid'ring duly, that a Prince's court
> Is like a common fountain, whence should flow
> Pure silver-drops in general.
>
> (1.1.5–12)

Consider the syntax of the second sentence. To what does the 'which' in line 9 refer? After some work, we shall conclude that it must be 'his royal palace' (l. 7). To deliver this logical connection with clarity the actor has to keep absolute poise, producing and then setting aside the 'dissolute and infamous persons' as if they were a parenthesis. In other words, Webster is scripting for Antonio an extremely poised, elegant and discriminating idiolect (see p. 45). The speech as a whole (we show here only an extract) flows gracefully, and divides into two contrasting halves: Antonio deals first with the ideal court and then with its antithesis. The very shape of the speech repeats his fountain image, suggesting not just a natural spring, but a graceful and delicate monument.

## Felicity conditions

When Kent challenges the wisdom of Lear's actions, he does a few things that we should by now be able to pick up on and describe with some ease. He uses commands ('See better' 1.1.157). He starts by calling his master 'Royal Lear' but soon descends to the more abrasive 'Lear' and 'King' (ll. 138; 157; 159). He is driven by his need to tell the truth (to observe the maxim of quality); but given the circumstances, his words break the conversational maxim of respect.

But Kent is, of course, doing his proper duty. He assumes that, as part of the aristocracy, he *must* correct the monarch when he is in danger of doing wrong. This is, indeed, part of the contract of mutual respect between them. Yet Lear has torn up that contract. His wilfulness has changed the conditions in which Kent now speaks. The warning has not been made in the happy – felicitous – circumstances in which it might succeed. And so Kent is driven, or drives himself, to an extreme.

So *felicity conditions* are key in life to making successful conversational gambits. And drama often depends on the mismatch between the illocutionary acts of characters and the conditions in which they make them. Two more examples are close at hand.

First, recall how Nora in *A Doll's House* boasts to Krogstad in Act 1 of her influence over her husband, who she hopes will employ Mrs Linde. Her bid for superiority misfires because, unknown to her, Helmer has just fired Krogstad, who now believes she has persuaded him to do this as well.

Second, let us return to *The Duchess of Malfi*. In the closing moments of the first act, the Duchess and Antonio perform a marriage ceremony on themselves. This is technically permissible in her society. She celebrates with the words: 'What can the church force more?' (1.2.404). As the play unfolds, we learn how infelicitous the circumstances for those words in fact are. The church – one of her two brothers is the Cardinal – can force her very brutally to submit.

In addition to felicity conditions, linguists refer to sincerity conditions – we are supposed to mean what we say – and preparatory conditions – we have to set the scene for our utterance to be successful (see Elam 1980: 161–3).

# Presuppositions

Kent, Nora and the Duchess all presuppose that they are safe to say what they say. It seems practical – pragmatic – at the time. They make the *pragmatic presupposition* that what they say will have the desired effect. So we have found two ways of saying the same thing. Another way of saying that much drama depends on a lack of felicity conditions for what characters say is that they make false pragmatic presuppositions.

Again, without losing ourselves in a forest of tables, lists and diagrams, let us see what other sorts of presupposition have been proposed, and what consequences these have for our analysis of dramatic dialogue.

Short (1989: 145–8) reviews work on **existential** and linguistic presuppositions. If we recall the example of *One Way Pendulum* (see p. 71, above), we witness the basic activity of talking about something in a way which takes its existence for granted. So *existential presuppositions* are at the heart of the way in which dialogue sets up the fictional world for us. A character says, 'I'm going to see the fairies', and we take it for granted – we 'suspend our disbelief ' – that there are fairies in their world.

It is a fact of life – or at least of the general arrangement of language – that we are more inclined to challenge what a sentence claims than what it takes for granted. So the very structure of sentences provides us with a way of *insinuating* things – literally, to 'curve' (*Oxford English Dictionary*) something into the conversation, to say something indirectly. If I say: 'My brother can beat your brother at football any day', you might think I am exaggerating or lying about his prowess. But you most likely accept that I have a brother in the first place. Disguise and deception are part of the common stuff of drama. *Linguistic presuppositions* play their important part in that game.

# Grice's maxims and the audience

We saw on p. 65 how an implicature passing from author to actor and audience can script, for instance, a character's discomfort. But we can usefully take things further than Short (1989) does.

There are occasions in plays – and sometimes plays as a whole – which we feel are sending a 'nod and a wink' to the audience. We raised this idea when discussing authorial signature (see p. 57, above).

At the opening of Joe Orton's *The Ruffian on the Stair* (1966), Mike is shaving at the sink. Joyce comes from the bedroom of the flat with a breakfast tray. The first lines are:

JOYCE:   Have you got an appointment?
MIKE:    Yes, I'm to be at King's Cross Station at eleven. I'm meeting
         a man in the toilets. *(He puts away his shaving materials.)*
JOYCE:   You always go to such interesting places. (p. 13)

Regardless of what implicatures we may later learn are passing between these two characters (and we learn of none), these opening lines set before the audience the proposition that 'meeting men in the station toilets is interesting'. To many in the 1966 audience, that statement would break the maxims of relation and perhaps manner. It seems not to be pertinent to anything, to be an obscure thing to be saying.

But for homosexual men in the audience, and other people who knew about 'cottaging' – meeting up in public toilets to find sexual partners and most likely to have sex there and then – the proposition would be hilariously, embarrassingly and dangerously clear. From their point of view – and, we can guess, Orton's – Orton is deliberately flouting the maxims of quantity and respect. He is insulting his 'straight' audience behind their backs, and saying much more than is 'necessary'.

There isn't really any implicature here in the strict sense. But Grice's maxims, when we apply them to the stage–audience axis, can give us access to the **rhetorical** attitude of a play or playwright.

What makes this example even more fun is that it is very similar in manner to Pinter's *The Birthday Party* (1958). Orton is making a pastiche. Pinter at that time was famous for producing sensations (implicatures) of hidden threat in his plots and situations. The idea of a ruffian on the stair in Pinter suggests a violent young outsider who will disrupt peace and maim individuals. Orton plays with the fact that, for some middle-class gay men, a ruffian on the stair suggests the convenient proximity of a 'bit of rough' – the cherished fantasy of a working-class sexual partner (see Shepherd 1989).

Here we see Orton working up a specific bit of irony, a sort of dare from the stage to the audience to see what he is really saying. But we can use Grice's maxims in more general terms, too, to think about the way that a play situates itself before the audience. Does it present itself according to the accepted conventions? Or does it 'go too far' or 'give too little' in some respect or another? Does it offend the sensibilities of the audience? And if so, why? Is it for the sake of it, or so that some other assumed maxim of theatrical communication ('truthtelling', say) can be maintained? Grice's maxims offer us a very useful model for spotting and then describing how some plays break the currently assumed conventions of the dialogue between stage and auditorium. And we might also say that such plays are 'speaking a deviant discourse' (see p. 55, above).

# The stylistics of theatrical prose and verse

When studying poetry, it is usual to call on *stylistics* – a variety of ways to analyse how the verse works. This analysis then helps develop and structure a commentary on the poem. Thus the commentary might attend to rhythm, alliteration, syntax (the way the grammar works), metaphor, simile and so on. All these contribute to the 'feel' of the poem as well as what it says.

Clearly such techniques will be of use when making a commentary on a piece of verse drama. What we find will not only tell us how the playwright is writing verse. Much more importantly, it will also tell us in some detail how meanings are being fashioned and how the playwright is making the actor speak. We have in fact already begun this work when we looked at Antonio and Lucky's speeches on p. 71.

The job of stylistics when applied to a dramatic speech, then, is to investigate it as a *theatrical* composition.

Stylistics can be brought to bear on any piece of writing, verse or prose. Whether or not we are students of English Language as well as drama, there is much that we can spot without specialist knowledge. The next two subsections demonstrate the sort of work that can be done.

## Prose analysis

At the opening of Tennessee Williams' *The Glass Menagerie* (1945), the character Tom Wingfield '*strolls across the front of the stage*' … '*stops to light a cigarette*' by a fire-escape … and '*addresses the audience*' thus (we have numbered the sentences for later reference):

(1) Yes, I have tricks in my pocket, I have things up my sleeve. (2) But I am the opposite of a stage magician. (3) He gives you illusion that has the appearance of truth. (4) I give you truth in the pleasant disguise of illusion. (5) To begin with, I turn back time. (6) I reverse it to that quaint period, the thirties, when the huge middle class of America was matriculating in a school for the blind. (7) Their eyes had failed them, or they had failed their eyes, and so they were having their fingers pressed forcibly down on the fiery Braille alphabet of a dissolving economy. (8) In Spain there was revolution. Here …

and the speech goes on. Let us comment on how it unfolds for an audience:

(1) 'Yes' answers nothing other than an assumed accusation or comment. The speaker is 'one ahead' of us, but at the same time seems defensive. He then says the same thing twice, with identical syntax, connected by a comma. Saying something twice can be for emphasis, but may also suggest redundancy, a waste of words. Maybe the comma produces a 'drift' in the sentence?

(2) Clear **metatheatrical** reference: this is about the show as theatre. So who is speaking? The author? Is this character its 'author'?

(3) and (4). Expand on (2). Again, two syntactically identical statements. This suggests a clear opposition, yet the line is difficult to grasp because the difference is mainly produced by the swapping of 'illusion' and 'truth'. The sentences mean the opposite of one another, but are very similar.

(5) and (6). Repetition again, 'I turn back', … 'I reverse'. These redundancies seem scripted to produce a 'poetic' or 'epic' feel to this speech as it goes on.

(6) But the repetition now supports a *turn* from the 'I' of the presenter – the pronoun is used six times – to what he is presenting. This sentence marks a point of division in the speech. While the sentences have so far been short, and simple in terms of both syntax and vocabulary, this one is long, a little more complicated, introduces adjectives ('quaint', 'huge') and a major metaphor. This metaphor is ironic – the positive idea of matriculation clashes with the conventional idea of blindness as a misfortune.

(7) Opens with another repetition/opposition structure ('them' – 'eyes') and then *flows* on through the comma, into an extension of the 'blindness' figure. Violence is connoted – 'forcibly' and 'fiery'. There are two disjunctions here. First, 'fiery' is unconventionally paired with 'Braille'. Second, the clear signal that both 'alphabet' and indeed 'fiery' suggest is paired with 'dissolving'. Both the long stretch of the metaphor across two sentences and these disjunctions may script two feelings: first, an ironic attitude on the part of the speaker; second, the bewilderment of those people from the 1930s (as opposed to the clarities of Spain).

Making sketch notes in this sort of detail helps us get close to the way in which the dramatic text is working on its audience. The next step will be to write an account of the speech using what we have identified. Clearly we cannot do this for the whole play. But, when commenting on a speech, we should always be ready to go into such detail rather than just repeating the surface meaning.

## Verse analysis

Let us return to Desdemona's speech that we first met in Chapter 1. Here it is in full:

| | |
|---|---|
| O God! Iago, | 149 |
| What shall I do to win my lord again? | 150 |
| Good friend, go to him; for, by this light of heaven, | 151 |
| I know not how I lost him. Here I kneel. | 152 |
| If e'er my will did trespass 'gainst his love, | 153 |
| Either in discourse of thought or actual deed, | 154 |
| Or that mine eyes, mine ears, or any sense, | 155 |
| Delighted them in any other form, | 156 |
| Or that I do not yet, and ever did, | 157 |
| And ever will – though he do shake me off | 158 |
| To beggarly divorcement – love him dearly, | 159 |
| Comfort forswear me! Unkindness may do much; | 160 |
| And his unkindness may defeat my life, | 161 |
| And never taint my love. I cannot say 'whore'; | 162 |
| It does abhor me now I speak the word; | 163 |
| To do the act that might the addition earn, | 164 |
| Not the world's mass of vanity could make me. | 165 |

The speech divides into four sections: 149–52 (urgency); 152–7 (composure – the start of the formal stage figure); 157–60 (eruption of urgency from within the composure); 160–5 (recomposure). The speech stages a struggle between urgency and an attempt to remain composed.

- Line 149 is shared with Iago, who has been winding Emilia up. Desdemona *interrupts* him, first with a cry of desperation and then with a direct address to him. The words go in different directions.

- 150 is end-stopped: this question could be a heading for the speech (for character and audience).

- Then 151 flows quickly into 152 through enjambment combined with simple words and regular iambic measure. The passage is marked by physical movement – gestures to Iago and to heaven, leading to the mid-line syntactical break at 'Here I kneel' (152). The new sentence forces a pause in the still-regular iambic measure. If the performer delivers the line at an even pace, the kneeling is a sudden drop to the floor; if she kneels as she speaks the first half of the line, the even measure times a slow sink down. Movement and short simple phrases are to be replaced with verbal elaboration.

- 152–7 are made formal, statuesque, by using pairs of lines similarly headed: 'If e'er'/'Or'/'Or' in an argument structure which holds back the main verb ('forswear'), which finally arrives, climactically, in a line starting with a reversed stress and with an internal rhyme (dearly/ forswear me). We *hear* the ornate syntax: the speaker has an articulate intelligence. Within the sequence its general shape of repetition and coupling is echoed in miniature: 155 'mine' ... 'mine' with another 'or'; 157–8 repeats the shape, now speeding up through the enjambment made swifter by the 'And'. This formal arrangement makes the temporary rupture more violent, with the parenthesis 'though he ... divorcement' at 158–9; it is as if the increasing pace of the overall rhetoric is fighting a battle to contain the emotion that motivates it. It briefly shows itself before the argument continues.

- After the climax of 'forswear me' there is a new stillness produced by the simplicity, the repetition of 'unkindness may', and the fluid link between 'my life' and 'my love'. Within that stillness is all the force of resolution – the change from 'defeat' to 'never taint', but seemingly understated (the 'And' of 162 has the force of 'But' or 'Yet').

- The crucial *forced* internal rhyme of 'whore' and 'abhor' across 162–3 is, cruelly, almost a pun: the word men use of women falls apart in her mouth. She is *wresting* composure out of the situation, speaking the dreaded word with fragile poise.

- 164–5 end the speech with sounds that make the words *solidify*, through two sequences of euphony: 'a*ct* / th*at* / might / add*it*ion' ... '*mass* / *make* / *me*' and through the huge syntactical inversion (in the shape of chiasmus: one word order mirror-images the other); which is

also coupled with the weird metre – the chaos of the opening of the
final line, and its 'feminine' ending. This is formal public composure
with a suggested mass of feeling, the chaos of stress, beneath it.

# Architectonics

Opening a copy of Schiller's *Mary Stuart* (1800), one is struck by the
physical shape of the print on the page. There are great slabs of speech.
Characters typically speak several verse lines at a time. This grandeur and
weightiness translate onto the stage. The play in performance often feels
solid yet also graceful, like a huge bridge or building might, defying gravity
by being massive yet also beautifully balanced.

Schiller's play and others of its type make obvious the physical feel of the
dialogue's outward shape, which in other cases might be, say, slabby, spiky
or sparse. An important part of the design of such plays is the *architectonics*
of the dialogue.

Contemporary plays have developed particular, and now characteristic,
architectonics. In *Blood*, as we noted earlier (p. 52), rap is used as an
expressive vehicle by a character alone on stage. As a formal utterance it is
distinct from the shape and mode of dialogue between characters. A similar
distinction between dialogue and other modes is used by Sudha Buchar's *My
Name Is...* (2014). Dialogue is not the play's regular mode. When characters
do interact it is often done within the context of them telling their own story.
This storytelling is set up as if they are talking to an interviewer (though
none appears onstage). The alternation between dialogue across stage and
address out from the stage may be said to be one of the regular architectonic
features of contemporary drama: see the section on 'Newer Kinds of Drama'
(pp. 172–3). Be aware that architectonic features may be obscured by stage
business, and even more so by film, where a sense of tension between 'across'
and 'out' itself tends to disappear.

# 4

# Plot and action

This chapter has four sections. In the first, we encounter ways of thinking about plot and action. We then turn to look at ways of modelling the action of a play, as a means to understand the way it works on an audience. The third section considers questions of storytelling, or narration. Finally, we turn to the distribution of characters across scenes and how this relates to the design of the action and its plotting.

## Plot, action and situation

### Action and events

What is action? Pfister (1988) suggests a simple and powerful definition: an action is something which changes the situation. Hamlet stabs Polonius through the arras and so has to go on the run. Lear divides kingly power and so the kingdom falls into disarray and he falls prey to his children. Pfister diagrams:

$$ S1 \xrightarrow{\text{action}} S2 $$

Hamlet's action above is purely physical. Lear's action is accomplished through words. And recall our discussion of speech acts in general: even a seemingly bald statement can change the situation. Cordelia's simple statement 'I love your Majesty/According to my bond' (1.1.91–2) has a devastating effect at the start of *King Lear* – because Lear takes the statement as an act of refusal. High dramatic consequences flow from revelatory statements in many melodramas. In Palmer's *East Lynne* (1874), Lady Isabel has left her husband and is assumed dead. But she returns disguised as a governess, Madame Vine, to nurse her dying child. Her cry 'My child is dead!' (p. 336) reveals that the mother herself is living. It begins the process of her discovery to her husband and their reconciliation before she herself dies.

Is, then, everything that is said and happens on stage 'action' in Pfister's terms? Usefully again, he says not. Consider a play like Beckett's *Waiting for Godot* (1955). The two characters say and do many things, but their situation remains the same at the end of the play as it was at the beginning. They are still waiting for Godot – waiting for something significant to happen.

But the audience do witness many events, from the trying on of boots to Estragon's attempt to hang himself. Similarly, while our day may have been full of events, we might still feel at its end that nothing has really happened: our situation has not changed, we have not changed the situation of others. Pfister uses 'event' to describe things said and done in a play which do not change the situation. His diagram is:

$$S1 \xrightarrow{\text{event}} S1$$

In *Waiting for Godot*, the fact that nothing significant happens is central to what the play is about. To some it suggests that there is no ultimate meaning or purpose to life, that, in the real world as much as on the stage, we while away the time thinking, arguing, struggling and looking for a truth which will never arrive. Meanwhile, Beckett refused to admit that his play was about anything at all. And so, to some, *Godot* also suggests that plays may appear to be significant acts of communication, but are themselves in fact just events. Taken together, of course, these two interpretations keep chasing one another round in a circle. If we believe life has a point and Beckett's play, by being devoid of meaning, successfully argues that life is pointless, it has challenged our belief. But how can a meaningless play argue anything successfully? This paradox probably contributes to the play's continuing fascination.

Mid-twentieth-century plays such as *Waiting for Godot*, which engage with the idea that life has no ultimate meaning and express this through the construction of paradoxical worlds (see p. 164) and dialogue (see p. 58), are part of what Martin Esslin (1968) dubbed 'Absurdism'. Absurdist plays question the value of human existence after 'the death of God' and the purposes of theatre itself.

The point of *Godot* is precisely that it consists *only* of events, and we expect plays (and life) to contain action. We can expect most plays, indeed, to be a mixture of events and actions. But what is a change in a situation? Does it include a nuanced change in the relationship between two characters? Must it contribute towards the outcome of the play, its dramatic resolution after the crisis? Suppose there is no crisis?

We need, then, to think of our event–action **binary** as a dynamic one. Most things that happen on stage in most plays can be thought of as having degrees of either event or action. We might even want to think of an 'action' as a special sort of 'event'. An event is anything that happens; actions are events which change the situation. This does not mean that Pfister's distinction is too simple or that it has collapsed. Rather, it can become a subtle tool for use in commentary and analysis.

# Situations and their elaboration

As we have already discussed, an obvious function of much dialogue is to elaborate character. Another function is exposition, establishing the situation from which the action of the play proceeds. But the changing situations throughout the action themselves are, in most plays, also elaborated. Whole scenes may be given over to this sort of function.

Nora's dance of the tarantella can be seen as a point of crisis. It perhaps moves the action on in the sense that the state of mind it expresses is one which cannot rest in its given situation. Readings of the play which concentrate on 'psychological development' will want to place this scene into a plausible scheme of the changes in her state of mind. Several critics at the time found Nora's psychological development implausible, mainly because they could not believe anyone could really come to leave home and children so precipitately. We could argue with them perhaps.

More recently, it has been argued that the tarantella scene is just one instance in many from the late nineteenth century in which women are represented as fundamentally 'hysterical'. It is a moment in the play when Nora is reduced to a gender stereotype. There is doubtless some truth in this.

But, especially if we think in terms of *gestus* (see below, p. 121), of something being shown to us with some deliberation, we can also see this scene as an elaboration of the situation. The scene explores not only Nora's mental state but also the interpersonal dynamics of power into which she has now fallen. At the most basic level, note how the two men conduct her movements. We may say that she 'expresses' something they cannot themselves see in front of their eyes. But we can also see – are made to see – that they are themselves part-authors of what she has to express. The scene in this sort of reading might be thought of as asking, 'Where are we now?'

Again, to claim that the tarantella scene is an *elaboration of the situation* does not say everything about it. It does not exhaust all other 'takes' on it. But it is an important take, and one we can keep in our repertoire of approaches to *any* scene. One possible way of looking at the tarantella scene is as a *tension* between Nora as biological stereotype and Nora as victim of the gender system. Perhaps it asks, 'Which is she? Can we decide?' If so, then we are starting to ask questions about the world-view, the ideology, of the play as a whole. (As your studies progress, you might come to note that, if that question is implied, it is one asked by men as subjects [as 'I'] about women as 'others', as objects of enquiry or pity.)

The *degree* of elaboration, through plot, event and scenography, may also give us an indication of the basic concerns of a play and the way in which the play persuades us to accept it as a way of looking at the world (its 'strategies of authentication'). Naturalism, for instance, elaborates scenes and situations both because it is interested in precisely *how* an environment affects 'agency' (that is, it is concerned with actual and possible behaviours, our ability to act in the world) and because the audience are required to believe in the stage as a direct replication of life. Not all plays have these interests.

# The theatre of situations

In *Huis clos* (1944), Sartre places his three characters in hell. At the end of the play they are still there. Their situation has not changed. But the play works on its audience with much more urgency than *Godot* does. The hell they are in looks like a middle-class drawing-room, which was also the typical setting of the well-made plays still dominating Parisian theatres (see p. 21). Each character spends their time justifying their past actions, or rather excusing them as being forced upon them by circumstances. They dramatize their lives. Sartre also engineers a fierce triangular battle for affections between the three. Each needs the approving gaze of another in order to feel fully themselves, yet also feels threatened by being looked upon critically, from 'outside'. This, implies Sartre, is the situation you are in, you people watching this play. Why not recognize the shape of your situation – which is as I have shown you here, you too are in a sort of hell – and change it? Some things, like our need for the approving gaze of others, are unchangeable. But we can be free if we just stop excusing ourselves and act honestly in the present. The door is open (the door to the room is open by the end of the play, but they dare not leave). Walk through it. The point to existence is what we make of it.

These **existential** arguments developed out of Sartre's experiences during the Nazi occupation of France in the 1940s. Paradoxically, he felt, the occupation freed him because he had to think about his situation in the immediate present, and act upon it. Several other of his plays work out the logic of a given situation. *Huis clos* is the most **parabolic** of his 'theatre of situations'. He is not interested in dramatic solutions or in a tidy conclusion to the plot, but in mapping out what a particular situation offers to or demands of human agency.

This emphasis at the level of a whole play is not unique to Sartre. Many of Brecht's plays can be seen as the elaboration of our situation within late capitalism, often through **parabolic** means, as in *The Good Person of Setzuan* (1943b). In this play, an important part of the situation is the binary gender system, the rigid ideological separation of 'male' and 'female'. The play concludes with a spoof happy ending which patently leaves the main character in the lurch. In similar territory, Caryl Churchill's *Top Girls* (1982) explores the situation of women faced with the opportunity to become powerful in a male-defined economic system. It opens in a mythic dimension, gathering together powerful women from history for a bizarre dinner party – and ends in realist mode in 1980s Britain. Again, there is no neat ending. Howard Barker's experiments in a 'theatre of catastrophe' deny the audience not only clear plot lines but also clear characters. In order for theatre to take its audience seriously, he argues, 'it must stop telling them stories they can understand' (Barker 1989: 13). A theatre of 'political reconstruction' (p. 17) must 'return the individual to himself' and ask: 'Are we thus?' (p. 20). Barker goes so far as to avoid a clarity of fictional situation in order to shock his audience into considering their own.

A similar use of what we might call scripted bewilderment can be found in Alistair McDowall's *Pomona* (2014). The narrative shows a young woman looking for her sister who has disappeared, possibly murdered, somewhere in a city. But the play unsettles our experience of this narrative in various ways. Its time scheme is disorderly in that scenes move backwards and forwards in time and the play seems to end where it started. It is sometimes difficult to know how one scene relates to the previous scene. Here is the complete text from the end of scene 13: '*Moe reaches, tentatively./ He stops breathing./ He holds her foot./ The world falls around them.*' Scene 14: '*The lights die./ Ollie is underground./ She walks down a long tunnel with a flashlight, breathing hard.*' Scene 15: '*Gale and Keaton. Silence. Gale:* She has / Left./ With the, the lap – My laptop.' (pp. 390–2) The author's note at the start says: ''There are no entrances and exits unless stated. They just/ Are.' We should note, because we return to it later, that the typography, the insistence on line breaks and spaces, is meticulously precise. This can shape, and unsettle, our reading experience. So too our relationship with the central character is unsettled in that, although she is played by a single actress, the script requires that there are two versions of her, as if identical twins but with no elaboration of discrete individual histories. Indeed her entire narrative hovers between reality and fiction. Twice she enters role-play games and it then becomes unclear how much of what we are watching is the fantasy of role-play and how much is offered as reality. This scripted uncertainty as to time and character and story is a way of articulating a particular version of 'urban' experience, an experience which combines constantly available information with the sense that there's too much of it to be fully grasped. It apparently offers endless openings and opportunities but at the same time placelessness and anonymity. McDowall's scripted bewilderment subverts the classic conventions of narrative and character in order to image a contemporary form of alienation.

# Modelling action

## Scales of action

We have moved from what constitutes an action within a scene of a play to considerations of whole plays. Can we then usefully think about scales of action? Pfister (1988) proposes we think in terms of *actions*, *action phases* and *action sequences*. Lear banishing Cordelia or Kent is an action. The division of the kingdom of which both of these are parts is an action phase. Lear's journey from belligerent father and king to his death as pitiful seer is an action sequence.

It will often be a matter of our own judgement what we call an 'action' and what an 'action phase' – just like the distinction between action and event. Any reading or account of an artwork emphasizes particular aspects of it, gives it a particular shape. We all have different pictures of the same play (e.g. Wertenbaker's *Our Country's Good*: see p. 198). Our interpretations give, as well as discover, shape; and Pfister's scales of action can help us to be sensitive to this.

## From Aristotle to the well-made play

Most of us use the word 'action' in more ways than we have so far described. Sometimes we use it to contain both action and event as defined above. Sometimes we mean just physical activity, either the actions a character is performing or the dynamics between bodies on the stage – the 'blocking'. These uses are fine, but we need to get used to being precise about how we are using the word at any one time.

A significant modern usage of the word 'action' we have not raised so far echoes its use in translations of Aristotle's *Poetics* (*c*.350 BCE ), part of which discusses the forms of tragedy and comedy in the Athens of the fifth century BCE. Aristotle writes that a proper tragedy has a beginning, a middle and an end. That sounds rather obvious, but let us pursue it.

First of all, Aristotle distinguishes between *drama* (such as Sophocles' *Oedipus Rex*) and the written or spoken story form, *epic* (such as Homer's *Odyssey*). An epic is inclusive and complex: it contains many stories, goes off at descriptive or philosophical tangents, has no single point of departure and no single point of arrival. The drama, by comparison, is concentrated and focused. It has a clear start and end, and concentrates on a single story. Remember that this is what *Aristotle* is saying about Greek tragedy. It is not a universal truth.

Second, Aristotle has a general philosophical position of the natural growth of things. If you take this seed, that sort of plant will grow. Plant it in clay and expect this sort of result. So situations, people and decisions taken in life have their natural development and conclusion. He is not talking either about plausibility or about fate, though many since have cited him as if he were.

For Aristotle, the drama is a place in which this natural growth of things can be re-experienced. This following-through of consequences constitutes the action of the play. By contrast, Brecht deliberately called his **dramaturgy** 'epic' to challenge what the Aristotelian formula had become by the twentieth century. He argued that it had become a formula for plausibility and for subjection to a supposed inevitability of things. Against an action of seemingly natural unfolding, Brecht developed his own formula of *montage* in which disparate and seemingly disconnected events contribute to the whole argument. Nevertheless, the argument remains *focused*.

While many treat Aristotle as if he were stating what a proper drama should be, the *Poetics* is much more descriptive than it is prescriptive. This, he claims, is what a tragedy is like if it is true to type. He might be describing a leopard. It seems unlikely, for instance, that he would think the emotional release he calls *catharsis* (see below, p. 88) very becoming for someone as civilized as himself. As Andrew Ford (1995) argues, Aristotle implies that this untidy affair is much more the thing for women and the lower classes.

Recall Scribe's insistence in 1836 that people go to the theatre to be entertained, not improved, and his formula for the 'well-made play' that included a simple action, intrigue and secrets, points of crisis and entanglement, and a just conclusion. The Scribean formula has helped set a particular shape of action in stone. We can find it at work in many of the most commercially successful plays of the Western theatre from the last 100 or so years. But let us be clear that it is (a) not true of all plays; (b) not necessary for a 'good' play; (c) a particular prescription that comes from particular cultural circumstances. But we can, indeed, find at work in *A Doll's House* five phases of action to fit the formula: *exposition – development and complication – crisis – dénouement – resolution*.

The play opens by letting us in on Nora's situation, which develops with the arrivals of Mrs Linde and especially Krogstad, and then winds up in intensity to a breaking point. Nora's departure gives the play a definite ending, at least in terms of pure action.

We might argue that this sort of shape works for many audiences because it gives them the experience of going on a journey. It can be a journey full of risks and incidents, but all is safely distanced from them, not only because they know it is really a fiction, but also because it is rounded off, satisfactorily done with by the time the lights go up at the end. But other shapes can offer similar pleasurable rewards. On p. 37 we saw how, in detective fiction, full exposition is delayed to the end. The process of tension and release gives pleasure.

Implicit in the model for the well-made play is a variation in the pace of action. Matters speed up in the third and fourth phases. Again, while not accepting the model itself as some sort of rule, it brings to our attention the *effect* of pace of action both throughout and at various moments in a play's duration.

## Shape of the action

Our discussion of Aristotle and Scribe raises the question of the whole shape of the action of a play. It is a shape which an audience carries away with them; which informs the way in which they relate to the characters; which affects their pleasure or displeasure. It is also intrinsic, as we saw with Brecht, to the way in which a play argues its point, if it has one – or to the way in which it positions its audience in relation to the events portrayed.

What, then, is the shape of the play you are reading now? Is it 'linear', following events one after another, or does it use montage? Is there a rise-and-fall pattern? Or is it like the medieval **morality** play *Everyman* (*c*.1498), which has a fall-and-rise pattern, even though it ends with a death? Is there a sense of strands being tied together? Does it feel satisfyingly closed off at the end, or is there a feeling of incompletion? Do we feel as if we are on a journey? If so, is it one of discovery or of inevitability? Are we mostly following the journey of one character? Does it mainly explore a situation? If so, do we get the sense of a satisfactory or niggling elaboration? Is it 'objective', or does it take a 'subjective' viewpoint, as in Tennessee Williams' *The Glass Menagerie* (1945)?

We shall develop some of these questions in the next few subsections. But the best beginning *always* is to take a blank piece of paper and *draw* the shape of the action as it strikes you.

Aristotle uses 'action' in the sense of the thing that has been done. For him, the action of the play is our experience of its unfolding to completion. We can retain this sense of the action as an impression of something done that we carry away from the theatre, but our feelings will not always be of completeness.

## Schechner's open and closed structures

In his book *Performance Theory* (1988), the North American academic and radical theatre maker of the 1970s, Richard Schechner, proposes we test two simple models on any play we encounter. Which does it fit? His model for the well-made play, which he describes as a *closed* structure, is roughly as shown in Figure 4.1.

A and B stand for two people, two forces or two ideas that are in conflict at the start. R stands for their resolution. This might be a happy outcome, but just as easily tragic. Resolution can include tragic recognition and death (see below, p. 88). In *A Doll's House* Ibsen teases his audience with happy resolutions, in which Helmer and Nora are reconciled, but also indicates a 'satisfactorily' unhappy one in which Nora drowns herself and Helmer recognizes his loss. Nora herself wants an impossible combination of the two.

Schechner's second model is for an open structure, shown in Figure 4.2.

Nothing has happened fundamentally to change the opening contradiction. There have been what he calls 'explosions' (E), but they have not changed the situation. We might as well therefore call Schechner's 'explosions' events. So this second model fits *Waiting for Godot*.

A significant feeling that we may carry away from many plays – especially from the turn of the nineteenth into the twentieth century – is a contradictory one that the thing is finished, but also unfinished. The opening contradiction is resolved, but not satisfactorily. At the end of Chekhov's *The Cherry Orchard*

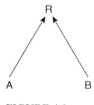

**FIGURE 4.1**

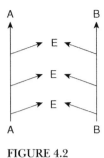

FIGURE 4.2

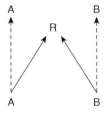

FIGURE 4.3

(1903), the aristocratic Ranevskayas have finally accepted that history has moved on and begun to abandon their pretence to power, privilege and wealth. The ex-serf Lopakhin moves into his historic inheritance by buying their cherry orchard for enterprising development. But Lopakhin is boorish and unfeeling. The orchard will be chopped down to make way for holiday homes. If the Ranevskayas' way was selfish, patronizing and ignorant, petty-bourgeois capitalist enterprise does not seem to promise humaneness much of a future either. The model, then, becomes a combination of the closed and open structures, where A might stand for stability and B for humane values, as shown in Figure 4.3.

The dotted lines show what Schechner calls the 'ghost' action (because it lies behind and disturbs the other more recognizable action). Which set of lines gets dotted depends both on the play and on the way we respond to it.

## Genre and structure

'Genre' roughly means 'kind'. We discuss the idea of theatrical genres in more detail later (see p. 210). Here let us note that many genres are characterized by a particular shape of action. Most obvious, perhaps, is romantic comedy, which begins in discord and ends in accord, corresponding to Schechner's closed structure. Especially if we concentrate on the young Athenians, Shakespeare's *A Midsummer Night's Dream* (1594) is a good example. The plots of many romantic comedies also briefly contain, and all suggest, a time of harmony before the disharmony. The feeling is that there is a natural order of things to be returned to. More factors – such as, in this case, a concern with sex and love – contribute to the profile of a genre, and genres have internal variations (a genre is, after all, simply a label given to a collection of similar things). But shape of action is often one of the fundamentals.

Spotting these shapes can help us unpick the way in which a complex play is working. Romance – an idealizing form, often set in **pastoral** or classical worlds – also works towards a final synthesis, a return to peace, order and union. In Shakespeare's *King Lear* (1605/6), Cordelia seems to enter a different world – that of Romance – after she is banished. France's vows to her (1.1.250–5) could be seen to announce this. While the play works like an Aristotelian tragedy, with Lear coming to recognition of his fault at the point of death, his reconciliation with the world couples with a Romance-genre reconciliation with his lost daughter. This contributes to the exquisite feelings on offer to the audience at the end of the play.

Plays that work towards a happy final synthesis are said to have a comic structure. This does not mean that they are all necessarily funny (consider Romance, e.g. *The Tempest* 1610/11), and not all comedies share the structure (consider satirical comedy, e.g. Jonson's *Volpone* 1606).

# Boal and coercion

Notwithstanding any details of the fictional world, a play structured so as to suggest that 'there is a natural order of things to be returned to' (see above) will tend to affirm any such feelings an audience has in relation to the real world. In *Theatre of the Oppressed* (1979), Augusto Boal suggests that Aristotle's formula for tragedy is *coercive* – that it forces people to conform to an existing order, by persuasion. He argues that the shape of action and the relationship between spectator and **protagonist** – that of empathy, where we 'feel with' the character – encourage our desire to conform rather than rebel or resist.

Aristotle suggests that feelings of fear and pity are aroused in the audience, to be purged at the moment when the hero suffers and then comes to recognition (in Greek, *anagnorisis*) of a personal fault or mistaken action (*hamartia*). The Greek word for purging (like lancing a boil or scouring a pot) is *catharsis*. An implication is that tragedy thus helps educate the spectator in the management of their emotion. But Boal asks, in relation to what? If injustice makes us angry, do we need to manage that anger, or exercise it in the real world in order to overcome injustice?

Central to Boal's argument is the notion of *ethos* (see p. 25 for personal ethical choices). A society's ethos is the way it expects people to act. The ethos of the tragic hero conflicts with the ethos of the society in the fictional world in one single but essential respect, the *hamartia*. According to Boal,

Aristotle assumes we will approve of the ethos of the fictional society. The *hamartia*, says Boal, is simply nonconformity. Regardless of the details of the fictional world, Aristotle's 'coercive system of tragedy' encourages us to regard all nonconformity as a fault.

Boal then goes on to look at other dramatic genres, to suggest that a similar coercive structure is at work in them, because they too work through empathy and catharsis and set part or sometimes all of the ethos of a **protagonist** against the ethos of a society. He asks, what relationship is set up between the ethos of the society, that of the **protagonist**, and that of the audience?

While Scribe (see above, p. 85) suggested that his formula was for the delivery of entertainment, he himself and, later, others used the well-made play to deliver moral messages in the so-called 'thesis play' genre. An example is Dumas *fils' La Dame aux camélias* (1852), also known as *Camille*. Boal (pp. 43–4) discusses this play in his scheme. The action is set in Paris and in the present of 1852. The heroine, Marguerite, is a high-class prostitute. Though she serves 'respectable' society, and it accords her the status of a celebrity, she commits just one 'sin' – of falling in love, and with an upper-class man. From this point her fortunes change: she is hounded, suffers and eventually dies. Boal describes her *hamartia* as 'negative' – it is the opposite, like a photographic negative, of the Aristotelian *hamartia*, because the audience will see love as a virtue and not a vice. But this means that, through empathy with Marguerite and emotional release when she suffers and dies, they will become critical of the social ethos of the fictional world. While they set out in Act 1 finding the stage world a pleasantly romanticized version of their own immediate reality, by the end they are forced to consider the hypocrisy and cruelties of their own social system, their own lives. The play has done *critical* work.

Note that Boal argues that *Camille* is coercive but that it does progressive work. It persuades through stealth, but persuades in the right direction. Questions of form have been central to arguments about politics and theatre since the 1920s at least. One regular topic is the extent to which an audience is 'led by the nose' by the form, or encouraged to think for itself. This debate has also been taken up by film and television studies.

# Tragedy and history

Not all tragedies comply with Aristotle's description – not even all Athenian ones. In *Modern Tragedy* (1966) Raymond Williams asks, 'What do we mean now by tragedy? What dramatic forms have expressed basic notions of the tragic in the past?' One half of the book sets out a very useful historical scheme demonstrating a variety of forms which embody changing cultural definitions of the tragic. Medieval tragedy allocates a role to Fortune, for instance, while **Neoclassical** tragedy is more secular; the understanding of what is involved in the 'fall of princes' changes as feudal society dissolves into a society of the mercantile city. Contemporary with Williams some scholars opposed the apparent cheapening of the idea of tragic experience by insisting that 'the tradition' (understood mainly as Athenian and Renaissance tragedies) pointed to an essential meaning of the tragic in life. Williams argues instead that 'all we can quite take for granted is the continuity of "tragedy" as a word' (p. 15). What counts as tragic experience changes with history; and so the dramatic form of tragedy also changes.

## Action and aesthetic design

We have been arguing that some shapes of action have an intrinsic argument. This is sometimes mainly to do with *aesthetics*: the neatly closed shape of a romantic comedy, especially if we are taken on a journey of delightful confusions in its middle, offers us a feeling of safety and completion. We might feel the same about a vase.

In some cultural circumstances, aesthetic questions become a self-conscious part of dramaturgical design. German playwrights of the 'Classical revival' around 1800 – **Neoclassicism** – wanted to recall the sense of rational order they saw in ancient Greece, an order they also saw embodied in its art. Schiller's *Mary Stuart* (1800), for instance, has five acts in emulation of classical precedent, but the dramaturgical design is made ostentatiously 'Classical' through symmetry.

Basic to the play is the clash between Mary Queen of Scots and Elizabeth I. Acts 1 and 5 centre on Mary, Acts 2 and 4 on Elizabeth; the central, third act stages their meeting (see p. 167). Schiller elegantly skews this symmetry by having Mary at the centre of Act 5 but offstage: her execution happens in neighbouring offstage space, creating a sense both of tension and of loss (see p. 145). Other energies are at work in the play: an urgent emotional register bursts out at times. The classicism is also at work in the verse form and in the mode of the actor's body that Schiller presumes (see below, p. 121). All such elements taken together communicate a sense of value and meaning to the audience quite independently of the story being told.

While Schiller uses aesthetic unity Gary Owen manipulates aesthetic contrast to provoke feeling. His play *Love Steals Us from Loneliness* (2010) is structured in three sections, 'Before', 'After', 'Before'. In the opening section a young woman has had an argument with her boyfriend, in the middle section we understand the boyfriend has died in a car crash, then we return to the conversation where we came in. Both 'Before' sections are written as realist dialogue between two people (including such touches as the woman taking a pee as she speaks). 'After' has more characters but they mainly speak out to the audience, from different and separate fictional places and across a rapidly extending time scheme. The aesthetic contrast between the sections works on the audience independently of the story, affecting their feelings about what had initially seemed a familiarly realist staging.

# The arrangement of plots and action sequences

All actions and events in *A Doll's House* contribute to the same action sequence. While Doctor Rank, Mrs Linde and Krogstad all have their own stories, and all experience change, their presence in the play is as counterpoints to and agents within the main story of Nora and Helmer. The play has a single plot, and part of its power is its focus on this single thread.

*King Lear* consists of a plot and sub-plot. As we suggested above (see p. 83), Lear's journey from belligerence in Act 1 to atonement in Act 5 is a single action sequence which constitutes the main plot. Gloucester's somewhat similar journey, less foregrounded by the play's design, is the sub-plot. Part of the play's power comes from the juxtaposition and combination of these two threads. As Pfister (1988: 219ff.) argues, the Gloucester sub-plot echoes and affirms the main Lear plot. The echoing structure suggests that a particular shape of experience (of unsettling and dangerous change; of the need for deep reassessment of our personal responsibilities) is all-pervasive, is a general truth of the times. Further, the doubling of the argument adds to the sense of weightiness: this 'truth' is a heavy burden.

Note how the two plots are interwoven: they occur in the same place and time scheme. The action alternates between the two plots. Sometimes they collide. This interweaving silently invites us to compare the two plot lines. In the last paragraph we highlighted their similarities; but there are also important differences, of which we shall here consider two.

First, the two men learn different, but complementary, things. We might say, for instance, that while Lear learns pity, and the need for it given humanity's weakness before nature, Gloucester learns the need for fortitude and the possibility of grace. Recall the scene at Dover, where Poor Tom (Edgar disguised) fools Gloucester into thinking he is taking a suicidal leap over a cliff, whereas he simply falls to the level ground. After this, he values life. By virtue of their differences within a single frame of reference, a similar experience, the two plot lines perform a *mutual elaboration* of the **existential** situation Shakespeare might be seen to be exploring in the play as a whole. The idea of blindness and insight which echoes between the two plots helps invite this sort of experience of the play.

But, second, the differences within the single frame of experience include a difference of character type and generic reference (the sort of play we might think we are witnessing at any one moment: see p. 210). Recall again the 'clifftop' scene. It is very bizarre and could, out of context, be a piece of clowning. And take Act 1 scene 2, in which Edmund fools Gloucester into believing Edgar plans to murder him. If we look freshly at it, without knowledge of the impending action, it has the shape of a comic scene, one as old as Roman Comedy. Gloucester is the old dupe, the *senex* or *vecchio*; we are invited to take delight in his gullibility and the wit of the young trickster who manipulates him. Yet this is nothing to do with 'comic relief'. This early, there is nothing yet to relieve. Rather, we might speculate that the pressure is to *feel with* Lear, *look upon* Gloucester, as an object. Gloucester is set up as an 'objectified' version of Lear.

But then look at the scene of Gloucester's blinding (3.7). Bloody and terrifying events which in a Greek or Roman tragedy might be reported are here done on stage, and done with slow deliberation. The scene often evokes deep uneasiness and deep pity. But Gloucester is not a tragic hero; he is a bit of an old buffer. In a way, this makes his suffering all the more distressing. There is not space here fully to pursue this line of exploration, though you might want to do so yourself. For instance, the argument becomes more involved once we suggest that perhaps Lear too is a 'bit of an old buffer'. The shape emerging is of two character-plot *potentials* (possibilities and expectations about what they are and might become) being set up and then made to collide, interweave and reflect one another. The bizarre but truth-bearing discourse (see p. 55) the Fool brings to Lear – which includes popular comic tales – is also brought onto the stage in the figure of the foolish Gloucester (who also reflects Lear himself). Consider, too, laughter as part of a tragic response.

We might also find thematic linkages – such as jealousy, lust and merit – between the plot strands in *A Midsummer Night's Dream*. But here the plots have roughly equal status; there is no hierarchical plot/sub-plot structure. Again, the plots interweave, and we have already noted the pleasure offered by their being skilfully juggled to mutual resolution. Indeed, the multiplicity of plots contributes to a sense of richness and variety; the play is like a big bag of toffees. In this case, then, a particular arrangement of plots supports the aesthetic, pleasure-giving functioning of the play; it declares itself as delightful artifice.

We have so far used 'plot' and 'action sequence' as if interchangeable, and legitimately so. We might in some circumstances want to distinguish between them. Let us again take our example from Pfister, perhaps to invite some further reading (see especially his discussion of Jonson's *Volpone*, pp. 213–16). Ibsen's early play *Peer Gynt* (1876) has an 'episodic' structure in which the **eponymous** hero has several unrelated adventures in different parts of the world. Each adventure has its own logic of cause and effect, so each is a complete action sequence. But linking them is Peer, and his quest to 'find himself'. This overarching quest narrative might be seen to constitute the single plot.

Webster's tragedy *The Duchess of Malfi* (1614) owes some of its power to a neat use of action sequences in relation to plot. The central figure of the Duchess has two foils (see p. 22), Cariola and Julia. Cariola the waiting woman is given the theatrical function of a presenter – she helps to display the Duchess to us. Julia, the adulterous wife, is placed within an independent action sequence – she aims to satisfy ambition by taking as a new lover the Cardinal, who then kills her. This climax to the action sequence forms an ironic parallel to the main plot involving the Duchess. For even though Julia almost takes on a male role in organizing her own life – she threatens Bosola with a gun so that he will have sex with her – she is still killed. But there is more than irony in the relationship between the main plot and Julia's action sequence. Just before her death she is told that the Duchess has been murdered, and then she is forced to kiss a poisoned Bible. This violent use of old-fashioned ceremonial is the sort of thing that tormented the Duchess. The deliberately neat parallel is set up with obviousness. It may be grim, but it also has a theatrical panache.

Let us recap. Some plays, like *A Doll's House*, have a single plot. Others, with multiple plots, may treat these hierarchically (*Lear*) or afford them equal status (*Dream*). In *Malfi* there is an ironic interaction between plot and action sequence. Multiple action sequences may be interleaved, each action sequence corresponding roughly to a plot strand (*Lear*, *Dream*). Or they may be given in succession, sometimes contributing to a single plot (*Peer Gynt*). Variations on these possibilities help construct meaning and contribute to audience pleasure and, sometimes, to a declared sense of 'theatricality', where, as in *Malfi*, the stage declares itself as a stage.

Webster has his Duchess of Malfi die during the fourth act. We might see her courtship and marriage, conflict with her brothers, persecution and murder as three action phases within an action sequence to be completed with Antonio's pursuit of revenge and the succession of their son as Duke as phases four and five. But with the Duchess's death the erstwhile melancholic misanthropist (and misogynist), Bosola, undergoes a fundamental change. He comes to see her worth and he, too, becomes her avenger. It is possible (we would invite such a view) to see Bosola as Webster's chief focus for the final acts of the play. His conversion and pursuit of revenge seem like a fresh action sequence, or a second phase in a two-phase sequence centred on him that only really emerges in the design of the play at this point. Although the Duchess dies, she does not learn through her suffering. But Bosola learns from it. It is as if he were a tragic hero by proxy. On this reading, Webster in fact gives the Duchess a subsidiary status in the play bearing her name.

While an inspection of plot (Duchess) and sub-plot (Julia) can help us to comment on Webster's thematic design and his management of events, a more thoroughgoing analysis may begin to lay bare the possibly unconscious ideological scheme (see p. 55) of the play: the male-centredness of a play named after a woman. Our use of Pfister's levels of action has helped us in this.

# Plays-within-plays, metatheatricality and levels of fiction

Shakespeare's *Hamlet* and *A Midsummer Night's* Dream both use the device, fairly common since the Renaissance, of the play-within-a-play. The 'Mousetrap' play which Hamlet uses to trap Claudius into guilty reflection works on the king because its plot mirrors his own story. In terms of the plot of *Hamlet*, this is perhaps all we need to say about it.

But there is, of course, much more to say, too, in connection with themes and theatricality. It is, after all, a very old-fashioned piece of writing that the prince has these *old-fashioned* players perform. And he himself has much to say about playing and its effects on our emotions (2.2.544 ff.). Right at the crisis point in this rather modern play, with its interest in psychological depth (see p. 41), comes a public pondering about the power of theatrical formulae which, though somehow outmoded, nevertheless persuade and move. Not only does Hamlet muse on this: we also witness the direct impact of what some might call 'crude' drama within the 'reality' of Hamlet's world. On a broader canvas, Phyllis Gorfain (1983) suggests that the play as a whole is deeply interested in the idea of *play* as inconsequential, or pretended, action. Thus Hamlet's playful stabbing through the arras which kills Polonius, his playing at madness which might as well be madness, the purposeful bit of play-acting he brings to court, and the playful duel which Claudius designs to be deadly, all contribute to this deeply embedded theme – of which the fact that *Hamlet* itself is just a 'play' is a part.

This last point links with our concern with the self-conscious theatricality of some plays. *Hamlet* can be seen as a very showy, highbrow piece which Shakespeare's company, the Lord Chamberlain's Men, were using to show themselves and their chief playwright off as ground-breakers. It is a tragedy, yes. But it is also a play *about* plays, and not just at the 'Mousetrap' moment. Where plays comment on plays and theatricality, they are said to have a *metatheatrical* dimension. Clearly, the mechanicals' play of Pyramus and Thisby helps give the *Dream* such a dimension too – as well as providing the means for us to be pulled between the snobbiness of their court audience, the workers' own sincerity and our own desire to laugh at their incompetence.

The fictional world of a play-within-a-play is 'below' that of the play which contains it: we take it less seriously as a fiction. So, too, are dream sequences realized on stage. Some plays – notably in the early twentieth century – play with this hierarchy. Strindberg's *Dream Play* (1902) is a case in point. Plays-within-plays change their status according to different historical practices and interests. In Shakespeare's time watching plays formed a part of court entertainment in which protocols of power and status were jealously observed. Strindberg's play appears on the back of a growing cultural interest in psychology and the life of the mind. By the twenty-first century, in McDowall's *Pomona*, the interest in virtual reality, in gaming and role-play, offers a new source for the blurring of kinds of fiction (see p. 183).

Our discussion here has links with the discussion of 'worlds' on p. 164.

# Story, plot and narration

## Story and plot

Sophocles fashioned the *plot* of *Oedipus Rex* out of a previously existing *story*. He could have made his play a different shape and still told the same story. Many other playwrights have told the same story, but in different ways. One of the means by which Shakespeare got to know about King Lear was probably the old play *Leir* (*c*.1590). Underlying both plays – which have different plots – is the same story. A dramatic plot, then, is the arrangement of a story for presentation on the stage (Pfister 1988: 197).

What that arrangement does and the motivations we discern behind it are every bit as important as the story itself. At this level of work, reading for the story is only a small part of our enterprise. Taking the hint from Aristotle, we can make the general observation that dramatic plots tend to condense the story, make it more linear and clarify or introduce structures of cause and effect. Often structures of coincidence, juxtaposition and irony are also introduced or developed. On such bases, thematic, moralistic, ethical or critical arguments may be built. As we have seen so far in this chapter, a particular shape of plot or arrangement of plots is arguably always meaningful in itself, and certainly contributes significantly to what this particular act of storytelling comes to mean to its audience.

Pfister (p. 196) tends to suggest that the story comes 'before' any plot. We have ourselves said that a story 'underlies' a plot. Temporal (before) and spatial (under) metaphors are useful, but we should be careful with them. Consider *A Doll's House*. Ibsen tells a story about a woman called Nora and her husband. We know from his diaries and letters that the character and her situation are loosely based on an actual woman he had heard about. Her real-life story and Nora's are similar, but not the same. We have seen how Ibsen was manipulating the conventions of the well-made play. Presumably, then, the events – such as discoveries and threats – and, indeed, characters (such as Krogstad and Mrs Linde) created in the fashioning of Nora's *story* out of the real woman's were determined by the sort of play Ibsen wanted to write. Nora's *story* depends on the plot-shape Ibsen had in mind. Once written, though, it can be told by other dramatic plots and in other media.

Stories only really exist as things told, that is, as real or imagined events given shape. Dramatic plots tend to tell stories, to embody them, in particular ways; they give a particular general shape to the world and the way we view it. For instance, they condense, and do not *usually* employ flashbacks, as novelistic plots quite frequently do. Different genres do the telling in their particular ways, and then individual plays have their own plot strategies. In some modern plays we shall encounter a deliberate tension between the formal telling of story and the embodiment of plot in dialogue. This tension is what gives the play its particular atmosphere and effect, and we need to be able to describe the shapes, the structure and contrasts, that produce it. We need to think of every play we encounter as a *specific embodiment* of a story. Our object of enquiry is that embodiment – the story-and-shape – not the story 'underlying' or to be seen 'through' the play.

# The telling of stories

During the 1980s the British theatre company Shared Experience became famous for their particular brand of 'storytelling' theatre. It is not that they narrated the events on stage as if speaking a novel. Rather, they acted plays – such as Shakespeare's *Cymbeline* – in such a way that they 'stepped back' from the action and characters, keeping their audience constantly and pleasurably aware that the actors had a story to communicate, a story to re-tell. They 'demonstrated' their characters, then, but not for Brechtian reasons of distanciation. The feel of their shows was, rather, that the audience were being introduced to a box of delights, intriguing, precious and beautifully fashioned. Delight was strengthened by the use of only minimal sets, costumes and props. This was theatre that was centred on imagination.

Part of the magic of those shows derived precisely from the fact that, for the most part, dramatic texts let the events narrate themselves. This, in turn, is one reason why plays tend not to use flashbacks, which in novels usually need the intervention of a narrative voice to place them in relation to the rest of the action. There is rarely a narrator-figure in drama, in contrast to the dominant practice in novels or short stories (see p. 22). A dramatic text is a script for a piece of collective storytelling, in the West since 1600 usually without a separable narrator.

We thrive on stories; we love to hear them. And *telling* stories is a deeply human activity. Each of us has a notion of the story of our own life, which helps us make sense of who we are; it is part of our identity. We make sense of the world by making or learning stories about the world, ordering our experiences into causes and effects. The practices of science and medicine depend on stories, as does commentary on the arts. We tell the history of the universe or evolution; connect in orderly fashion the nature of the virus, methods of infection, life habits, symptoms, the action of drugs (they change the situation), likely outcomes for individuals and the likely demographic scenario to come. And we sort artworks into movements or models of cultural production (Chapter 8), linking them to events at large.

Just as theatre and playing can become part of a play's concerns (**metatheatricality**), some plays script a concern with our need for and delight in telling stories, of setting out a narrative, of making the disorderly confusions of real life settle down into an acceptable or pleasurable pattern. Prospero's account to Miranda of their past history early on in *The Tempest* can be regarded *either* as a rather heavy-handed bit of exposition on Shakespeare's part, or as a bit of lengthy exposition which also *characterizes* Prospero's driving desire to have the record put straight, the story properly told – and concluded. The events on the island which he controls are part of his making the story he wants to tell happen. Caliban has his own story to tell; it contests Prospero's.

# Live and narrated action

Prospero's account to Miranda is the major piece of exposition in Shakespeare's *The Tempest*. It gets the story so far established, so that the action can meaningfully start. It helps simplify what has to be presented on the stage: exposition facilitates the condensing of the action (see p. 95 and p. 45, above).

But in this play, and most others, the situation after the opening is changed by events which happen offstage as well as on it. We learn about offstage happenings by hearing characters tell one another about them – or, in some plays, by being told by a narrator. In nearly every play we meet there is both *live action* and *narrated action* (see Pfister 1988: 204–11). Again, we can put the fact that things are made to happen offstage down to the condensing principle of drama: to have everything necessary to the action done on stage would often be confusing and would make for very long plays.

## *Condensation, decorum, emotional effect and aesthetic thrill*

When Hamlet is sent off to England it is a ruse. Rosencrantz and Guildenstern are instructed to murder him at sea. By his good fortune, he accidentally discovers the plot, kills them instead, and returns to Denmark finally to avenge his father. The episode is one of several making up his journey from feckless melancholy to death in vengeance. But it is an entirely narrated episode. Since all the live action takes place at Elsinore castle and its precincts, we might guess that the action is narrated for the sake of *condensation* of the plot. The focus is kept tight.

Playwrights have other reasons for choosing to have action narrated rather than witnessed directly. One is *decorum*. It may be decided that what needs to happen in the course of the action (say, a murder or a rape) should not be shown, lest it disgust, alarm or perhaps excite an audience – or lay open the players to abuse. The eighteenth-century London stages of Covent Garden and Drury Lane, while busy with comedy, farce and spectacle as well as the odd tragedy, were resolutely decorous in this sense. This decorum was part of the theatres' role of contributing to the **Town**'s civility.

A second reason is *emotional effect*. A narrated event works directly on the hearer's imagination. Especially if the language in which it is narrated is vivid and evocative, an audience may become more emotionally disturbed than they would were the events staged instead – because the real thing can never be as weird as what we imagine.

This seeming paradox – that absent action can be brought somehow closer through words, that the insubstantial can give the effect of substance – can also deliver an *aesthetic thrill* to an audience. Right at the heart of conventional Western theatre is a paradox: *all* of the events before us, whether enacted or narrated, are both there (we witness them, believe what we see and are told) and not there (they are fiction). The aesthetic thrill depends on this paradox.

Several of the plays of the Roman writer Seneca (*c*.4 BCE–65) involve very bloody and terrifying deeds, but almost all of these are narrated rather than enacted. It is supposed that Seneca's plays were written to be read aloud rather than performed, but they were nonetheless one of the major influences on the Renaissance revenge drama, especially that sub-genre since called the 'tragedy of blood'. An important early example is Kyd's *The Spanish Tragedy* (1585–7), where we see Horatio killed and then see his father describing the corpse. Renaissance plays actually stage the blood and gore, but at the same time, as we suggested above, there is an aesthetic effect to be had by narrating action – this is not merely redundant description. Thus in Kyd's play, as in other Renaissance plays, there is an interest in the *interplay* between the direct experience of violent, live action and the narration of the violence and its effects.

West (1991) suggests that both the 'realist' David Garrick and later the 'classical' Sarah Siddons in the second half of the eighteenth century were appreciated for their art in consciously presenting their role while displaying true emotion. The actors were to be passionate but not to be overcome. This serenely poised management of emotionality was itself decorous – the actor was a model of both restraint and honesty, a model citizen. The narration or recall of extreme events provided effective moments in which to stage this ideal, and some plays – Hannah Cowley's *The Fate of Sparta* (1788) is one – were scripted specially to deliver that effect.

We might say that Brecht contests the dominant conventions of Western theatre by having all the action in some sense narrated even while it is enacted. The actors 'demonstrate' the action, put it at a distance from them and us (see p. 32). In Brecht's play *The Mother* (1932), the characters/actors stage a 'Report on the events of 1 May 1905' (scene 5). Here, not only do the performers 'demonstrate' the characters; those characters themselves also report significant past events in which their comrades died. The characters narrate the events as they act them out. The scene is very difficult to stage without making it sentimental and, indeed, 'epic' in a very un-Brechtian sense – it all too easily becomes monumentally moving in conventional terms. The combined emotional effect and aesthetic thrill of action *narrated* within the fictional frame are difficult to overcome.

A final example of the power that can be obtained from combining the live and narrated, the substantial and the insubstantial, is Caryl Churchill's *Escaped Alone*. The play consists largely of conversation between four women flowing continuously over several afternoons (we analyse the interesting formal aspects of this conversation on pp. 65–6). The conversation moves across various fairly local topics, both received from media discourse and emerging from the personal lives of the women. At regular junctures one of the women, Mrs J, addresses the audience (a shift handled clumsily in the first production). Her speech is rather different from the general conversation: 'The hunger began when eighty per cent of food was diverted to TV programmes. Commuters watched breakfast on iPlayer on their way to work. Smartphones were distributed by charities when rice ran out' (p. 22). Unlike the incomplete sentences of the women's conversation Mrs J's language is more formally presented, is **rhetorically** arranged. Her stories about a dystopian future are clearly both fictional and yet, in a sense, possible. They contrast sharply with the pace and references of the general conversation, which is recognizably 'real', in the here and now of the women's lives. But there is one other mode of speech. Each of the other women at one point departs from the conversation to tell a story about her own life – about a fear of cats, about depression, about killing a partner. These stories are different from Mrs J's. They express individual feelings, and their **syntactically** fluid language is more of a piece with the conversation. So there are three contrasting elements to the speech, two of which are narrated (indeed the whole play begins like the telling of a story). The aesthetic thrill, and indeed horror, work at two levels, with a sort of inevitable connecting logic. The stories by individuals indicate the depth of alienation and distress that underpin the casually drifting surface of a 'normal' conversation while the stories told by Mrs J foresee a world of cataclysmic alienation and collapse which can never be recognized by those trapped into the 'normal' conversations of the everyday here and now. The relationship between one mode and the other cannot fully be articulated, an inability marked in a speech which is eloquent precisely because it enacts the failure of eloquence. Towards the end Mrs J simply says 'terrible rage'. Then repeats it twenty-five times. The overall effect of this careful aesthetic design is a wonderful but terrifying example of the effectiveness of combining interaction and narration.

## *Stageability, liaison, argument and pleasure*

In Act 3 scene 2 of *The Tempest*, Ariel makes himself invisible and plays tricks on Stephano, Trinculo and Caliban to begin punishing them for attempting to usurp Prospero's authority. The local action ends with them following the sound of Ariel's music offstage. We next hear of them much later, at 4.1.171–84, when Ariel recounts to Prospero what we have already seen – and then briefly continues their story: they have been dragged through hedges and finally 'left ... I'th'filthy-mantled pool' (l. 182) near to Prospero's cave. And then, almost immediately, they arrive on stage, '*all wet*' (l. 193 SD) to suffer even further manipulation.

Let us comment on this sequence of staged and narrated actions. What strikes us first? Perhaps it is indeed the *pleasure* the audience is set up to get from the appearance of the bedraggled bunch in Act 4. What delivers that pleasure? The moment is clearly one to be exploited for direct comic effect, signalled by the rare stage direction at l. 193. But there is also a structural pleasure scripted, which is again to do with the *interplay of presence and absence*. Crucial to this is the way in which what Ariel narrates is much wilder than what we witness in the first onstage action. We see something; it is elaborated in our mind's eye, though we lack direct contact with it. Finally we witness the results – we are rewarded by the 'true' presence on stage of the object of our delight. Note that the shape here is a **crescendo**.

A more banal – though also important – consideration is the question of *liaison*. The interplay of live and narrated action sustains the continuity of the servants' plot line across its interruptions by other plot lines. The audience are kept up to date, given sign-posts, reminded where they are in each story. But we can take this further. Prospero is also kept up to date. He needs to know what has happened. This is on the one hand a matter of plausibility – he is supposed to be in control, after all. But it is also a matter of what Prospero represents: he is indeed 'the one who needs to know'. Recall our remarks about him on p. 96.

We have just described how a plot line is sustained across its interruption by others. The other side to this coin is that those interruptions are made possible: the audience can concentrate securely on several matters at once. We have here an especially interesting case of interruption, since it is Prospero himself who halts the betrothal masque, having suddenly realized that 'I had forgot that foul conspiracy / Of the beast Caliban and his confederates / Against my life' (4.1.139–41). The interruption pits the 'light' of love, sex and marriage against the 'dark' of conspiracy. Yet what we get from the conspiracy sub-plot at precisely this moment is broad comedy. By the play's ending, Prospero has forgiven all. We might see the comic pleasures to be had in the servants' plot line as part and parcel of this scheme of forgiveness.

Yet more banal – and this time, surely, not very important at all – is the question of *stageability*. It would be difficult to make a scene within the originally prevailing stage conventions which satisfactorily showed the physical punishment of the servant characters. It might also be difficult given the actual technical facilities. But surely much more important than either is the audience's delight in *cruelty at a safe distance*.

One of the ways in which *Richard 3* and its eponymous hero work their sinister charm at the opening is by having Richard, once his exposition is over, both say what he plans to *do* and then immediately do it. He tells us he plans 'To set my brother Clarence and the King / In deadly hate the one against the other' (1.1.34–5). As Clemen (1986) notes, Shakespeare is here making use – perhaps ostentatiously and playfully – of the medieval 'planning monologue' usually delivered by the Vice. For our present purposes we might also call this, in more general terms, *anticipatory narrated action*. The rush of audience pleasure comes from the 'rhyme' of narrated and staged action – when Clarence immediately enters and the duping begins; an action is described, and then it happens. And that pleasure is intensified by Richard's announcement of Clarence's entry: 'Here Clarence comes' (l. 41). He is in control, and so are we: rhymes make us feel secure. The pleasure puts us in a particular relationship with the duping of Clarence – one that is progressively to be disciplined as the action unfolds.

Pfister (1988) uses the terms 'scenic realisation' and 'narrative mediation' where we have used 'live action' and 'narrated action' respectively. While we have suggested that Shakespeare sets us a snare in the devilishly attractive Richard, Pfister sets out a sophisticated account of the trick played on Malvolio in Shakespeare's *Twelfth Night* (1602), involving both anticipatory *and* retrospective narrated action. We witness the tricksters plan, carry out and then reflect upon the deception. We take delight in the plan and execution on the terms just argued. But that reflection is a sobering experience for characters and audience alike, especially since it is prompted by the more serious, high-ranking characters (pp. 209–11). There is, then, a *moralizing* potential in the interplay between staged and narrated action. Pfister also makes a very good account of Leicester's soliloquy during Mary's execution in Schiller's *Mary Stuart* – a case of *simultaneous* narrated action (pp. 205–7).

## Character perspectives and choric functions

When Ariel reports his tricks on Stephano and the rest, he does so with a vividness that expresses his own pleasure. The same goes for his report of his management of the opening shipwreck: 'the fire and cracks / Of sulphurous roaring the most mighty Neptune / Seem to besiege' (1.2.203–5). This is not instruction to a scenographer, nor is it merely narration – the intensity of these lines comes from a *character perspective*. This is *his* point of view. Narrated action – or 'narrative mediation', in Pfister's terminology – is always potentially from the point of view of a character as much as a message being sent by the playwright. With this example we can go a step further. This particular perspective is one which the character is forced to present: Ariel is eager 'To answer thy [Prospero's] best pleasure' (1.2.190).

In Shakespeare's *Antony and Cleopatra* (1606/7), Enobarbus makes his famous barge speech (2.2.195 ff.). The events he describes predate the play's beginning, but, strictly speaking, this is not exposition – it does not affect our understanding of events. Most regularly, the speech gets trundled out in commentaries as 'evidence' of Cleopatra's character or as 'evidence' of Antony's besottedness. But it is much more than either of these. Especially if we note Enobarbus' competition with the Roman officers, the speech tells us a great deal about Enobarbus himself. Played well, the speech is *simultaneously* deeply engaging for the audience and patently obvious as a piece of private enthusiasm.

When, in *Hamlet*, Gertrude describes Ophelia's death, she describes something that obviously neither she nor anyone else has witnessed. While this would be an impossibility or a deception in real life, Shakespeare's stage was not concerned with plausibilities of this sort. She appears here as *chorus*. The events need to be told. Again, while questions of stageability are perhaps pertinent, they are hardly of great importance. The events are all the more pathetic because distanced from the stage; Ophelia's presence is truly 'lost'. Perhaps also these words produce more pathos than words delivering onstage action, or silent action, possibly could. But most important of all, surely, is that it is *Gertrude* who is at the staged centre of pathos; she is here the subject of empathy, the one who truly and deeply feels. This does not 'mean' that she is guiltless. It contributes to the range of quite separate attitudes the play invites us to take towards her.

A modern use of narrative as a sort of chorus, and certainly as a necessary telling of traumatic events, comes at the end of Dalia Taha's *Fireworks* (2015). The play is set in contemporary Palestine where two families, like the rest of the population, are under siege from Israeli armed forces and subject to regular bombings. The play depicts the ways they cope: dreaming of going away, hoping the war will soon be over, viewing the air-raids as 'fireworks' and telling stories of a heaven where all is at peace. The children absorb the brutalities of warfare into their daily games. At the play's end on the holiday festival of Eid one of the two children is killed during a game. The other child, in her holiday clothes, tells us a story as if it is twenty years later. Her story is of a girl who refuses the assurances that the dead will be happy in heaven: 'the girl thought he's not in the sky, and he's not happy. He's right there, in front of her. She can see him whenever she shuts her eyes.' (p. 78) It's precisely the formal device of the story that has the force to refuse illusions and insist on facing the actuality of death.

As we shall see in chapter 7, the interplay of narrated and live is a device particularly used in late-twentieth and early-twenty-first-century plays.

## Silent narration

Plays, for the most part, tell their own story without the aid of a narrator. The narration is done through the way the scenes succeed one another – *silent narration*. We have seen how narrated action as well as staged action contribute fundamentally to this.

While admitting that what we see and hear on stage is a realization of a script for performance by those who have 'interpreted' or 'produced' it, we can distinguish between staged and narrated action in an important way. The experience of an audience is generally that staged action is there for us to interpret; and we select what we concentrate on, shift our focus. By contrast, narrated action forces our focus in one direction; and it carries its own interpretation of the events reported. It is an account, it has a perspective (Pfister 1988: 204). This perspective can act on us without our knowing it. When it is apparent it can sometimes feel as if the author is making a direct intervention. Thus Cranmer's prophecy about the future Elizabeth I in *Henry 8* (1613) can be taken to be Shakespeare's compliment both to the memory of that queen and to the popular daughter of James I. This experience of a shift in focus can happen of course without a sense of the author intervening, but the move from a sense of interpreting to that of listening can still be palpable. It works that way in Churchill's *Escaped Alone* (see pp. 98–9). As we watch the conversation among friends we look in from outside: the deeper preoccupations of the characters emerge within the flow of the conversation sequentially across the scenes. This flow is frequently broken by Mrs J's direct address to us, compelling our focus on her visions of a future collapsing world.

When looking at silent narration we must be aware how it operates in a filmed play. In film the scenes tend to flow on from one another more smoothly than on a stage, so the sense of inevitable logic of narrative is stronger: we are more vulnerable to the effects of silent narration. But it is also the case that film can powerfully control our focus. Where four characters are having a conversation, as in Churchill's play, the director can instruct the camera to close in on a particular character or sequence of characters. It could also isolate Mrs J (as the original stage director did). When the camera moves and selects a character so it leads our focus as audience. This in turn affects our sense of the relationship between and status of particular characters. This is an instance where film brings its own text – the scheme that organizes camera movement – to the text of the play.

# Character and scenes

## Character distribution

Different plot lines in the same play will involve different sets of characters. These sets may cross over significantly, as is the case with the Gloucester and Lear plot lines in *King Lear*. Goneril, Regan, Cornwall, Albany, Kent and Edgar for a start are all significant players in each. Or the sets may be more or less discrete, with only one or two characters participating in more than one. Such, for instance, would be the case for Hal in *1 Henry 4*, if we say there are separate 'Falstaff ' and 'Henry' plot lines as well as 'worlds' (see p. 164).

Clearly, a useful way to get hold of the plotting of a play is to look at the character distribution scene by scene. The upper table in Figure 4.4 tabulates the distribution of characters from about midway in Shakespeare's *The Tempest*. Whether or not we decide to give separate (sub-)plot status to Prospero's dealings with his daughter, the underlings and the shipwrecked aristocrats, the table helps us get a hold on the design of the play's action. At a glance we can see that either Prospero, Ariel or both are involved in every scene: Shakespeare structurally foregrounds their control of events. Act 3 focuses first on the young lovers and then the servant class. Note who is the agent of control in each: Ariel deals with the underlings. Some sort of dramaturgical decorum seems to be in operation. Then in 3.3, both Prospero and Ariel deal with the aristocrats. In the single scene of Act 4, which contains the betrothal masque, Prospero has the spirits perform for Miranda and Ferdinand, but the servants also appear; perhaps there is some sort of contrast being scripted. And then, in Act 5, all three groups are brought together.

|  | 3.1 | 3.2 | 3.3 | 4.1 | 5.1 | Epilogue |
|---|---|---|---|---|---|---|
| PROSPERO | X |  | X | X | X | X |
| ARIEL |  | X | X | X | X |  |
| MIRANDA | X |  |  | X | X |  |
| FERDINAND | X |  |  | X | X |  |
| ALONSO |  |  | X |  | X |  |
| SEBASTIAN |  |  | X |  | X |  |
| ANTONIO |  |  | X |  | X |  |
| GONZALO |  |  | X |  | X |  |
| ADRIAN |  |  | X |  | X |  |
| FRANCISCO |  |  | X |  | X |  |
| OTHERS |  |  | X |  |  |  |
| CALIBAN |  | X |  | X | X |  |
| TRINCULO |  | X |  | X | X |  |
| STEPHANO |  | X |  | X | X |  |
| MASTER |  |  |  |  | X |  |
| BOATSWAIN |  |  |  |  | X |  |
| 'IRIS' |  |  |  | X |  |  |
| 'CERES' |  |  |  | X |  |  |
| 'JUNO' |  |  |  | X |  |  |
| 'NYMPHS' |  |  |  | X |  |  |
| 'REAPERS' |  |  |  | X |  |  |
| SPIRITS |  |  | X | X |  |  |

|  | 3.1 | 3.2 | 3.3 | 4.1 | 5.1 | Epilogue |
|---|---|---|---|---|---|---|
| Prospero/Ariel | X | X | X | X | X | X |
| Lovers | X |  |  | X | X |  |
| Servants |  | X |  | X | X |  |
| Aristocrats |  |  | X |  | X |  |

FIGURE 4.4 *Character distribution by scene in Shakespeare,* The Tempest, *Acts 3–5 and Epilogue. The lower table is a condensation of the first and reveals the patterning of the action more clearly: see p. 103.*

The Tempest is tragi-comic – it stages the happy resolution of deadly conflict. It is also a Romance: the healing action takes place in an idealized or exotic world, and the play invites our celebration of it as pure invention. One of the ways it does this is by being so clearly *designed*. The plot lines are not merely interwoven: they are woven together in a patterned way – lovers; servants; aristocrats; lovers and servants; all three groups. This patterning is illustrated in the lower table in Figure 4.4.

If you know the play, or want now to read it, you might easily make further comments on the basis of Figure 4.4. But we can also go further with this sort of mapping, as Figure 4.5 will demonstrate. To get there, we need first to ask a question.

# What is a scene?

The scene ends when the lights go down. The mother has died in the daughter's arms and *'the light fades to nothing'*. Or no, the scene ends when the curtains close. The colonel lies dead on the floor and the smoking gun is in the butler's hands: *'curtain'*. Or the king says, 'To battle!' and everyone leaves the stage. *Then* the lights go down or the curtain closes – or both. But what happens on the Elizabethan or Jacobean stage, where there are no front **tabs** or lighting board? What is a scene, and when?

The original texts of several Renaissance plays do not mark scene divisions; others do. A good rule of thumb for editors wanting to insert scene divisions and numbers is that a scene ends when the stage empties. In the Renaissance, you clear the stage so that the next bit of action can begin. The exits are part of the plotting.

We shall see in Chapter 6 (see p. 140) how the flat-and-relief system of shutters, developed after the introduction of scenery in the Restoration, tends to make the change of scene principally a change of location. And persons may be left or discovered on stage at the end or opening of any scene given in relief, upstage of the closing and opening shutters. The later practice of drawing a front curtain between scenes facilitates both scene changes and having the stage unemptied at the head and foot of *each* scene. Sophisticated lighting does the same job as the curtain. From the mid-nineteenth century onwards the scene might change before our very eyes, as part of the entertainment.

Any playtext we meet will observe conventions of scenic division that are tied up with the technical development of the stage. We should note these. Scene divisions are also, of course, an important part of any play's design, as we saw on p. 103. The scene changes when the feel as well as the logic of the action demands it. These breaks are part of what the audience is to experience: something has been established or accomplished; so the scene ends and we all set off to another situation, a fresh episode.

In all that we have so far said in this subsection, the change of scene is tied to a change of situation on stage. For playwrights, actors and audiences in seventeenth-century France, this sense of a new stage situation was felt to occur with the entry or exit of a character – any character except perhaps servants. In the rather formal and statuesque proceedings of the **Neoclassical** stage, then, each new combination of characters is marked – and this includes the playscript – as a new scene.

We can take any dramatic text and divide it into 'French scenes'. It turns out to be a useful exercise. It is useful to production managers and directors in planning whom to call for which rehearsal, for dividing the play up into manageable bits of action. Within the scope of this book, it is especially useful for getting a closer take on the patterning and design of a play's action.

| | 3.1 | | | 3.2 | | 3.3 | | | | | | 4.1 | | | | | | | 5.1 | | | | | | | Epilogue |
| --- | --- | --- | --- | --- | --- | --- | --- | --- | --- | --- | --- | --- | --- | --- | --- | --- | --- | --- | --- | --- | --- | --- | --- | --- | --- | --- |
| | a | b | c | a | b | a | b | c | d | e | f | a | b | c | d | e | f | g | a | b | c | d | e | f | g | a |
| PROSPERO |  | U | X |  |  |  | U | U | U |  |  | X | X | X | X | X | U | X | X | X | U | X | X | X | X | X |
| ARIEL |  |  |  |  | U |  | U | X |  |  |  |  | X |  |  | X | U | X | X |  | M |  | X | X | X |  |
| MIRANDA |  | X |  |  |  |  |  |  |  |  |  | X | X | X | X |  |  |  |  |  |  |  | X | X | X |  |
| FERDINAND | X | X |  |  |  |  |  |  |  |  |  | X | X | X | X |  |  |  |  |  |  |  | X | X | X |  |
| CALIBAN |  |  |  | X | X |  |  |  |  |  |  |  |  |  |  |  | X |  |  |  |  |  |  |  | X |  |
| TRINCULO |  |  |  | X | X |  |  |  |  |  |  |  |  |  |  |  | X |  |  |  |  |  |  |  | X |  |
| STEPHANO |  |  |  | X | X |  |  |  |  |  |  |  |  |  |  |  | X |  |  |  |  |  |  |  | X |  |
| ALONSO |  |  |  |  |  | X | X | X | X |  |  |  |  |  |  |  |  |  |  |  | M | X | X | X | X |  |
| SEBASTIAN |  |  |  |  |  | X | X | X | X | X |  |  |  |  |  |  |  |  |  |  | M | X | X | X | X |  |
| ANTONIO |  |  |  |  |  | X | X | X | X | X |  |  |  |  |  |  |  |  |  |  | M | M | X | X | X |  |
| GONZALO |  |  |  |  |  | X | X | X | X | X | X |  |  |  |  |  |  |  |  |  | M | X | X | X | X |  |
| ADRIAN |  |  |  |  |  | X | X | X | X | X | X |  |  |  |  |  |  |  |  |  | M | M | X | X | X |  |
| FRANCISCO |  |  |  |  |  | X | X | X | X | X | X |  |  |  |  |  |  |  |  |  | M | M | X | X | X |  |
| OTHERS |  |  |  |  |  | X | X | X | X | X | X |  |  |  |  |  |  |  |  |  |  |  |  |  |  |  |
| 'IRIS' |  |  |  |  |  |  |  |  |  |  |  |  |  | X |  |  |  |  |  |  |  |  |  |  |  |  |
| 'CERES' |  |  |  |  |  |  |  |  |  |  |  |  |  | X |  |  |  |  |  |  |  |  |  |  |  |  |
| 'JUNO' |  |  |  |  |  |  |  |  |  |  |  |  |  | X |  |  |  |  |  |  |  |  |  |  |  |  |
| 'NYMPHS' |  |  |  |  |  |  |  |  |  |  |  |  |  | X |  |  |  |  |  |  |  |  |  |  |  |  |
| 'REAPERS' |  |  |  |  |  |  |  |  |  |  |  |  |  | X |  |  |  |  |  |  |  |  |  |  |  |  |
| SPIRITS |  |  |  |  |  | M | M |  |  |  |  |  |  |  |  |  | M |  |  |  |  |  |  |  |  |  |
| MASTER |  |  |  |  |  |  |  |  |  |  |  |  |  |  |  |  |  |  |  |  |  |  |  | X | X |  |
| BOATSWAIN |  |  |  |  |  |  |  |  |  |  |  |  |  |  |  |  |  |  |  |  |  |  |  | X | X |  |

FIGURE 4.5 *French scene analysis of Shakespeare, The Tempest, Acts 3–5 and Epilogue. Key: M – mute; U – onstage unseen by other characters.*

# French scene analysis

Figure 4.5 presents a French scene analysis of the same portion of *The Tempest* as tabulated in Figure 4.4. It is, then, a more thoroughgoing picture of character distribution. We now have the second half of the play divided up into about 25 episodes, or bits of action, and we can see at a glance who is involved in each.

The episodes we have identified are tabulated in Figure 4.6 (see p. 108). Note that we have given each French scene (or episode) a brief title or summary, and selected a key quotation – sometimes two – for each. This work of analysis, basic commentary and selection made us pay close attention to the whole of the text, and gave us a working focus (the French scene) at every moment. Nothing could pass us by. We now have an overview of the play's structure, a handlist of its episodes and key quotations which we can put to use in an essay. Composing the titles and selecting the quotations started the work of detailed commentary on the play – we had to decide what was significant. For instance, for 4.1a we have tried to encapsulate the contradictory nature of the episode – the union Prospero blesses is scripted also to be a trading in women between men. We have similarly foregrounded what looks like deliberate contradiction in 5.1e. Would your choices have been the same as ours?

Figure 4.5 is a bit dazzling at first sight. It makes little sense on its own – the tabulation of Figure 4.6 helps open it up. But Figures 4.5 and 4.6 are of much less use to you than the tables you will make for yourself – for it is in the act of *making* a French scene analysis that we encounter a play's detailed action-design at close hand. The two tables took one of us about three hours to draw. In the course of doing that, enough notes were made to fill a chapter if they were written up. French scene analysis is good preparation for an essay then! The next job would be to select what was useful to attempt the task set by the essay.

Rather than write such an essay here, let us develop just a few points – mostly about the play's design – and leave the rest for you to discover. For instance, we now have 4.1 divided up in such a way that we can see the order in which the two groups of lovers and servants appear. So should we say that there are really two scenes here, not one? Or that the sequence we noted in Figure 4.4 of 'lovers; servants; aristocrats; *lovers and servants*; all three groups' should really go: *lovers*; *servants*; aristocrats; lovers (4.1a–d); servants (4.1f, a–g); all three groups? Not at all. It is indeed 'lovers *and* servants' (4.1a–g) because the stage never empties; Prospero and Ariel remain on stage (4.1e). The scene continues; the two episodes are held together. So the play is designed with even more exquisite playfulness than we had already established. There is a break but not a break. This works on the audience.

Note, too, the 'rhyme' between 3.2a,b and 3.3a,b: in each, we see a group of usurpers divided among themselves; and then a trick is played on them. We might from here develop a commentary on the sequencing, rhythm and build-up of the stage tricks and spectacles in the play.

3.1a    Ferdinand *solus* and the logs – 'most poor matters/Point to rich ends' (3–4)
3.1b    Prospero watches the lovers – 'Fair encounter/Of two most
        rare affections!' (74–5)
3.1c    Prospero *solus* –'So glad of this are they I can not be' (92)
        . . .'For yet ere supper-time must I perform/Much business
        appertaining' (95–6)
3.2a    Usurping servants divided – Cal.: 'Let me lick thy shoe. I'll not serve him' (22/3)
3.2b    Ariel further divides them – 'Thou liest' (43); then once
        reunited leads them astray with music – Cal.: 'The isle is full
        of noises' (130 ff.)
3.3a    Aristocratic  usurpers divided – Seb.: 'The next
        advantage/Will we take throughly' (13–14)
3.3b    The false banquet
3.3c    Ariel as Harpy – 'You are three men of sin' (53ff.)
3.3d    Prospero takes stock – 'My high charms work' (83ff.)
3.3e,f  Processional exit of the aristocrats – Alonso leaves
        distracted; his usurpers follow; Gonzalo and Adrian
        comment, 'All three of them are desperate' (104)

4.1a    Prospero blesses the union – 'as my gift, and thine own
        acquisition/Worthily purchas'd, take my daughter' (13–14)
4.1b    Prospero instructs Ariel ('What would my potent master', 34;
        'Do you love me, no?'48) and Ferdinand ('do not give
        dalliance/Too much the rein' 51–2)
4.1c    The betrothal masque
4.1d    Prospero cuts the masque short – 'I had forgot' ... 'Our revels now are ended'
        . . . 'We are such stuff' (139 ff.)
4.1e    Ariel reports on the servant usurpers
4.1f    *Enter – all wet* and the washing-line gag
4.1g    Prospero takes stock ('At this hour/Lies at my mercy all mine enemies' 261–2)
        and promises Ariel freedom

5.1a    Prospero takes stock ('Now does my project gather to a
        head', 1) and decides that 'the rarer action is/In virtue than in
        vengeance' (27–8)
5.1b    Prospero *solus* – 'But this rough magic/I here abjure' (50–1)
5.1c    Aristocrats in the charmed circle; Prospero rehearses
        forgiveness; Ariel despatched to find the mariners
5.1d    Prospero accuses and forgives – 'Welcome, my friends all!' (125)
5.1e    Ferdinand and Miranda discovered: the game at chess – Mir.:
        'Sweet lord, you play me false' (172); Seb.: 'A most high
        miracle!' (177)
5.1f    Ariel brings on Master and Bo'sun – Alons: 'there is in this
        business more than nature/Was ever conduct of'(243–4)
5.1g    Ariel brings on the servants – Pros.: 'this thing of
        darkness I/Acknowledge mine' (275–6); Ariel set free

Epil.   'Prospero' *solus* as character/servant-performer – 'Let your
        indulgence set me free' (20)

**FIGURE 4.6** The Tempest: *tabulation of episodes identified by Figure 4.5.*

In 4.1c, the betrothal masque, we have a group of onstage spectators. But note also that within this group Prospero is then scripted to become the subject of Ferdinand and Miranda's gaze in 4.1d. The audience's gaze is similarly led; and the audience are thus encouraged to look at Prospero and not *with* him.

We found it difficult at times to decide whether or not to start a fresh French scene – especially when Ariel left or entered the stage. While the play is divided very definitely into episodes, Ariel is scripted to flit in and out of them. Our 'difficulty', then, in fact leads us to an important feature of the play's design, which the last sentence encapsulates.

One place where we decided to make more French scenes than strictly necessary was at 3.3d–f. The sequence in which the aristocrats leave the stage seemed to us important. And we have deliberately used the word 'processional' in our summary title (Figure 4.6) to underline the formal nature of this play.

We have left the betrothal masque undivided for now. But it has its own rhythm, its own aesthetic, which the author is quoting – it is a pastiche of a real court entertainment, and recognizable to the original audience as such.

French scene analysis helps us to see more clearly the way in which the stage empties and fills (see p. 167). We can see, for instance, that the stage fills – with the spirits who deliver Prospero's masque – in the action phase concerning the lovers. Writing 'M' for 'mute' can be a revealing exercise. For instance, we might note while reading *A Midsummer Night's Dream* that all the humans are gathered together for the festivities of the last scene. If we are canny, we might also note the ungenerous way in which the aristocrats are made to poke fun at the mechanicals, introducing a 'minor key' into the romantic comedy ending. But a French scene analysis (in the absence of a walk-through) will quickly demonstrate that Helena and Hermia are scripted to be mute for this scene. Why? What shall we do with this in our production?

And just one more teaser. Note that in 4.1c we have included 'Ceres' but not Ariel. In 4.1e, Ariel says he wondered whether to remind Prospero about Caliban 'When I presented Ceres' (l. 167). One editor, Kermode (1964), asks, 'Why does Ariel mention this?' (p. 105n.). Our work here surely helps us towards the answer he misses – the line is part of the stage trickery and wonder being worked on the audience. We as spectators learn that we have been watching Ariel without knowing it. Productions which choose to make Ariel apparent as a player in the masque miss this opportunity for playful wonder.

## Agon and contradiction

By 'protagonist' we mean the main character in the play. But in fact the word comes from the Greek *proto*('first') and *agonistes* ('actor' or 'combatant'). Aristotle and others tell us that Athenian tragedy evolved out of a religious ritual in which a chorus narrated mythic events. Eventually, the convention developed that one of the chorus would stand out and set up a dialogue with the rest of the chorus. Later on, the **protagonist** began to impersonate people in the story. This is our real **protagonist**, the *first actor*.

But what of this idea of the agonist? Actor and combatant are, in ancient Greek, embraced by the same word. Tied up with this word for actor is the idea of struggle. The actor is not so much an impersonator as the one who struggles.

It is very common to say that struggle, or *agon*, is at the heart of drama. The hero struggles with his adversary, or Fate, or his inner nature. Many plays can indeed be understood in this way. But we might also take the cue from our short account above and say that at the heart of drama is dialogue – not simply speeches, things said by characters, but *debate*, question and answer. Plays struggle – explicitly or implicitly – with ideas and beliefs; one of the most important things about characters is the differences between them. And plays set up a dialogue with the audience, airing differences of idea and belief.

We would be mistaken to think that all drama derives from ancient Greek ritual, or any ritual at all (see Schechner 1988: 1–6). But we can usefully think of drama as something which deals in oppositions, in *contradiction*, difference. A good way into a play is to think about what it sets up in opposition to what: within characters, between characters, between ideas, between itself and the audience, between itself and other ways of telling stories.

A focus on contradiction will help us maintain a sense of plays as *dynamic* artworks, things that are moving because they are on the move.

# 5

# The actor's body

When a group of people sit in chairs and read a play 'round the room', they shut out of their activity a key element that is scripted by the dramatic text – the staged body. In this chapter we shall look at the scripting of the body, asking how the actor's body is told to move and how it is invested with significance. Second, we look at what assumptions are made by the dramatic text about the body: how different sorts of performance possess, and promote, different feelings about the actor's body. Finally, we address the fact that theatre brings real bodies on stage and real bodies in the audience together – in a uniquely productive way.

## Stage directions

We have already said early in the book that stage directions give instructions as to when, where and how the actor is to move. A typical direction might be: '*Sits R[ight], and with a pair of scissors seems busily engaged in trimming the flowers in pots on stand.*' This is an instruction for the actress playing Lady Audley in Hazlewood's *Lady Audley's Secret* (1863: 252); she has just been threatened with blackmail by the drunken gamekeeper who has seen her murder her first husband; now, as the husband's friend enters, she assumes her mask of innocence. With this context in mind we can see that the stage direction scripts a multi-layered picture: trimming flowers is, on the surface, a proper pastime for a Victorian lady, but the actress has to 'seem' to be doing it – we have to watch it as a polished performance of how to be a Victorian lady, done by a character who isn't one. Furthermore the requirement to be 'busily' engaged allows the actress to show hints of that violent energy that killed a husband: it's not just the scissors but also the meticulous concentration that suggest the murderous calculation. This quality, together with the skill of the performance and the decorative charm of the 'lady', gives special charisma to Lady Audley. So the stage directions can script much more than the mechanics of movement or emotional expression: they can give an aura of energy or specialness to an individual.

In the same way a stage group can be organized, not merely mechanically but also into relationships of power and energy. Take an incident in the second scene of D. H. Lawrence's *The Widowing of Mrs Holroyd* (1914): Mrs Holroyd's husband has come back from the pub with two women friends; as he goes to fetch them a drink a rat runs through the open scullery door into the kitchen where they are all sitting. The rat runs under the sofa, centre stage at back; one of the women gets onto the table, downstage and slightly to the left of the sofa; the other woman later scrambles onto the armchair near the table, clinging onto her friend's skirts as she does so; Mr Holroyd, moving upstage, begins to approach the sofa, on which his wife sits. She has this direction and line: '*bunched up on the sofa, with crossed hands holding her arms, fascinated, watches her husband as he approaches to stoop and attack the rat; she suddenly screams*: Don't, he'll fly at you' (p. 159). The group has been organized so that the two drunken women are slightly to one side, in undignified postures. This leaves the serious, central focus on Mr Holroyd's approach to the sofa and his wife. Her attitude is defensive, vulnerable; his is that of the hunter. For a moment there is silence as she watches in fascination. The stage directions have produced a statement about division of gender roles: male as hunter, female as vulnerable, defensive, but fascinated by the hunter. We know, however, that Mrs Holroyd resents and is unhappy with her husband: the actress is invited to time the suddenness with which she shouts out against the tension of the silence, for that shout can indicate not just a fear *for* the husband but also an anxiety at having him so near. The mechanics of this everyday realistic incident are thus scripted by the stage directions, but so too they script a deeper statement about sexual antagonism between two characters within a context of 'natural' (as the play has it) gender roles.

## Implicit stage directions

We said much earlier that many plays, especially Renaissance ones, contain implicit directions for actors. To remind us of that point, and to extend it a little, let us look at a moment in Middleton's *Women Beware Women* (?1621). Bianca has been tricked into a situation in which the Duke can sexually assault her. She reacts with shock to his sudden appearance and he says: 'Prithee tremble not./I feel thy breast shake like a turtle [dove] panting/ Under a loving hand that makes much on't' (2.2.320–2). Clearly his hand is already on her breast, which he can feel panting – but it is more cruel than that, for he insists on making 'much on't', fondling it as one might stroke a captive bird. At the same time, in his speech, the **syntax** is smooth and untroubled, evoking its image of a turtle dove. The very fluency of the verse rhythm produces a breath pattern in the actor which displays bodily control. The mode of speaking thus also scripts the body, producing the power which compels Bianca's 'submission'.

The scripted action here portrays a turning point in Bianca's story. But it is also useful to focus on how the bodies are scripted over a whole play. A good example is supplied by Shakespeare's *King Lear*. In the ceremonial opening scene the bodies are required to move with the public display and formal measure of a state occasion. Halfway through the play, the clothes are drenched with water, dirtied or torn off the bodies. One of the elderly bodies is bent over, in the stocks; another is imprisoned in a chair, while his eyes are gouged out. The movement across the stage is the uncertainty of the blind or speediness of the mad. At the end of the play bodies are left to litter the stage, their dead weight insisted upon in the image of a pietà (the dead Christ on the Virgin Mary's lap), from which this time there is no resurrection. We could say that the scripting requires that the actors' bodies become steadily more clumsy and move irresistibly from the stature of upright dignity to being folded over and brought close to the ground. This scripted action for the body clearly reinforces the play's bleak picture of human life.

# Costumes and props

## *How props and costumes function*

There are two other methods by which the actor's body is instructed or controlled by the text – through what it is required to wear and through the stage props it has to deal with. A stage prop, most broadly understood, is a part of the setting that is specially distinctive in that it can be used or handled.

One of the reasons a dramatist is interested in specifying costume and props is that these can be used to give information to the audience. Shakespeare insists on what Hamlet wears when we first see him: the second scene of the play presents Claudius in the middle of his court, but in the festivity one figure stands out, because he is wearing black – Hamlet. The costume is a neat way not only of indicating that Hamlet is in mourning, but that he is different from the rest of the world around him. Claudius too can also be made to stand out, by ensuring that he has a crown on his head. Dressed like the rest of the court, Claudius is part of his community but, as crown wearer, he is the ruler of it. Hamlet's difference is more fundamental, in that spiritually he isn't even part of this community. He stands out even more than Claudius does. His separateness and the political threat of that will constitute a major part of the play's narrative. All of this is indicated by use of costume (blackness) and prop (the crown).

So a major function of costume and prop is **semiotic**, making meanings for an audience. The props that the playscript insists on are thus usually more than mere parts of the scenic setting – they come to our particular attention because they carry meaning. We can see this if we go back to the direction that asks Lady Audley to trim flowers (quoted on p. 111). It is unsurprising that she should use a tool to do her domestic gardening. But in the hands of the murderess the activity of the scissors becomes grimly significant. The activity offers us a message that Lady Audley is attempting to behave like an aristocratic lady, but that there is an undercurrent of violence to her. The prop stands out because it has semiotic force.

But it has a second quality. In doing the trimming, the actress has to concentrate her energies into the use of a small instrument – the scissors. Earlier she had employed very large gestures, so now her body seems constrained in its size. The use of the prop imposes a discipline on the performer's muscles. Alongside its significance, its intellectual effect, it has a physical effect. This ability to change how the performer has to move gives the scissors power as an actual object – the precise operation of its mechanism, its shape which is sharp at one end, all of these real physical characteristics have to be respected by the performer. Part of the force of the prop on stage is that it is a real object with specific shape, size, weight. Its reason for being there is to be the real thing.

So, with regard to the performer's body, the use of costumes and props can control movement. A corset or neck ruff pulls it tight at particular places, coping with a long dress or trailing cloak requires speed and balance of movement to be regulated. For handling a sword or, as in Stephens' *One Minute* (2003), a pool cue, you need to use different muscles and ranges of movement than you do for handling a fan. This produces different images of how the body relates to the space around it – the person wielding a sword, or drunkenly flailing a pool cue, seems to extend out into space, pushing into it, slicing through it; the person fluttering a fan seems to be drawing inward from the space, enclosing themselves, keeping their hand close to their face. These images then imply different things about the body making the movement – a person reaching into space feels more active and expansive than a person drawing back from space, a difference that has been often ascribed to the sex of the person. So the use of prop or costume can affect not simply how the actor moves but also how the audience feels about that movement, and about the character that makes it. The playscript which requires particular props or costumes is by this means constructing a relationship between audience and character which need have nothing to do with narrative information.

## *Historical varieties*

So far we have spoken of props and costume in general terms. But we now need to note that they are used differently, they have been controlled by different conventions, at various periods of dramatic history. The actual words we have been using – props and costume – tell us something of this varied history. 'Props' is short for 'properties', objects that belong to – are 'proper' to (French 'propre') – the person who is using them, and this tends to be the sense in which the word was used on Shakespeare's stage. Prospero has his staff, the object that marks his magical power; Richard 2 has his crown. In the famous scene of the formal deposition of Richard he hands his crown to Bolingbroke, but it is not an instant act. He holds out the crown and, while Bolingbroke extends his arm to receive it, Richard pauses there, calling our attention to the visual image which he likens to a well with two buckets – while one goes up the other goes down. And he still doesn't hand it over. When Bolingbroke asks whether he is going to do it, he hesitates again, and then finally hands it over. It is an extended business, and the tension in it derives precisely from the fact that it is uncertain where the crown belongs. The longer it is held in the air, the less status it seems to have. It is as if it isn't really an object in its own right, but depends for its significance in being placed on someone's head, belonging to someone. Shakespeare is using the theatrical characteristic of the property in a way that implies a political point. The same question that the crown prop provokes may be asked about the monarchy, which the crown stands for – does it have an intrinsic value or is it open to power struggle, a contest over belonging?

The word 'costume' also has a history. It tends to denote the characteristic dress of a country or period or class of people. This usage dates from the early nineteenth century. On Shakespeare's stage they would have used a different word: 'attire'. The structure at the back of the stage in the Globe was called a tiring house, where actors put on their attire. This word is much less specific than costume: costume is to do with suggesting categories and conformity, 'period costume'; attire is just something you wear. And that openness, without bothering about uniform characteristics, seems to have marked its use on the Renaissance stage. There is a manuscript drawing thought to be an illustration of Shakespeare's early play *Titus Andronicus*, which is set in ancient Rome. In the picture two men wear doublet and hose, two have breastplates and Roman kilts; there is a woman in an elaborate dress with long hair, and a man in a sort of short toga with a wreath on his head. This is clearly not period costume, but it is also not haphazard. The least important characters, soldiers, are wearing Elizabethan attire; the most important character is the most Roman (we know about the importance because we can relate these figures to the narrative of the play). Other differences are marked as well: the men in breastplates are of fighting age, younger than the man in the toga. The woman, acted by a boy, is in a lavish dress. This indicates that she is decadent and corrupt – like her hair she is 'loose'. So the use of Renaissance attire here is motivated not by the desire to create atmosphere, to suggest a category like nation or period, but by the need to communicate information – about status, age, occupation, morality. This is not creating a realistic world, it is *emblematic*.

Even when 'costume' becomes the norm, that's to say when a designed clothing scheme is regularly used to suggest where and when the play is set, there remain different conventions to its usage. In melodrama, for instance, the villain tended to wear black and the innocent heroine was in white. This convention lasted into Hollywood westerns, where villain and hero are indicated by clothing colour. At his first appearance the villain is clearly marked, and his clothing makes him look similar, and links him, to a whole range of melodramatic villains. What we are looking at is not so much an individual as a type (see p. 28), and we expect him to behave according to type. Indeed, when one nineteenth-century actor tried replacing the traditional black wig with a blond one, the audience expressed their hostility. This story suggests that audiences take pleasure in characters that behave according to type – like watching an acrobat or stunt rider, you want to see them do what you know they have the potency to do. This sort of response to *typification* needs to be borne in mind when a playscript seems to start piling on a whole series of predictable details: it may be trying to generate a particular sort of pleasure.

## *Realisms*

It has been argued by Stanton B. Garner Jr (1994) that with realism the whole relationship between acting bodies and props is fundamentally changed.

To begin to illustrate this, let's revisit the Shakespearean stage. In the text of *King Lear* the Duke of Kent is put in the stocks in Act 2 scene 2; in the next scene we are with Edgar alone; then we return to the Duke of Kent. It is supposed by editors that the stocks were not moved from the stage and brought back on again, but that they remained on stage, with Kent asleep in them, while the intervening scene was played. There is no lighting or flown scenery to mask these stocks. So we have to assume that the audience, seeing that nothing was happening in them (Kent being 'asleep'), agreed to ignore them. As a prop the stocks seem to be both there and not there: their physical existence becomes apparent only as and when the human action requires it.

By contrast consider the props that appear in the opening minutes of Lawrence's *The Widowing of Mrs Holroyd*. She enters with a basket heaped full of washing from off the clothesline. From these she 'lifts out a white heap of sheets and other linen, setting it on the table; then she takes a woollen shirt in her hand'. This is still slightly damp, so she spreads it on the back of the rocking chair in front of the fire. She is then interrupted, but after a brief conversation she 'continues placing the flannel garments before the fire, on the fender and on chair-backs, till the stove is hedged in with a steaming fence'. In semiotic terms, whiteness is to be a key element of the play. As it appears here, we see the stage becoming whiter: the work of the woman seeks to remove the dirt of the coal mine, but the evidence of that work takes over the living space, changing the function of furniture – it's slightly claustrophobic. We might also note that the stage is giving over real time to the display of woman's work, in all its difference, and seriousness, and effort.

But we haven't yet articulated what Garner says was really new about this sort of staging. We get close in noting that the stage activity takes real time. The actress is not pretending to work, she is actually spreading clothes on furniture. Her body has to strain and bend in relation to the weight and quantity of the washing. And – crucially – Lawrence imagines it steaming in front of the fire. So, even when the action moves elsewhere, the washing carries on with the process of drying. It seems to have an existence of its own in a way that Kent's stocks do not. The stage is interested in, and requires, their dampness, whereas Shakespeare's stage was not interested in the quality of metal in a gold crown.

There are two consequences from this realist use of props. The first is that these objects really are the things they claim to be, and the presence of a collection of such objects on a stage gives to the stage a feeling of particular detail, of differentiated surfaces, of material density. These objects are not just signs. And the second consequence is that, with all these real objects around, we become more conscious of how the actor's body relates to them. They demand of the woman playing Mrs Holroyd an effort of work as a performer, and, within the fiction, they show how the character is surrounded by, caught up in, her daily chores.

The props, so to speak, *ground* the body in the efforts of their own material existence. They also do a second thing – they seem to extend the body's influence on the space around it. In *Widowing* as Mrs Holroyd spreads clean washing around her the outside world comes in through the door in the shape of Blackmore in his pit-dirt. A limit is set upon her *spatial expansion*. Contrast this with scene 12 of Brecht's *Life of Galileo* (in the third, 1953, version of the play). The new Pope, Urban VIII, is receiving the Cardinal Inquisitor. The opening stage direction says that 'in the course of the audience he is robed'. The scene demonstrates how the Cardinal Inquisitor persuades the Pope, who has an interest in science, to take action against Galileo. There is no other mention of the costuming activity until just before the end of this three-and-a-half-page scene: 'The Pope is now in his full robes.' And the Pope concedes that 'at the very most' Galileo can be shown the 'instruments' of torture.

To read the dialogue alone is to see how one man cleverly persuades another. But what is happening visually tells us something more. The Pope is becoming a physically more substantial figure as he is robed. Those robes literally extend his body into more of the space. What this signifies is the movement between the intellectual individual who was Cardinal Barberini and the public function which is Pope Urban VIII. Fully robed as Pope, Urban takes a decision against Galileo which has nothing to do with science and everything to do with the institutional authority of the Church. At the same time, the man wearing the robes does his best to limit the punishment. He will show Galileo the instruments, not use them; but showing the instruments is still the first step in the process of enforcing the Church's will. This unresolved tension between person and function is staged by the costuming activity. The scene as Brecht writes it, with the robing continuously accompanying the dialogue, shows that rational argument is caught up into institutional positioning in the process of human and historical decisions.

Brecht's scene demonstrates how costuming is a political process. We can understand how the authority of the papacy is being built before our eyes, through the robing, and at the same time we feel the force of that robed body as a spatial entity. We are here a long way from any assumption that the prop is simply a property, something that 'naturally' belongs to the character. Props and costumes do something to the body that handles or wears them. The robes put upon Cardinal Barberini institutionally transform him into Urban VIII. As he stands there passively, the robes seem to have the more forceful existence. In a similar way Paul, in Stephens' *Motortown* (2006), discusses society: 'The only thing we can do is feast ourselves on comfort foods and gobble up television images. Sport has never been more important.' He then talks about internet porn. His analysis is cynical, eloquent and blunt to the point of violent: the poor he says 'have tiny parameters of possibility and a miniscule spirit of enquiry or investigation. They would be better off staying in their little holes and fucking each other. And killing each other. And the girls are so vapid.' (pp. 171–2) In part what is violent about this is the articulate handling of linguistic register. This is underlined and elaborated by Paul's activity. Wearing half-moon glasses he uses a tiny screwdriver to adapt a gun that Danny has bought. The work is very detailed and meticulous, and continues while Paul talks. Where it is all leading is the modification of the gun into a functioning weapon. When he has finished Paul hands Danny something with which he can kill people. The making of the gun sets the context for, and reveals the potential violence lurking in, the meticulous articulation.

The relationship between body and object became the stock material of realism's wildest comic form – farce. In farces objects commonly get lost and turn up when you least want them. This sort of comic business depends on a disruption of the old assumed relationship in which props are simply there to be used and handled by characters. In the first act of Pinero's *Trelawny of the 'Wells'* (1898) Ablett has turned up to wait at the farewell dinner of a group of theatrical friends (see also p. 205). He has arrived in his waiter's outfit, only to discover that he has brought two left gloves: 'During the rest of the act he is continually in difficulties through his efforts to wear one of the gloves upon his right hand' – and it keeps turning up where he doesn't want it. Objects are getting out of hand, so to speak.

While the farce object's refusal to comply is hilarious, that refusal takes on a more sinister potential in one of late twentieth-century drama's favoured props, the mobile phone. For example: in Hussain's *Blood* (2015) Sully is forcibly split from his girlfriend Caneze, beaten up and taken to Pakistan. He is told not to contact her. In a sequence of scenes she rings him, he turns his phone off (because he has been warned she will be injured if he contacts her), he twice picks up his phone then puts it down, she waits for texts. The phone comes to represent not an everyday mechanism of communication but something which has been diverted from its purpose by the violence its use can unleash. Every time it is not used it evidences the invisible network of relations in which Sully and Caneze are caught. This begins to suggest something of the potency, and dramaturgic eloquence, of fairly 'ordinary' props.

Stanton Garner develops his argument by suggesting that in the second half of the twentieth century the realist stage, rather than discussing, and joking about, the relationship of body and props confronts the body with objects that have no clear function in relation to it. By way of example, he analyses Pinter's *The Caretaker* (1960) which has a lengthy description of the setting, including 'a couple of suitcases, a rolled carpet, a blow-lamp, a wooden chair on its side, boxes, a number of ornaments, a clothes horse, a few short planks of wood, a small electric fire and a very old electric toaster'. These objects were clearly once owned and used, but they no longer have a functional relationship with humanity. Instead we now only notice that they are clutter. Not only do they not have a function, but there doesn't seem to be any order in the piles of them. Garner remarks that the character Davies 'struggles to find a place for himself in this de-functionalized environment' (p. 114). His placelessness is imaged in the story by the missing papers that would prove who he is. What Pinter is suggesting is a world where the human being is no longer in control of his environment, not able to make sense of it. At the same time he becomes aware of the limits of his body, its vulnerability to an outside world which surrounds him with clutter. Human control has lost the things which were, in a different sense, its props.

How do you make sense of a stage piled with rubbish? What is it for? For an audience as well as for Davies this is unsettling. Pinter's plays were labelled 'Absurdist' early on, because their world didn't seem rational. It also seemed peculiarly modern in its unsettled view of humanity. It is a long way from props as properties. But that distance shows rather vividly how in different periods of drama props and costumes are handled very differently. And not only that, but in their different handling can be seen images of the relationship between bodies and objects. This relationship comes from, and suggests, philosophical ideas about human beings and their worlds. Props and costumes are thus much more than performance accessories.

## What scripts assume about actors' bodies

At the start of this book we glanced at the matter of conventions of performance, and said that in any one period there would be the dominant conventions, residual ones from a previous time and emergent ones. The scripting for the actor's body may assume an already-existing convention for playing; it may wish to challenge this convention, or it may seek to develop a new one. If one is merely reading stage directions it is not always possible to visualize that familiar actions may be done according to very different conventions, that standing and walking may entail different attitudes in different theatres. In some respects this understanding of the different conventions which are being scripted only comes from knowing a little about various theories of performance, as we shall show later. But it is also possible, first, to see how the dialogue text assumes, and scripts, a particular sort of bodily action.

## The bodies assumed by dialogue

In the scene from *The Widowing of Mrs Holroyd*, above, the script assumes that Mrs Holroyd's line will be shouted as if it had been dragged out of her, impulsively, by the crisis. The actress will have worked hard to produce a sense of a person in the grip of circumstances. Contrast with this Lady Bracknell's response, in Wilde's *The Importance of Being Earnest* (1895), on hearing that Jack has lost both his parents: 'To lose one parent, Mr Worthing, may be regarded as a misfortune; to lose both looks like carelessness' (p. 360). Clearly this line is not trying to imitate realistic speech, nor even to sustain characterization. Its manner is derived, residually, from comedies of wit, within which the performer herself displays conspicuous skills in timing and verbal acrobatics. Wilde's line assumes, and reinforces, a poised body, which holds itself back through the network of pauses on the punctuation marks until the punchline is delivered. The punchline is expected because of the balanced **syntax**; but it is also expected because the speech requires the performer's body to move between personal conversation, with 'Mr Worthing', and public address. That public address is produced by the lifting of the head and upper torso as the performer breathes in time with the syntax. It is this technique which Wertenbaker uses to show how Liz's body can be transformed from that of a convict into something more 'civilised' when Liz says: 'Your Excellency, I will endeavour to speak Mr Farquhar's lines with the elegance and clarity their own worth commands' (*Our Country's Good* 1988/1991: 83).

This scripting that holds the body in equilibrium contrasts, deliberately, with the sudden distortions and extensions of the body required by melodrama: 'He is gone – gone! and no one was a witness to the deed!' (*Lady Audley's Secret* 1863: 248). To say the second 'gone' with the necessary additional emphasis the performer has to organize her muscles to produce the right sound, which, quite apart from any added gestures, creates the apparent size of melodrama. It was in a bid to limit that size, and the distorted body, that Robertson used the everyday furniture in *Caste* (1867), directing that an actor 'has been twisting about' with a chair during a speech (p. 139): to have to act with the chair is to limit the size of the body's movements, and concentrate them on an everyday object. In a similar way Shakespeare ended the performance mode which Marlowe had scripted in *Tamburlaine* (*c*.1587), where the long sentences flowing across several verse lines require a great deal of breath, and breath control, having the effect of inflating the body (as for an opera singer) and causing it to walk with a strutting movement: Hamlet, by contrast, has lines with numerous breaks in them.

## Bodies scripted by theories of performance

In 1803 the German theatre director Goethe developed rules for actors, which were based on the idea that graceful performance would be developed by the study of classical statues (see Nagler 1959: 428–33). This body is assumed by the plays of Goethe's contemporary, Schiller: in a work such as *Mary Stuart* (1800) this classical body is under threat from a newly emerging passion, the tension between the two inhabiting the performed text of the play and giving it its force.

In scene 4 of Brecht's *The Good Person of Setzuan* (1943b), Shu Fu the barber ejects Wang the water seller from his shop, and then strikes Wang's hand with his curling iron. When Wang asks others sitting outside to act as legal witnesses, '*all are … eating. No one looks up.*' They are deliberately ignoring him. Much in the way that we saw Desdemona composed into a formal picture on p. 6, Brecht here composes a clear picture of social attitudes. The Unemployed Man, Grandfather and Sister-in-Law selfishly fill their bellies while ignoring someone else in need. Brecht called such a picture a *gestus*. Willett (1977: 173) usefully glosses this word as referring at once to 'gesture', a physical attitude, and 'gist', a main point. The gestus of eating the rice physicalizes a typical social attitude. Brecht wants us to ask where this attitude comes from. The class and employment status of the characters will matter.

Now, just before Wang asks for witnesses, two contrasting propositions are put to him. Shen Te says he should see a doctor, quick. But the Unemployed Man says, 'He doesn't want the doctor; he wants the magistrate! The barber's a rich man, and he ought to get compensation.' Both Mrs Shin and Wang think this is a very good idea. Wang enthusiastically says, 'It's already very swollen. Would it mean a pension for life?' Fearing that the swelling may be going down, but reassured by the others that it hasn't, '*Holding his hand very carefully and still looking at it, he hurries off.*' It is a moment of great comedy, a gift to the performer. But it is also, of course, a very fine gestus. Wang carries his hand *both* as a precious part of his body that has been wounded and hurts, *and* as a precious object that he can use to get cash. With great economy, Brecht physicalizes the contradiction between going to a doctor for the sake of health and going to a judge for compensation – between the value of the hand in terms of its usefulness, and its exchange value, its price. For Brecht and other Marxists, capitalism reduces everything to its exchange value and prevents us from seeing the real use-value of things. This threatens our well-being and perhaps our survival. Wang is about to endanger/ruin his body for the sake of profit. In this comic gestus, Brecht not only uses the actor's (Wang's) body to deliver the gestus. The body is also the direct subject of the gestus. Marxism is about human survival.

There is another gestus on stage too. We saw in Chapter 2 how Brecht wants his actors to *demonstrate* the character they are showing. They take up an attitude to the character, and to the audience, and they do this for a reason. Brecht's theatre deliberately seeks out its social purpose. Underlying the gestus of Wang's hand is the gestus of the Brechtian performer. The performer makes clear in her or his attitude the social relationship that is being sought between stage and audience. Whenever we read or perform Brecht's plays, we need constantly to keep both these levels of gestus in mind.

# The body and the audience

## *The body as a specific object of attention*

We have established how dialogue, stage directions and conventions of playing can variously script the state, bearing and conduct of the actor's body. We have also looked at the relationships between props and costumes and the actor's body. Let us now begin to think more explicitly about the audience, and the various ways in which the staged body may be regarded and experienced by them. And let us start that journey by looking at occasions when the body is foregrounded by the dramatic text.

In certain sorts of theatre and many accounts of plays and performances, it is as if the body is principally there to carry the story, to deliver the dialogue. We might say that the body is a 'vehicle' for them. The banal realism that succeeded high Naturalism is one sort of theatre that seems to invite such a reception – the audience take no special notice of the body before them. Some commentators have pictured this as the audience 'looking through' the actual body on stage to the story, to events that might as well be happening in a book. They say that the body becomes relatively 'transparent'. And, even in formal modes of production like the Neoclassicism of Goethe and Schiller, the mode of the body can still become for an audience a sort of carrier wave for the message of the play or its recounting of events. Even such a formalized body can for some in some circumstances be regarded simply as a transparent sign vehicle – like these marks on this page or screen that you are making sense of now. Look for a moment at the marks themselves.

We have looked (see p. 116) at how stage properties can become foregrounded as objects in their own right. In a similar way, bodies onstage are sometimes scripted to become foregrounded as bodies. In those moments we have examined – Lady Audley cutting flowers; Mrs Holroyd tensely immobile; Bianca assaulted by the Duke – it is as if the stage bodies become more concrete for us, more immediate. Even after such moments, they can readily recede again to the function of transparent sign vehicle – if our habits of **reception** help incline us that way. Yet there are plays and other scripted events in which the apprehension of body as body is especially foregrounded, and sometimes in a sustained way.

Consider again the Duke's assault on Bianca in Middleton's *Women Beware Women* (?1621). As she struggles, he advises, 'This strength were excellent employ'd in love now, / But here 'tis spent amiss … / I'faith you shall not out, till I'm released now.' (2.2.328–31). While the lines work as implied stage directions to prescribe the struggle, they also act discursively as part of the whole play's concerns with desire, power and responsibility. The Duke insists on his authority to prescribe the conduct of Bianca's body. Note especially how he twists the language of courtship. He aligns her struggle with his supposed metaphorical imprisonment in love for her. He has the power to use language to excuse and mask physical domination. More than this – the word 'release' strongly connotes ejaculation. He will rape her. These few lines encapsulate the distance between her human (bodily) integrity and his brief pleasure that rests on absolute power, as well as the distance between the mask of language and the materiality of the body. But there are of course more than 'lines' here. Let us not forget that the audience are scripted to witness the assault: there is a physical discourse of desire and power at work throughout the play. The lines script a physical action directly concerned with body and selfhood – and they steer our response to it.

We noted on p. 12 how stage directions entirely displace dialogue in Act 3 scene 3 of Galsworthy's *Justice* (1910). The young man Falder, with whom the play positions us to sympathize, is in prison – a place that the play suggests will simply brutalize him. The directions closely choreograph a sequence of movements: he is first 'seen standing motionless, with his head inclined towards the door, listening' (p. 261). His state is labile – a spring of energy interrupts the increasingly intent listening, only to give way to a collapse into despair. His relationship to objects in the cell is alienated – his finger runs along the distempered walls; he looks dumbly at his sewing work. At the end of the scene, he hammers in frenzy at the door, joining the clamour of other unseen prisoners. At one point, Falder moves 'like an animal pacing its cage' (p. 261). The gestus (see p. 121) points two ways: to natural vitality denied; and to humanity reduced to the animal. This scene, written directly as physical action, scripts a body bereft of all significant action. While Aristotle favoured empathy based on our perception of ethos (see p. 88), he admitted that it can flow from the spectacle. And here is a special kind of spectacle, of a body deprived of ethos: it has no intercourse with others, nothing meaningful to do, no prospect of projecting itself into the world.

## *The stage body and the body of the spectator*

Let us now approach more directly the relationship between the stage body and the body of the spectator. The medieval Corpus Christi cycles evolved out of annual processions celebrating the fundamental truth of the mass – that the ceremonial bread transubstantiated into the flesh of Christ, the wine into his blood. The cycles consist of plays that sequentially tell the Christian history of the world, from its creation to its end. The earliest-written and religiously central plays are those telling of the birth and death of Christ, whose self-sacrifice on behalf of humanity was seen as making sense of the whole narrative. The York Crucifixion (C15) is one of the most famous, especially because of the graphic manner in which it deals with Christ's body. Most of the dialogue is given to the four Soldiers who conduct the crucifixion. Jesus himself speaks just twice. When he is brought on by his executioners, he announces that he will die to save mankind. And later, when sardonically asked by the Soldiers what he thinks of their handiwork as they raise him on the cross, he forgives them, as the Bible records. But, in accordance with this being a theatrical, **rhetorical**, occasion, Jesus has more to say. He instructs the audience to 'Behold mine head, mine hands, and my feet' (l. 255) – they must take care not to waste his suffering.

This injunction to learn from Christ's suffering is made in the context of the audience having just witnessed scenes of the utmost cruelty. At the start, the Soldiers congratulate themselves for having prepared well for the killing. The cross lies on the ground ready, and, when Jesus is brought on, they tell him to 'bend thy back unto this tree' whereupon they set out to 'fetter him' (ll. 74, 78). Speaking about rather than to him – and only as an object, and one about to suffer – they squabble and vie with one another to tie his hands, and to stretch his 'limbs on length' (l. 85). The language redoubles the action for the audience, as well as scripts it for the players. A nail will, one says, stand fast 'through bones and sinews' (l. 103). But they cannot nail him completely yet: the body does not fit the cross. 'It fails a foot and more' because 'The sinews are so gone in' (ll. 107–8). So they decide to tie cords, 'And tug him to, by top and tail' (l. 114). An extended sequence of stretching the body to fit the cross ensues so, as they say, that the job will look well done and Jesus suffer the more. When they have done, 'asunder are both sinews and veins / On ilka side' (ll. 147–8). Finally, the cross is raised. The Soldiers argue over it, one complaining of exhaustion and another that his back aches. They celebrate the fact that dropping the cross into the mortice will break all his bones; and, in a final ghoulish moment, they scrabble around for wedges as the cross sways in a hole made too big for it.

We might accurately say that the York Crucifixion makes Christ's bodily suffering insistently present to its audience. But there is more to the 'truth' of the presentation than this construction of immediate bodily presence. There is, for its audience, the embodiment of an ethical truth. While the Soldiers complain about their labour, Christ dies patiently to save them from sin. And while the Soldiers 'know not what they do' (Bible, Luke 23 v. 34 – echoed in l.261, 'What they work, wot they not'), the audience by deliberate contrast are in a position to know that Christ has died for them. Their sin and their complaints about their own suffering as it were repeatedly crucify Jesus. It is especially poignant that, in line with the plays being presented by the appropriate trade guilds, the York Pinners – makers of nails – were responsible for the Crucifixion play. The immediate physical labour of the everyday is brought, in a confessional manner, into the centre of the play. There is a declared bodily contract between stage and spectator.

We can only speculate, but the play seems especially constructed so as to prompt a **kinaesthetic** response from the spectators. They stand and watch a precious body being stretched and broken. Their bodies have particular investments (they have a special interest) in the body – even bodies – on the stage, and will respond accordingly. In the case of this late medieval audience, we might identify some obvious cultural factors that structure that investment. Included in these is a religious belief in the inseparability and indeed interpenetration of the everyday and the divine. One's body is part of God's universe: it is on loan from God. The relationship between the spectator's body and that of Christ is already culturally scripted. And it follows, of course, that the body of the amateur player personating Jesus on the pageant wagon is also part of God's universe. Again, we can only speculate on the degree to which that body becomes apparent in itself to any one fifteenth-century spectator. But insofar as it is present, then added into the mix is the 'doubleness' of that body as tending towards both the representational/sacred and the communal/profane that we note below (see p. 205).

We should take care not to suggest that, ultimately, 'ideas' shape the body. In the eighteenth century, idealist philosophers developed the model of a radical and hierarchical separation between mind (above) and body (below). And, while many cultures and moments within them assume some sort of division, most assume at the least some interplay between the 'two'. A Marxist, for instance, would say that a particular thought is produced in the context of particular physical practices – a peasant woman thinks differently from her sister who works in a factory. A prevailing sense in Western theory now is of mind as a bodily activity. It is bodies that do the thinking. We live in our bodies: or rather, we are our bodies and what our bodies do. Theatrical reception is an activity of the body.

There will, then, be a number of **determinations** on the scripted encounter of stage body with the body of the spectator – not only in the York Crucifixion but also, say, in Bianca's rape or Falder's incarceration. Included in these determinations will be the cultural status of the actor's own body. The Restoration actress was subjected to the prurient gaze of men in the audience; Renaissance players were blamed for telling untruths by the very fact of personating others – hence their bodies were subject to laws of containment; young men playing women on the Renaissance stage were variously celebrated or condemned as bodies of ambiguous gender (see p. 200).

We should note, lastly, here that this relationship of the various bodies becomes very different when you watch plays on film or DVD. Sitting effectively alone in the dark and physically overwhelmed by a film screen, many audience members feel as if the screen person 'flows into' them. Here, perhaps even more than on the stage, lighting, sound and other aspects of design condition our reception of character and body. In some periods, music has been so continuously present as not to be consciously noted by most cinema-goers, while it has been a key element in determining reception.

What similarities and differences are there between this sort of film and say a realist play? Watching bodies on the screen is not like looking at them on a stage; for one thing, they cannot look back. The actor will undoubtedly have played the scenes in a scattered order, according to the logistics of the shooting script. Further, script here and in television has a different status and function from the dramatic text. It is developed through its various forms from outline through treatment, script and storyboard, as the production develops. Even where the play exists, it has added to it a script for camera and effects. Watching movies, the focus of our attention is directed by the camera and the edit. We look from 'impossible' angles. There is often a strong pull away from scenes of interpersonal action to scenery as a thing in itself. It is worth bearing such considerations in mind when watching films of plays. Often perfectly good works of art in their own right, they work quite differently from stage productions, and to a quite distinctive script.

Watching television can place us in a different relation to the screen and our surroundings from cinema, and so conditions our **reception** differently. Not only is the screen smaller, even in the case of large TV screens which offer more 'immersive' viewing,, but the focus can also be different: we might chat or do the ironing while watching, or pop to the kitchen to make a drink. We no longer share the same rhythm as the staged action. DVD and some televisions allow us to control and selectively replay the flow of events, changing our experience of narrative, and of the interplay between the past-tense of story and the present-tense of viewing. Further, DVD permits not only this but access at any point to actors, directors, writers and designers who will talk about and show aspects of the production process, other versions of the story. Any of these considerations affect our experience of 'drama' in non-theatrical media.

## *The stage and the body in culture*

From noting how various stage bodies are scripted to behave and appear, we have moved to considerations of the relationships between stage bodies and spectating bodies. And we have noted that, in order to delve into these relationships, we shall not only need to consider the direct scripting of the body and the prevailing stage conventions. We shall also need to think about the ways in which bodies are lived in the culture; and about any number of abstractable sorts of response between the stage body and the spectating one, from kinaesthesia to fantasies of identification, as well as the cultural or personal status of the player.

Let us turn, then, to the ways in which bodies are lived in the culture – and approach the question through the theatre. We said above that the theatre of banal realism invites its audience to regard the stage body as relatively transparent, to disregard it as a body. We can think of this in terms of what we have called authenticating conventions (see p. 36). The calm and decorous body of the banal realist stage was then accepted as the appropriate vehicle for the drama – 'unnaturally' large gestures or vocal range would be deemed excessive. As Peter Womack (1996) has wittily argued, the 'realism' of this drama in terms of plot is not simply to do with the accurate mimicry of life. It is about being 'realistic' about life, not expecting too much from it – about the virtues of making do as opposed to struggle. And this sense is carried too in the bodies both on the stage and in the auditorium. The audience sit in silence, mostly formally dressed, composed in the theatre and satisfied with life outside it.

We began here by also mentioning the **Neoclassical** stage and its own sense of decorum. As we noted in connection with Sarah Siddons' Neoclassical performance in Hannah Cowley's *The Fate of Sparta* (1788) (see p. 98), this decorum is based on a tension between truth to life – especially with respect to emotional states – and the civilizing restraint of artistic composition. This was echoed in the bodily attitude of many in the middle-class audience: the cult of sensibility had encouraged an openness to experience and a directness of emotion – but always conducted with discretion, restraint (see Barker-Benfield 1992). We can picture the audience response to the play as being structured by this tension. At another tragedy, for instance, a parson caused deep offence by giggling – until it was understood that he was overcome with emotion, that the giggling was a symptom of his desperate containment of grief.

It would, of course, be quite wrong to assume that all conventions of playing directly mirror the dominant bodily habits of a culture. The stage is precisely a place culturally licensed for extraordinary behaviour. But there will always be a discernible connection between the corporeal regimes of a culture or subculture (what it is proper for bodies to do) and what it expects or allows its players to do with their own staged bodies – and this forms part of the relationships of bodies across the theatrical divide. This connection, and the expectations to which it gives rise, are put under particular pressure in plays dealing with non-dominant or minority groups. The most obvious case is that of the disabled performer. In her plays for such performers Kaite O'Reilly produces texts that collide with normative assumptions about corporeal regimes. One of the monologues in *In Water I'm Weightless* (2012) says: 'I've been undressed too many times / roughly / not out of urgency, or eagerness – desire / just rush. / Clothes yanked over my head'. Another starts: 'I wonder sometimes about my fictional limbs' (pp. 163, 147). These assume and require a certain sort of body for the speaker, and only work that way. Dominant attitudes to theatrical casting are explicitly mocked. One performer itemizes roles: 'Whether it's a horror flick or not, I'm always the monster', or doing 'a "crip" cameo' to highlight accessibility issues about 'the pig pen', scripted by 'a wheel-chair using writer on an equal opps, inclusive, cultural diversity attachment'. Such casting both stereotypes people by their disability and conceals the aesthetic, emotional and physical skills of non-dominant bodies: 'I wouldn't be in any other skin. I love this body. It works. It really, really works for me.' (pp. 166–7) Assumptions about the bodily behaviour of young Black British people are a less obvious, though persistent, case. A teacher of voice and acting at London's Central School of Speech and Drama, Claudette Williams, has argued that too much training of young Black actors assumes that they don't need the skills of classical acting since their main roles will be in dramas about the inner city. The young Black actor, Williams argues, should also have access to, and facility in, the norms of the classical body and voice which would enable them to play Hamlet and Hedda Gabler.

We should note here that, while much less developed than in the East (see e.g. Barba and Savarese 1991), actor training in the West is both a training in skills and a training in bodily value. The 'conventional' acting student is taught both how to do things, and – whether consciously or not – how to use their body in a way that audiences will approve. This double training is more apparent in conventional dance, such as classical ballet. The ballet dancer's general demeanour is valued as well as the more obvious aspects of their technique, the dancing itself. But that general demeanour is indeed a technique, and it is learnt. In the 1930s Norbert Elias mapped how our everyday bodies have become increasingly constrained with the development of industrial and commodity culture. Rules of civility – sometimes as explicit as the etiquette of the table or of meeting the monarch; sometimes as implicit as the niceties of the social kiss or handshake – determine what our bodies can be or do. Not just performers, we all have learnt techniques of the body. Dancer-choreographer Pina Bausch set out in the late 1970s to challenge both these regimes. In her 'dance-theatre', the performers abstract and physically quote versions of their own 'automated' social behaviour. Bausch set out to free the dancer's body so that it might directly intervene in our everyday bodily habits. Her work is one of the influences on what we now call 'physical theatre' (see Servos 1984).

## The phenomenal body

But, just as we have thought about stage properties as objects in their own right, let us now think about the bodies on stage as things in their own right – things that are 'simply there' – and see where it leads us. There is in fact a branch of philosophy called phenomenology that deals with our direct confrontation with the world, before even our habits of perception intervene to construct orderly data for us to process. Think of the infant before he or she has even learnt the activity of looking or recognizing what they see. Similarly, theatre phenomenology has concerned itself with our confrontation with the stage 'before' we simultaneously make sense of it. Theatre **semiotics**' attention to signs in the theatre ignores the important fact that the stage and its persons are fundamentally first of all there confronting us. So thinking in a phenomenological way about theatre can help us think about the 'thereness' of stage objects (see p. 116) and persons.

In an earlier section (see p. 82) we mentioned Sartre's play *Huis clos* (1944). Its three principal characters are caught in an intolerable yet inescapable **economy** of looking and being looked at. Basically, each needs to know that they are seen by another in order to feel that they truly exist, that they are a subject. Yet the gaze of the other simultaneously threatens to reduce them to the status of an object. The very thing that sustains their sense of selfhood – being regarded by another – also threatens to annihilate that sense. The economy of the gaze in *Huis clos* embodies one aspect of Sartre's existentialist philosophy – he holds this relation to be true of all subjectivity. Sartre uses his play to suggest things about bodies and subjects in general. His thoughts about the gaze closely coincide with what the phenomenologist Maurice Merleau-Ponty had to say about intersubjectivity – the relationship between subjects. We strive to take perceptual hold of the world, and to hold others in that grasp, but the gaze of another reduces us to the status of object.

What have these thoughts about intersubjectivity in general to do with the theatre? In relation specifically to economies of the gaze, Stanton B. Garner Jr (1994) points out that, in conventional Western theatres, the audience is positioned so as to feel invited or powerful enough to hold or capture the stage and its bodies in their gaze, to reduce them to the status of object. But the stage is precisely a bodied space. And so, even without 'direct address', the bodies on the stage insist on their own subjectivity, implicitly at least threatening to return an objectifying gaze – even indeed by ignoring the audience's own presence. Because of the special physical and cultural relationship between stage and spectating space, the theatre is, Garner suggests, a privileged apparatus for apprehending this deep intersubjective dimension of our being in general. So one important aspect of any relationship between stage body and spectating body is this heightened sense of the **contingency** of both those bodies' status as subject.

So we have established a general principle about how conventional Western stages work intersubjectively. But we can go further. Because that fundamental relationship between stage and spectating space is **articulated** differently in different cultural moments, theatre phenomenology can help us think about the ways in which different stages construct different senses of that 'thereness'. It can help us, for instance, to get at our experience of stage aura, of the performer's 'presence'.

## Presence, absence, life and death

Perhaps on reflection it is meaningless to write about the 'transparency' of any stage body. One fundamental thing about the theatre is that we are brought into sustained and often deeply sensual relationships with a particular set of bodies. But which bodies? The bodies of the actors or the bodies of the characters? Think of the character's body, and the body of the actor becomes somehow ghostly, indeed transparent. But the character's body is not, of course, itself there. The playing of roles on the stage renders the status of the body **liminal** – constantly unstable, on an edge. In the circulation between personator and personated, the body perpetually slips between presence and absence. We can think about this slippage with the help of a Renaissance ghost.

Ghosts tend to have an uncertain status in the fiction. Hamlet worries about whether the apparition he sees is actually his father's ghost or the work of the devil (*Hamlet* 1601 Act 1 scene 3). But, in *The White Devil* (1612), Webster engineers an apparition that works in a deeply **metatheatrical** way. Duke Francisco is visited by the ghost of his sister Isabella, and her visit sets him on a vengeful path. But Francisco has himself summoned up his dead sister's presence 'in a melancholic thought' (4.1.101). Is the ghost in the fiction real or imagined? Who is doing the imagining? And how real is Francisco? Who and what is actually 'there'? The moment is not simply a play on our 'suspension of disbelief ' – it tangles intimately with our experience of embodiments on the stage.

And there is more. Immediately after the ghost leaves, Francisco declares, 'I am in love, / In love with Corombona' (4.1.120-1). But these words in fact declare a deception that he is about to conduct, playing the part of suitor so as to achieve his revenge. While he will play the part in 'public' as the play unfolds, Francisco puts on the deception here alone – except of course for the audience. And in that split second, as the actor personates a social individual adopting a false persona, the audience suffers a further **liminal** moment. Who, precisely, is acting? Webster slices together the instability of the stage body with the idea of the projected self as deception.

Even given suspense and emotional engagement, narrative drama tends to invite a sort of past-tense **reception**; it is as if events were being recounted, told over, rather than happening in the present. This tension between present and past tense – being in the direct presence of something no longer there – together with the tension between presence and absence of the body just noted, has led several commentators to suggest that Western theatre is at a very fundamental level to do with life and death. According to this perspective, one of the deep reasons why we go to the theatre is to experience a cycle of re-animation – the stage life that constantly disappears also constantly reappears. The experience compensates for real loss. And the corollary of course is that we learn to cope directly with loss, to rehearse death – precisely by experiencing that infinite number of extinctions.

# 6

# Spaces

This chapter develops ways of thinking about the significance and use of space in the theatre, and especially how dramatic texts script space. A good reading of a dramatic text – whether for commentary or for production – needs to pay attention to this aspect as much as to character or dialogue.

We start by seeing how an emphasis on space can develop a commentary on *A Doll's House*, thereby teasing out some questions and concerns that we might apply to other plays. We then set out these and more considerations about space systematically, to provide a kind of checklist. Within this second section you will find examples and models that will contribute to an understanding of *historical* developments in the theatre. In the short final section we introduce one further historical playing arrangement and look at the idea of taking a historical overview.

## Space and *A Doll's House*

### Spaces in the world and on the stage

The opening stage direction provides a detailed description of a room. The room is similar to those lived in by many people in Ibsen's audience. The world of the stage directly mirrors the world of the audience. We can be more precise. That audience can tell, as soon as the curtain goes up, just what sort of middle-class people they are about to meet with on stage. These people are not rich, but they are somewhat comfortable and aim to rise.

In the course of the play, several of the items described will be used by characters, others not. The sofa will provide a place for intimate conversation between Nora and Christine; the piano will be played for Nora's dance of the tarantella. But, also, these are people who can *afford* a piano and a sofa – as well as the displays of ornaments and leather-bound books which remain untouched during the performance.

The set is a replication of the world, but also a machine for acting. It represents a single room, but contains within it distinct areas in which the action will be focused. We have mentioned the sofa. Also, as George Bernard Shaw famously celebrated in 1913, the table becomes the place where Nora faces Helmer squarely in Act 3 to insist on an adult conversation (see Shaw 1957). A lamp provides stage focus for it.

The lamp also perhaps signifies Nora's wish for clarity. And we may feel that the sober conversation mirrors the one Ibsen is conducting with his audience. It is as if he, too, were sitting seriously at a table.

There are four doors. They help plausibly replicate a **bourgeois** apartment; but two, perhaps three, are significant to our further understanding of this design as an acting machine. In the next two subsections we shall look in some detail at their scripted use.

If the single setting provides several foci for the action, it also changes during the play. The Christmas tree takes up a prominent position, is at first bright and cheerful, but suffers decay in tune with Nora's development. She also brings in parcels; fills the room with her children and shared laughter; fills it again with her desperate dancing. At times there are several people on stage at once, at others only one. While this has much to do with the logic of the action – who needs to encounter whom for the plot to work – the *feelings* of fullness and emptiness (see below at p. 167) are important to what the play comes to mean to its audience.

When, early in Act 1, Helmer admonishes Nora for wasting money, she crosses to the stove as if for comfort. Commentaries on the play often note this. If we are working well, we will also note that Nora has already been scripted to put her parcels down on the table next to it. Shopping and the warmth of a hearth are scripted to coincide – and in the precise context of Helmer's line, 'A home that is founded on debts and borrowing can never be a place of freedom and beauty' (p. 25). Moreover, Helmer is then scripted to follow her to the stove. Dialogue, as we said in Chapter 1, tends intrinsically to suggest blocking, who moves where and when. But in this act, for instance, Ibsen takes care to script Helmer's pursuit of Nora about the stage.

We have said that the world of the stage in this play is continuous with the world of the audience. Let us now also say that the lit stage is separated by a **proscenium** arch from the audience, who sit in relative darkness. They are segregated according to how much they can afford for a seat. The theatre in which they sit is a valued and central cultural institution, though one in which battles are being fought about what sort of play should be put before them. Plays – especially this one – have an afterlife in the press and in earnest debates in homes and cafés (see p. 193). They can be read as well as seen.

We started this subsection with the sentence, 'The opening stage direction provides a detailed description of a room.' We then raised questions about the room the stage set represents, its relation to the audience and its status as a machine for acting. But we also need to note the following: it is a living room that is scripted (not a castle chamber, desert island or town square); and it is described, and in detail. To questions about the specific features of scripted space we can add useful ones about what *categories* of space are scripted, and about the extent to which they are scripted at all.

This brief beginning can help us develop a commentary on *A Doll's House* as a dramatic script, that is, as a set of instructions for producing activity on a stage. We can also use it to think more generally about what can be usefully noted about the scripted space in any dramatic text, the spatial conditions for which it is written, and the significance of the extent to which it explicitly scripts space at all.

Let us make a sketch summary of what we have raised so far with the spider diagram in Figure 6.1. Be aware that the diagram sketches the way *we* have raised the issue of space just here. It is simply an example and *not by any means the only diagram possible*. Argue with the diagrams we present! As you continue with the chapter, you will find that there is more you can add. You will also probably find that a single two-dimensional diagram cannot do justice to all of the questions you will come to ask about space. But you will find it useful – especially when you plan a piece of writing or a presentation – to make this sort of sketch as a way of thinking about those questions and planning a route through them. What spider diagrams would you make in order to analyse other aspects of production, such as the acting or lighting or sound?.

We shall now look a little more closely at *A Doll's House* to develop our understanding of space and to see how this can help us arrive at a commentary on the play as a whole.


## The door slams

When Nora leaves the doll's house for the uncertainties of an independent life, she does so offstage. Ibsen is scripting the use of the stage space here with some precision. Nora says 'Goodbye' and '*goes out through the hall*'. Helmer sinks down in a chair by the door; looks round and gets up, realizing fully that 'She's gone!'; and then '*A hope strikes him*' that, after all, a 'miracle of miracles' might save their marriage. Then, '*The street door is slammed shut downstairs*' (p. 104). What can we say about this use of space?

Let us start with the fact that Nora leaves twice. She leaves the room, then the house. In the time between, Helmer is given a moment of remorse and hope. But if this is a signal of his reformation, it has come – for the time being, at least – too late. The sound of the door, its very hardness communicating a sense of brutal finality, cancels his hope.

Or we might shift our focus and consider Nora herself. The sound of the door slamming suggests that she has crossed a space of potential indecision. Both the hardness of the sound and the fact that it signals a second act of departure speak her resolve.

Either of the last two paragraphs might have been prompted by a description in a novel. But if we imagine ourselves sitting in an auditorium, there is a basic effect to be noted, quite apart from our engagement with

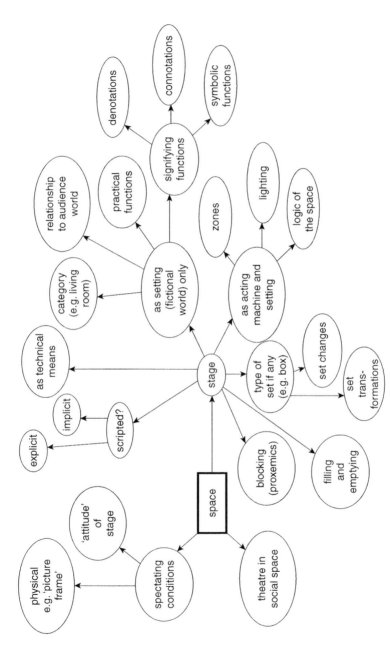

**FIGURE 6.1 _Thinking through space. What spider diagram would you draw? In what areas of this one are signifying, mechanical, phenomenal or aesthetic functions available for commentary?_**

the story. We are being left. Dialogue has frozen and the stage is emptying. We cannot see Nora's important final act. We as spectators are cut off from it.

The stage conditions for which the play was written are significant here. In a darkened auditorium before a lit stage, audience members can sometimes feel very alone, and at others very together. The impact of an offstage sound effect in these conditions is likely to be intensified. Here we enter the territory of theatre phenomenology (see p. 128). Plays are written for particular types of theatre, and script or help determine the *phenomenal* character of the stage for their production; so we can take a phenomenological perspective on the dramatic text. Undergraduate students will find Garner (1994) a useful introduction.

Let us also consider audience expectations (see p. 210). We have learnt that Ibsen is manipulating the established conventions of the 'well-made play', to an extent depending on this formula but also disrupting it to provoke thought. A conventional happy ending might have Nora return from the hall, to be clasped in Helmer's arms as they weep and resolve to find their miracle together. The period between Nora's stage exit and the offstage sound effect of the slamming door is the time – we might even call it thinking space – in which that audience expectation is raised, in order to be dashed.

Our account here so far has tended to suggest that Nora's exit is unpleasurable for the audience. Expectations of a conventional happy ending are dashed. The stage cools and empties before us. We are left in Helmer's sad company. Against this we have written one paragraph concentrating on Nora's resolve. Yet some in that original audience, and certainly many in audiences since, will have taken sufficient pleasure in Nora's resolve as to override any sense of difficulty or loss at the play's ending. Who is in the auditorium matters, as do possible differences between them (see p. 207). Some, indeed, might see Helmer at this point indulging himself again in self-dramatization. We might decide to *play* it that way, in any case. Nora heads for a new reality while Helmer indulges in his one-man play – a slightly different way of thinking about his being scripted to be left alone onstage.

The sound of the door slamming has a finality about it, and the play, indeed, ends with it. But where can Nora go? How might she survive? Is Ibsen contriving to ignore this very real question, as some have argued? Or does he script things so that such a question is begged? Can our discussion so far help with this question?

Our attention to this one organization and use of stage space has raised some questions of interpretation. Or, to put that in a better way, we have found that our interpretation of the play's ending needs to include attention to the scripting of stage space. The question is not what happened in the story or what the characters are feeling, but rather, what is scripted to happen on a stage in a theatre. At the most basic level, Ibsen has scripted an effect, a '*coup de théâtre*'. The double exit, and especially the offstage sound effect, constitute a basic structure which will move, startle or interest an audience irrespective of the fictional situation. We need, then, to think about the way this works *with* the fiction.

While we might come to some conclusions about the ways in which Ibsen was aiming to work on his audience, we would then in any case need to accept that what is scripted seems designed to produce contradictory responses in individuals or between individuals (see p. 209). A useful essay would develop this sense of contradiction.

Last, we have again raised the question of Ibsen's manipulation of audience expectation. A spectator who becomes conscious of this will experience the fiction as if it were in inverted commas, something quoted from somewhere. Another way of saying this is that it is 'distanced'. We might sometimes find it useful to use our category of 'space' in this sort of metaphorical way, too.

## Living rooms and the logic of spaces

There is only one set in *A Doll's House*. It represents a living room, the space which Raymond Williams (1980) has identified as characteristic of plays from the Naturalist movement which Ibsen helped inaugurate. Williams suggests that the living room is a significant setting for two reasons. First, Naturalism was typically concerned with the problems of the **bourgeois** family, and the living room is the place in which significant interactions between husbands and wives, parents and children, family and servants can be played out. Second, Naturalism was deeply and often pessimistically concerned with the notion of 'determinism'. That is to say, the plays mostly express the feeling that our past actions, genetic inheritance and environment all conspire to limit our ability to take control of our situation and change it – or ourselves. The living room, then – especially when realized as the **box-set** developed in the nineteenth century to depict domestic interiors realistically – is also symbolically a trap.

In this early Naturalist play, Nora and the audience come to see the living room – and hence her marriage of which it is the centre – as such a trap. It looks like an ordinary middle-class home, but in fact it works more like a doll's house. Her cultural environment blocks her self-realization as a person, reducing her to the status of an object. At the end of the play, she leaves this restrictive environment. The audience are never taken anywhere else.

There is, then, a basic *logic of space* at work in the play. There is a single and limiting space from which the protagonist finally breaks free.

Let us now pursue this idea in more detail. When Nora exits to the hall at the end of the play she enters a space we can glimpse through one of the upstage doors. Through the other upstage door – on the other side of the piano – is Helmer's study. Let us think briefly about her passage through each of these doors.

At the opening of the play, we have something like the reverse of its ending. The stage is empty. An empty stage feels dead. The entry of actors will animate it, bringing 'presence' to the stage. We hear a doorbell and a door being opened. Our expectations of stage presence are then fulfilled when Nora enters: through the open hall door we see servants whom she controls. The hinterland space between the living room and the outside world is active, bright, visible to us, and in Nora's control. She moves with ease and confidence, and we can see, and therefore sense, an ease of access between this domestic world and the outside.

Contrast her relationship to the door to Helmer's study. Ibsen might have scripted her to arrive home to be greeted by Helmer in the living room; but, with great economy, he scripts space to set up the logic of their relationship from the start. Having entered the domestic space with bright ease, Nora then '*tiptoes across*' to the study door, '*listens*' and then remarks, 'Yes, he's here.' They then conduct an affectionate conversation through the door. She does not open it. Eventually, Helmer comes out of his study to join her (p. 24).

Nora never, in the course of the play, opens the door to Helmer's study. It is easy to remark that this is the way things were in those days. But, in order to think and write adequately about this as a piece of drama, let us note how Ibsen specifically embodies this social fact on his stage. Here at the start, Nora makes a *verbal* crossing of the barrier she cannot cross physically. She knows what lies beyond the door and confidently pitches her voice through it. But she will not do this again. From this point on, the space works to entrap her – or perhaps to confirm the entrapment of which she had been oblivious or which she had hoped to deny.

If Nora is progressively trapped in the room, then Helmer moves with ease between it and its hinterlands, including his study. We quickly come to see his seemingly free and natural movement from space to space as a privileged use of private space. There is some poetic justice, then, in having him left trapped alone in his nest at the end.

Poetic justice is partly a matter of the audience's moral and ethical sensibility – they may feel it proper that he should be abandoned. But it is also a matter of the play's design – Helmer's isolation mirrors Nora's earlier entrapment, and the audience may derive dramatic pleasure from this, a sense of completeness. So this is partly an *aesthetic* matter.

## Meetings, perspectives and entrapments

If the living room is the typically preferred location of Naturalism for the reasons Williams states, it is also simply a plausible place in which a variety of people might meet. **Neoclassical** drama of the seventeenth and eighteenth centuries similarly used town squares. Especially if we make use of 'French scene' analysis (see p. 107), we quickly see that Ibsen has a succession of individuals interact with Nora in this first act: Helmer, Mrs Linde, Krogstad and Doctor Rank. Their movements into and out of the main playing space are an important part of the play's local design – especially if we think about Nora and space.

After Helmer goes back to his study, Mrs Linde is announced and a conversation ensues in which there is some exposition – we hear about Christine herself, and get hints of Nora's secret. But note especially in this context that Mrs Linde also talks about a life beyond Nora's. This is a woman of the world, one with a perspective on life. It is not a comfortable one. Nora's perspective on life at the beginning is that things will turn out right. By the end of the play she looks towards an unknown future in which she seeks self-fulfilment. But here Ibsen sets up a perspective beyond the doll's house which is painful: it is as if he sets up these two perspectives in dialogue with one another. In some later plays, he scripts space so that there is a *physical* perspective, a 'beyond' to the present action (see p. 147, below).

Krogstad's entry into the room is also from the hall door, but contrasts with Mrs Linde's. His arrival disturbs both women. Note how Nora pushes him back out into the hall, taking control with some desperation, for him to enter Helmer's study from there. She is defending her space.

So we learn that Helmer's study has two doors – one into the hall, and the other into the living room. Why? Clearly, there is a technical convenience for Ibsen here. For instance, Doctor Rank, who pops out when Krogstad joins Helmer, must have entered the study directly from the hall. There is no special dramatic reason for this. The succession of meetings with Nora is simply thus made more plausible.

The concrete arrangement of the Helmers' flat in the fictional world is that both study and living room give off a hallway, and that there is a connecting door between them. But in terms of their marriage, and in terms of the theatre, this is not a symmetrical arrangement. Helmer has use of the interconnecting door while Nora does not. Moreover, we in the auditorium are trapped in the living room with Nora. Helmer's study is out of Nora's reach and ours. His space connects independently with the outside world as well as with Nora's. Entries into the stage space disturb or impinge upon her. There is no orderly procession through the hall door. Rather, just as there might be in a farce, there are multiple unannounced comings and goings involving three doors. The technical solution is exploited dramatically.

If the short flurry of comings and goings creates a sense of unease, Nora recovers by playing with her children. Note how she again takes control of the space by making a mess in it, using furniture to hide under and laughing. But, when Krogstad enters again, Nora's response is to send her children back into the room off**stage left**. Persuaded by the arguments of her husband and Krogstad that her secret actions mark her as a moral reprobate and hence a danger to her children, she sends them there to protect them from herself as much as from Krogstad. She isolates *herself* in the room. She (and this does not *necessarily* mean Ibsen) fears that the sins of the parent would pass on to the child: she shares a deterministic attitude.

From this point on until her departure, the hinterland spaces of the study and hallway will take on a threatening aspect for Nora, accentuating her entrapment.

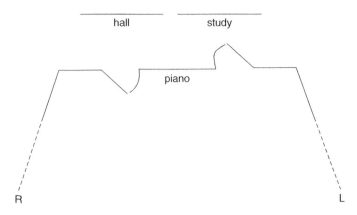

FIGURE 6.2 *Sketching the box-set.*

# A systematic approach to space

In this section we list and explore a number of considerations which can keep us alert to the ways in which space functions in the theatre, and how these functions are scripted or assumed by the dramatic text. We shall be concerned with three intersecting notions of space – the *fictional space* (the place of the action), the *theatrical scene* (what is put on stage to represent this, the set) and the *stage* itself. We begin with an important question.

## What sort of stage are we on?

In the last section we saw how the set Ibsen scripts for *A Doll's House* not only (a) represents something but also (b) works as a machine for acting, (c) engenders feelings such as claustrophobia in the audience and (d) contributes to the sense of the play as a work of art. The same four aspects – (a) *signifying*, (b) *mechanical*, (c) *phenomenal* and (d) *aesthetic functions* – will be pertinent to any set we encounter.

Rather than read the dramatic text 'transparently', looking for the story, we need constantly to hold in mind, as we say in Chapter 1, that plays are scripts for activity on a stage. The *way* in which the fictional location is represented – a **box-set**, say – depends upon the type of theatre the play is written for and the technical means developed within it. The type of set also constrains what sort of acting machine it can be. The box-set invites use of hinterland spaces, for instance. And both the type of set and the relationship between stage and auditorium help shape what sorts of phenomenal and aesthetic effects are possible. Those aesthetic effects – the feelings evoked in the audience – are closely tied up with the way in which the audience are placed to view the stage, which we shall call the *spectating relations*. A lit stage separated from a darkened auditorium by a 'picture frame' invites an attitude of easy ownership of what is looked upon, like a picture on the sitting-room wall.

Let us look briefly at a stage arrangement likely to be as yet unfamiliar to a majority of readers of this book, in order to demonstrate further the importance of relating the type of theatre a play is written for to a consideration of the mechanical, phenomenal and aesthetic functions of the set (if there is a set at all) – functions which are fundamental to the play's meaning in performance.

If you pick up a copy of *The Colleen Bawn* (1860), an Irish melodrama by Dion Boucicault, you will see that it opens outside Mrs Cregan's country-house residence; then the scene is '*The Gap of Dunloe (1st grooves)*'; and then '*Interior of Eily's Cottage*'. The first and third scenes require some depth of stage – in the first, someone comes on from rocks at the back, and later we look across the lake to a light signal from the distant headland; in the third we are inside a cottage room on the headland. But the scene between them only requires a two-dimensional landscape painted on two large shutters (or flats) which can be pushed on from the wings either side, guided by grooves in the stage; these grooves are the ones nearest the audience, the first of several. The second scene is thus called a 'flat scene', and it contrasts with the 'set' or 'relief' scenes, where three-dimensional furniture is set and free-standing pieces can give the appearance of depth or relief rather than flatness. The shutters needed to be closed after the first scene so that the third one could be set up in its place. This basic mechanical arrangement governed the organization of stage space for about 200 years. But the interplay of 'flat' and 'set' scenes was usually much more than a mere technical necessity. Very early on in its introduction, in the Restoration, the interplay was invested with significance. Thus in the precise middle of Etherege's *The Man of Mode* (1676) the stage is opened out to its deepest, to show the open-air pleasure grounds of The Mall. For the central character this is the moment at which he loses his control on the action, which is imaged as his losing control on the space. Our sense of him changes as he is moved from playing on the front of the stage, close to the audience and more or less at one with them, to being tucked away several metres back, peeping round bushes. The interplay of 'flat' and 'set' scenes makes the depth rather than the width of the stage important; the spectating relations are shaped, first, by the audience's proximity to or distance from the action and characters and, second, by the different feelings produced either by looking *at* a platform lit by the same light as the audience or looking *into* a separated world.

## A simplified historical scheme

There is no need to absorb an entire history of Western stages before continuing with this chapter; and this is not the place or opportunity to write one. You will, however, find it rewarding to become progressively familiar with such a history as you read more plays. A succinct and clear overview of a number of the main issues to do with space is offered by Balme (2008) and a useful compact history is Wiles (2003). These complement Wickham's classic account from 1985 while Leacroft (1988) remains an excellent source of detailed architectural drawings. The story Richard Southern tells in *Seven Ages of the Theatre* (1962) remains very suggestive in various respects.

Let us pick up on Southern now, in order to lay out a map useful to our immediate purposes. Please refer to Figure 6.3 as you read. Southern helped design several of Britain's regional repertory theatres in the 1960s and 1970s, and wanted to get away from the restrictions of the proscenium-arch theatre and *back* to the openness and accessibility of the Renaissance stage. The audience are thus, for instance, again wrapped around the stage. But the technical advances of four centuries also allow such a modern stage to be used very flexibly – scenery might fly in and out, multiple levels be built or the space be left relatively bare. We shall assume you have some familiarity with the **box-set–proscenium**-arch arrangement, the Renaissance open stage (such as at the Globe) and modern flexible stages.

Scenery arrived on the English commercial stage in the Restoration, after theatres reopened in 1660. Its use had already been developed at court, for masques. These elaborate performances of song and dance, performed by members of the court itself, celebrated the monarch as fount of wisdom, authority and justice. He or she sat in a central position before the spectacle. The discovery of perspective techniques in painting – where the flat canvas looks as if it has depth, and the viewer feels as if they are looking into a distance – had been developed in Italy and the technique emulated in theatre scenery there. The English court masque adopted it, and then the new theatres after 1660 picked up on the fashion. The introduction of scenery on the English stage introduces a change in spectating relations, and new theatres were built to accommodate it. The audience feel centrally placed to look in on the action – and, indeed, spectacle – and often through it to vistas beyond.

The theatre borrowed perspectival painting itself, producing the illusion of depth on flat canvas. But depth was also suggested by painted flats or shutters run in grooves from the wings, narrowing down into upstage space.

## Two aspects of the theatrical scene: backdrop and environment

'Scene' now means two things: a division in the text, like an act; or what the ancient Greeks called *skena*, the thing acted in front of, on a stage. The Restoration theatrical scene was originally a backdrop to the action, which was played downstage. Notwithstanding the stage–auditorium division, the scene was in one space (upstage), actors and audience in another (downstage). The upstage cloths and flats were usually painted so as to give a generic indication of location – a view of an Italian city, for instance. Thus the same scene might do for several plays. A single theatrical scene

**FIGURE 6.3** *The development of Western playing spaces. (i) The late medieval/ early Renaissance booth stage mainly consisted of a temporary platform erected in a public space – playing was both on the platform and on the ground before it* (Castle of Perseverance; Everyman); *(ii) the Elizabethan open-air amphitheatre developed the booth stage idea in a permanent structure, with the audience on three sides at several levels and musicians in a gallery above the stage* (Tamburlaine, Hamlet); *(iii) the Elizabethan hall theatre had a similar stage design within a covered room, with most of the audience end-on (apart from a few sitting on the edge of the stage itself )* (Tempest; Duchess of Malfi); *(iv) the Restoration theatre*

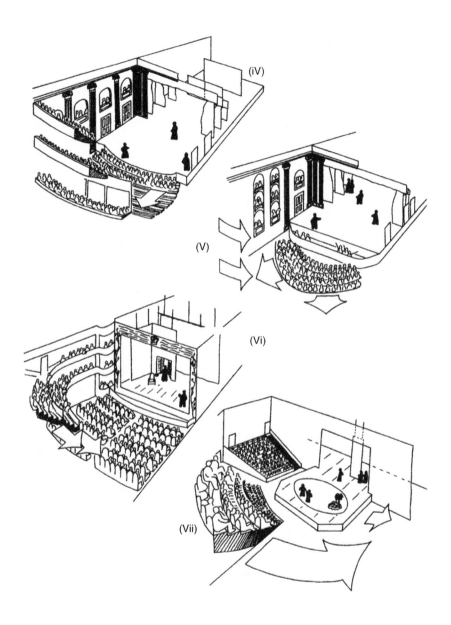

divided the space into three sections, with audience at one end, the 'scene' at the
other, and between them a forestage or proscenium with audience on either side
of it (Man of Mode; Rover); *(v)* in the second half of the eighteenth century the
pit, in front of the stage, took over some of the area occupied by the proscenium,
becoming the focal point of the auditorium (Tale of Mystery); *(vi)* by the late
nineteenth century there was no proscenium space shared with the auditorium,
the action happened behind the proscenium arch (Doll's House; Cherry Orchard);
*(vii)* mid- to late-twentieth-century theatres once again offered a facility for playing
both in front of and behind the proscenium arch (Hostage; Escaped Alone).

might also be perfectly acceptable as backdrop for several locations within the one play – it merely indicates the generalized place. Where a cloth *and* flats are used, the scene is potentially a three-dimensional place: thus instead of acting *in front* of it, the gradually developing practice of moving upstage to act *within* the scene, especially in tragedy, culminated in the theatrical scene being understood as an environment for the action.

From here we can trace a double movement: the progressive retreat of actors and action away from the space of the audience, coupled with the envelopment of the action by the scene. It is the culmination of this process with the **box-set** which Southern found so limiting. The flat-and-relief staging with which we opened this section occupies a substantial part – some 200 years – of this process of change.

Our historical sketch has distinguished between two aspects of the theatrical scene, as:

- backdrop to the action, or
- environment for the action.

Yet even acting within the scene can retain a sense of the scene as backdrop. In specifying the set for *A Doll's House* in so much detail, Ibsen firmly establishes it as environment, in contrast to the domestic box-sets that his theatre could easily have furnished from stock (perhaps with shelves painted on the walls). Thus our backdrop/environment **binary** has historical significance; but it is also a useful tool for thinking about any theatrical scene we encounter.

Use of the scene as environment is not confined to Naturalism. Consider Act 3 scene 1 of Lorca's *Blood Wedding* (1933), set in a forest which we suggest below (see p. 160) might also symbolize psychic or bodily interiors. German Expressionism provides similar examples. Even though the effect is managed literally through the use of backdrops, consider how Mathias in *The Bells* (1871; see p. 148, below) becomes 'enveloped' within the courtroom. The way a scenic device works depends on the context of its use. Again, in Sheridan's *Pizzaro*, performed at Drury Lane in 1799, there was a famous theatrical *coup* when the hero escaped from his captors: having left the stage, he reappeared high up on a fragile bridge over a cascading torrent. This was no mere perspective backdrop to the action – it now shaped it, making it more perilous, helping to establish the development towards an increasingly spectacular stage practice. And that rather extraordinary form, British Pantomime, often switches quickly between scene as backdrop and scene as environment. We might see this as part of the form's self-conscious and pleasurable 'theatricality'.

## Space and the persistence of its meaning

The last three subsections are all very well, but plays survive their original conditions of performance. We regularly see Renaissance plays designed for an open stage with minimal scenic apparatus done in **proscenium**-arch theatres and on modern flexible stages. Surely we need to get back to the story and the characters, and not get bogged down with details of stage history, details we cannot reproduce? Well, we certainly do need to find ways of remaking old plays for modern conditions. But a central part of the play's meaning is the way it was originally designed to work on stage. We do not necessarily have to replicate this, as if we were in a museum; but the mechanical, phenomenal and aesthetic functions we can see at work in the text are *part of the play's production of meaning* and so are a fundamental part of the materials we are working on when we restage plays from the past. The French term for the way in which a play is staged is *mise en scène*. A good challenge for modern directors and designers is not simply to find a *mise en scène* for the action and characters of a classic, but to find one for its originally intended *mise en scène*. The last three subsections are important!

## Three regions of fictional space

We can distinguish between:

- *onstage* fictional space: the space of immediate action, directly represented onstage (e.g. the Helmers' living room);
- *neighbouring offstage* fictional space: implied as in direct continuity with this, immediately offstage (e.g. the room offstage left where the children go);
- *distant offstage* fictional space referred to elsewhere in the world of dramatic reference (e.g. the bank or Christine Linde's shop and school).

We have also used the term *virtual* space to denote locations implied or referred to but not seen.

## Logic and status of the onstage fictional space

In this long subsection we follow a journey through a number of scripted theatrical sets and stage arrangements, to pick out significant general shapes and to see how these are made to work on an audience. Its aim is to stimulate similar investigations of your own. Our main focus is on the onstage fictional space. But we also look outwards to offstage space; and we look at moments where the stage ceases its function as representing a fictional location to become, literally, a stage. Thus, we begin with questions about the *logic* of the theatrical scene – its basic design and how it works – and go on to look at occasions when the *status* of the stage as fictional space is made to collapse.

## *Focus and tension*

We noted above how Ibsen creates a number of different *foci* for the action within a single stage set. This variety helps hold interest and assists plausibility, but these concerns are perhaps subsidiary to the main project of limiting the action to a single oppressive environment.

For much of Jonson's *Volpone* (1606), the protagonist's bed is the focus for the action. If we consider the original production conditions, we can see how strong a focus it is, being set on a bare stage. It is also of course Volpone's lair (see p. 148, below), and the 'stage' upon which he acts the dying man.

A scene may set up a *tension* between two or more foci, so that our attention moves between, say, a plinth in the middle of the stage, a window high up, and a downstage commentator. These are the arrangements for the penultimate scene of Arden's *Serjeant Musgrave's Dance* (1959), where the plinth is a combination of clock tower, lamp post and market cross. Various different figures speak from this platform, beginning with civic dignitaries. Acting as an onstage audience and commentator is the cynical figure of the Bargee, placed downstage. Whenever we are drawn to concentrate on Musgrave, our attention is likely to be distracted by this other focus, the Bargee: and his gaze is also fixed on Musgrave, but with a consistently sceptical attitude.

After the civic dignitaries have left it, Musgrave moves onto the plinth, from where he begins to conduct what appears to be an army recruitment meeting, until he suddenly displays the skeleton, dressed in red uniform, of a comrade killed on army service overseas. When this is identified as the remains of Billy Hicks, a native of the town, the only woman on stage gets up in alarm and then leaves. Not long after, she appears at the upper storey window with Annie, the woman who loved Billy. Up to now our focus has been moving between the passion of Musgrave and the cynicism of the Bargee. But now our sudden movement to a new focus, the window, produces a forceful and significant extension of the spaces of the stage. For looking down from that high window onto an all-male scene are two women. The axis of tension has shifted; and a realization of how the stage has been gendered is produced by this sudden shift in the **focal economy**.

With this shift the sense of the whole scene changes. Up to now, we have moved between Musgrave's religious passion and a cynical reaction to it; but when Annie appears the Bargee takes a ladder from the plinth to the window. Then shortly afterwards he joins Musgrave on the plinth, and Annie begins to climb down the ladder. The window is not forgotten, for the other woman later throws a bundle from it to Annie. The bundle, as Annie reveals, is another uniform of a dead soldier, its red colour duplicating the colour draping the skeleton on the plinth. Not only is the tension now between two sorts of passion, male and female, but also the centrality of the plinth with its red uniform is undermined by the repetition of that colour elsewhere. For the first time in the scene Musgrave's passionate singleness of purpose is confronted – as it were, *de*-centred – by another passion. Thus the tension between foci organizes, in a persuasive way, representations of gender and religious zeal – even without our needing to hear any dialogue.

In *The Dumb Waiter* (1960) Pinter plays games with dramatic tension by having the lift device, set at the margin of the onstage fictional space, periodically erupt into noisy action and so shift the attention of characters and audience to the sinister virtual space. This repeated tension between onstage and offstage space, together with the lack of any significant clarification of the situation offstage (the controlling environment in which the two men find themselves), puts deliberate strain on dramatic plausibility. Thus the physical tension also creates a tension between the 'transparency' of the events onstage – their acceptability as a representation of real life – and their status as pure invention.

## *Perspectives*

Offstage virtual space in *A Doll's House* is established by the set (doors) and by the dialogue. Since the Restoration, upstage painted scenes and backcloths have not only helped establish the onstage fictional space but often also presented vistas into the distance. We might usefully call this type of offstage virtual space *perspectival* space.

A perspective might merely enrich the specification of the location: parkland stretches out below the mansion window. But it will often have a symbolic function too. All four acts of Ibsen's *The Pillars of Society* (1877) are set in the garden room of a house. An upstage vista presents the garden, a gated fence and beyond this a row of brightly coloured houses in the town. People move about and chat in the distance. The play is concerned both with the confinement of women and with 'floating coffins' – unseaworthy ships, cynically used for the sake of profit. The vista might at first suggest a communal spaciousness, the easy connection between families. More abstractly, it might also suggest a space beyond present confinement. Yet, especially as the fourth and final act is set in gloomy twilight, the houses beyond finally suggest merely another wall. This town, this culture, is enclosing, petty and mean. It blunts perspective. But it also looks back at the protagonist in just, but ironically unwitting, accusation. Karsten Bernick is a cheat. In the final act, the town is illuminated and a huge transparency dominates the vista, proclaiming Bernick as a 'Pillar of Society' (p. 108); and this emblazoned trust in him is more than he can bear.

As Oswald drifts into syphilitic dementia at the close of Ibsen's *Ghosts* (1882), '*The sun rises. The glacier and the snow-capped peaks in the background glitter in the morning light*' (p. 97). There are suggestions perhaps not only of nature's implacable law but also of a desire to reach out beyond the confines of present life.

The idea of reaching out beyond the confines of the present is staged with a grim – if spectacular – concreteness in the final act of the 1871 melodrama *The Bells*. Mathias is about to go to bed; he pauses to celebrate his triumph in escaping any exposure of the murder he committed several years before. He exits and puts out the light. Then suddenly, out of the darkness, where once the bedroom wall had been, a courtroom crowded with officials stretches out in front of us: Mathias is sitting in its centre. This sudden new perspective was managed by having the bedroom wall painted realistically on a gauze screen. Behind the screen was a black curtain and behind that the courtroom was set. When the black curtain is raised, we can see through the gauze, as if through a haze, into the courtroom. This haze, combined with all the new colour, the shadowy crowd, the new lighting and – especially – the new depth of the stage, is like a dream. The perspective effect has done two things. First, it has moved us from everyday reality into psychic dream space; second, it has changed the audience's relationship with the stage – the familiar dimensions of the domestic interior have suddenly and inexplicably extended, the clearly defined stage picture has given way to something hazy and indistinct; while we still watch Mathias we are *also* in his head. So, when stage perspective opens before us, it can suggest much more than literal distance; furthermore, it can alter our sense of our relationship with the stage.

## Character lairs

What makes this moment so unnerving in the narrative of *The Bells* is that Mathias' bedroom, his private territory, becomes hugely public. A stage area that gives a character special status may be called a *character lair*; it is an area that literally belongs to them and to no one else. No other character in *Volpone* lies in the bed, for instance; Nora does not enter Helmer's study.

Such a connection between an area and a character can be apparent even when the stage space is less concretely defined. For instance, Brendan Behan's play *The Hostage* (1958) has as its central situation the imprisonment by republicans (IRA) of a British soldier in a room of an old lodging-house in Dublin. At the opening of Act 2 the house is in darkness, the soldier is confined to the room and two IRA men are on guard duty outside. We become aware, however, that all the other occupants of the house are concealed in the shadows looking for an opportunity to slip past the guards and get into the soldier's room. These attempts continue, with varying degrees of success and comedy, for the rest of the play. The soldier's room exerts a fascination on the occupants of the house.

For the soldier, the room is a prison: left on his own for the first time, he runs round it searching for possible escape routes. Later there are sounds of a parade outside: all the other occupants of the lodging-house suddenly appear, and they crowd at the windows to watch the parade go by. As it passes, they read out what is on the banners. Now these windows are imaginary. What the audience actually see is two groups of people standing at the front of the stage looking out into the auditorium and acting as if they are peering out of windows. Where they are standing is, apparently, a passageway in front of the room where the hostage is – but there are no walls between the passage and the room. As the occupants continue to watch it the soldier-hostage comes down to the front of the stage and explains to the audience the political circumstances giving rise to the parade. He is ignored by everybody else. Then he returns to his room and shortly afterwards four people manage to slip past the guards and get into the room, where they crowd round the soldier and paw him. Back in his room, his 'lair', he acquires a sexual attraction.

The usefulness of the character 'lair' within a generally flexible stage space becomes very apparent where plays with a simple stripped-down mode aim to show large-scale events. Bhuchar's *My Name Is...* (2014) presents the break-up of a family and removal of a child from Scotland to Pakistan. Only the main three family members, parents and child, are shown. They each tell their stories, which interweave, and they are often onstage together, while being in separate fictional places. Thus Suzy, in her council house in Scotland, says: 'I didn't realise he would take them to Pakistan./ Get married again ... have more children.' Farhan, in his drawing-room in Pakistan, replies: 'Suzy willingly left the children with me. We had an agreement. She said...' 'You're a better person than me. You keep them as Muslims.' (p. 31) The slash indicates that Farhan breaks into Suzy's speech and overlaps it. This overlapping, and, elsewhere, the technique of talking for someone else, taking, or supposedly taking, their words, makes the flow of speech both intimately close and yet not necessarily reliable, as if something is unverified or missing. Combined with the mode of speech, the device that enables the stories to be closely juxtaposed while insisting on the painful, unbridgeable, separation between characters is the lair.

## *Levels*

The area around the soldier in *The Hostage* is apparently charged with special attractiveness because people are generally desperate to get into it, but there is otherwise very little that concretely defines it. We shall return to this particular use of the stage later (see p. 153, below). For now, however, let us move back a little to look at a physical tension between two foci, and especially how the stage may be organized so that we are compelled to watch the *contrast* between one special space and another. A very familiar example of this involves another confined character, Juliet, who can only have a conversation with her lover Romeo by talking to him from her balcony. The contrast between these two spaces, and the tragic separation between them, is forcibly suggested by the use of different *levels*. She is high up, he is down below.

The stage Shakespeare used did not have the facilities for large scenic constructions. Built into its basic architecture, however, there were two distinct performing spaces – the open stage and, above it, the minstrels' gallery. Difference of level was thus a forceful way of suggesting not just separation, but difference between two situations. For example, in *Troilus and Cressida* (*c.*1600), Cressida observes the Trojan soldiers returning from battle from above, in her balcony. Her descriptions of them are witty, but she is nevertheless physically separated from the public world in which the men move. She talks, they fight. The contrast in levels suggests two aspects of Cressida: an innate intelligence on the one hand; a vulnerable, ornamental, status as a woman in a male world on the other. Similarly, we might say that the narrow space of Juliet's balcony, which also frames her as a static image, contrasts with Romeo's freedom of movement and activity on the open stage below, a contrast which defines the supposed difference between their genders.

This use of levels can still be found in the more complex scenic constructions of the modern stage. We have already noted one such use in *Serjeant Musgrave's Dance*. A more famous example is Arthur Miller's 1949 play *Death of a Salesman*. The opening stage direction describes a '*small, fragile-seeming home*' – almost dream-like – over which towers a '*solid vault of apartment houses*' (p. 7). Much of the narrative is clinched in this one contrast of levels: the traditional American Dream faces extinction in the face of modern capitalist development.

The home itself is presented schematically. We see three rooms at once, each set on a different level; there are no realistic walls between them. In Act 1, as Happy and Biff talk in their bedroom (a raised platform), they and the audience hear their father Willy mumbling to himself in the unseen parlour below. The parlour is the bedroom's understage: it is as if his embarrassing presence undermines them. After some time, light fades from the bedroom and rises on the kitchen, set at stage level and downstage of the bedroom, into which Willy has now emerged. He continues his private musings. The use of levels helps us observe divisions between sons and father, shared and solitary space; it also facilitates a cinematic cross-fading between spaces.

But this schematization of spaces and use of levels rather than more realistic walls also means that the actors can use the same stage space in contrasting ways. The long opening stage direction includes the instruction that '*Whenever the action is in the present the actors observe the imaginary wall-lines, entering the house only through the door at the left. But in the scenes of the past these boundaries are broken, and characters enter or leave a room by stepping "through" a wall on to the forestage.*' The forestage serves both as backyard and as '*the locale of all Willy's imaginings*' (p. 7). Thus, Willy's reminiscent musings become at first a conversation with his absent and merely imagined sons in younger times. But then the young Biff and Happy actually appear on stage, and we move into Willy's mind. We have established two ways in which the levels act as a contrasting device. Here we see that they also contribute to a *fluidity*. In the fantasy mode, walls melt. In the play as a whole, the division between concrete reality and Willy's fantasy also melts.

During the play, space can be real or imagined, present or past, but the character is not necessarily in control of the shifts between one and another. Past events can emerge, unbidden, as a sound cuts across speech or a new area of stage is suddenly illuminated. Respect for fixed boundaries makes the present feel claustrophobic. But the fluidity of the past can feel as much threatening as joyous. Because their focus on, and use of, the levels and areas seems to be led by the lighting, the characters appear to be in the grip of something larger than themselves, not so much entering spaces as being drawn into them. The characters are positioned in time as much as space by the levels, just as the home itself, the 'dream', is positioned by the property development that towers over it.

## Simultaneous action

When the levels represent different rooms, it is possible to show two apparently unconnected sets of activity which happen at the same time – to stage *simultaneous action*. This was present, in a sense, when Cressida talked about the soldiers below her. But a much more startling example is the rape scene from Thomas Middleton's *Women Beware Women* (?1621). While the owner of the house, Livia, plays chess with Bianca's mother-in-law below, Bianca herself is taken upstairs supposedly to look at paintings but in fact to be seduced by the Duke – or raped if she fails to comply. Livia knows all this; the mother-in-law does not. As audience we watch both areas of action simultaneously, and the scene gains its ironic strength from this simultaneity. As a game of strategy, tactics, power and capture, the chess game acts as an ironic image for what is going on without the mother-in-law's knowledge. But, more than this, the two women's *pursuit* of the game, their cool absorption in it, becomes an even stronger metaphor for the amoral manipulation of women's bodies and emotions as a means to advancement within a social hierarchy. Here, simultaneous action works to produce an attitude in the audience towards something much bigger, and more intangible, than the spaces themselves – it is an attitude of ironic recognition of the mechanisms of male-controlled society.

In a later play, we can see how very different technical resources set up simultaneous action, and produce a different attitude in the audience. In 1881 George Sims, the author of *The Lights o'London*, used lighting to direct the audience's attention to three locations at once: '*The lights have been lit in the Hall and the Lodge by this time so that the triple action can be seen by the audience*' (p. 115). In the Lodge, Bess prays for the success of Harold's interview with his father; in the Hall, Harold's father looks over his dead wife's letters and resolves to pity Harold for her sake; between the two, on the lawn, Harold, who has just quarrelled with his father, faces his future as an outcast. This 'triple action' has, again, an ironic effect, since the audience know more than any one of the characters. But that effect also produces an attitude towards the relationship between person and place – the audience feel that if the characters were not so irretrievably locked into their specific places, they could solve the problem. The staging makes us long for a movement between places, for things to be unfixed rather than fixed. The clear separation between Lodge, Hall and lawn feels as if it belongs to an unnecessarily constrained old order, whereas what the audience is enabled to see – with the newest stage technology – is the possibility of a modern world which, in its very fluidity and interrelationship, could resolve the crisis.

If we now recall *Salesman*, we can compare how the stage **articulates** different feelings about fluidity in relation to historical change at different moments in history.

## Unstable space

Simultaneous action is, literally, action in two or more places at once. We began with 'character lair', where we focus on the relationship between character and a fixed point in space. Then we looked at 'levels', where two or more characters are connected across contrasting spaces. And we arrived at 'simultaneous action', where the spaces are contrasted but the characters are not explicitly connected. In this case our feelings about one space – say, that of the hostess's chess game – can change drastically once the action begins elsewhere: it gets less cosy when a rape starts happening upstairs. The chess game that had seemed so hospitable comes to seem treacherous: it may be said to occupy *unstable space*.

A play can make space unstable without setting up simultaneous action. For instance, in the third act of *The Duchess of Malfi* (1614), we see the Duchess in her bedchamber chattering to her husband and her maid-servant while she arranges her hair. The activity requires the stage properties – brushes and mirror – associated with private space and leisure time. But this is more than mere privacy: it is also the space of self-definition which she has claimed at the play's beginning. Her companions leave her as a joke and then, unseen by her while she chatters on, her murderously jealous brother Ferdinand enters, carrying a dagger. This unannounced penetration of the privacy changes our feelings about the space: it seems vulnerable, entrapping, dangerously cut off from public space. By exploiting the onstage–offstage boundary, Webster stages a struggle between the Duchess's attempts to create gentle order and attack on it from without. That attack comes from her brothers, who in their turn see her project as disorderly: it does not fit with their plans for her to marry in the interests of their dynasty. The stage oscillates between gentle orderliness, tyrannical control and a frenzied brutality. At the play's end, the stage is littered with bodies.

In the modern theatre, with its greater range of precisely controllable effects, space can of course also be made unstable by light and/or sound. For example Neilson's *Penetrator* (1993) opens with 'The sound of rain and the occasional passing car. A deep, ominous bass rumble.' This effect recurs later in the play. Tadge has appeared **in** Max and Alan's flat: 'Darkness. Deep ominous bass. The sound of laughter through walls.' 'Somewhere in the dark, Tadge listens, his eyes wide.' (pp. 61, 94) Here we are now more clearly in Tadge's head, but the effect, rhyming with the opening, suggests that he has brought with him into this cosy familiar flat something of the unfixed, potentially violent space from which he came, and thereby dangerously altering the flat's atmosphere.

## *Carnival*

We have already noted in our discussion of *Death of a Salesman* that the same spaces could shift between past and present; they acquire different values in different time schemes. But there are nevertheless, as we noted, certain rules to be observed by the actors in relation to space and time. The potential instability is limited by these rules. In circumstances where there are no such rules space can become very unstable. We can also phrase that back to front: where space seems very unstable, there appear to be no rules. These are the circumstances of *carnival*. Carnival is the time in the religious year when the usual rules about moderation and restraint of appetite are in abeyance. In medieval Europe carnival was supposedly a time when all normal social hierarchy was turned topsy-turvy, when transgressions were licensed and order disintegrated into sensuality and laughter. In such a rule-bound art form as drama, it is rare to find carnival on stage, especially in scripted form. Nevertheless we have already bumped into an example, and we are now going to return to it, since it forms an appropriate final sequence to our consideration here of fictional space.

When we looked at *The Hostage* earlier we noted the soldier's prison/lair. In doing so we began to suggest the fluidity of the stage space – the lack of walls, the mimed windows. This fluidity is particularly apparent when the parade goes by. The occupants of the lodging-house stand in a passageway watching a parade that supposedly passes through where the audience are sitting. While they do it the soldier walks from his room, through an imagined wall, and talks, through another imagined wall, to what he sees not as a street but as a real audience. But he talks with reference to a parade which occupies the same area as the audience. Used in two different ways simultaneously, the stage space retains its fictional dimensions even while these are revealed as unreal. This is more than a matter of the space temporarily becoming what anybody decides to treat it as – which would be the case on the Shakespearean stage. Here it is always two things at once, superimposed on top of one another, never properly separable: a lodging-house in Dublin, and a stage here and now. This doubleness also affects the show's original pianist, Kate: her piano is half on-, half offstage; she is only a musician, not a character in the lodging-house; she is literally present when people are fictionally 'alone' on stage; she is asked to supply music for songs, and also to lend money to buy cigarettes; a half-offstage piano is a place where people hide from an IRA guard. The fictional space is unstable, but so is the division between fiction and immediate reality (we return to this instability on pp. 172–3).

Simultaneous and contradictory use of the stage as fictional location and as literal stage smashes the conventional rule by which we customarily keep these two functions of the stage apart. The stage becomes crazy;

it challenges our sense of the serious. The carnivalized stage can be seen as an undercutting of the self-seriousness of dominant forms not only of representation but also of belief. This can be a pure gesture of refusal to be serious: Behan was certainly something of a joker. But it can also be a **rhetorical** gesture suggesting that getting to or near the truth is not a simple matter. Getting at the reality of things – such as the common history of Britain and Ireland – is risky, confusing and contradictory. No presently existing maps and rules are of use.

## *Hinterlands*

We looked in the beginning of this chapter at *buffer zones* or hinterlands to the main space of the action, such as the Helmers' hallway. They **mediate** between the onstage fictional and offstage virtual spaces, but are rarely there just for the sake of plausibility. They most likely contribute significantly to the action.

One example of this sort of contribution can be observed in the second act of Sean O'Casey's *The Plough and the Stars* (1926). The scene is a pub, with a counter coming down the depth of the stage on audience left and windows onto the street at the back. Outside in the street a political meeting is being held: this is Dublin late in 1915, with Irish republicans and nationalists about to rise up against British rule. We can occasionally see the speaker at this meeting as a silhouette against the window. At a point almost halfway through the act there are two groups of people, at either end of the bar, arguing with one another. One group consists, loosely, of nationalists; the other group (of two) consists of the pro-British Bessie Burgess and the vaguely Marxist Covey. The woman in each group is not only very vocal, but her anger is particularly focused on the other woman, whose conduct and propriety are criticized.

Their argument is suddenly interrupted, and silenced, '*when the tall, dark figure is again silhouetted against the window, and the voice of the speaker is heard speaking passionately*' (p. 169). When this brief nationalist speech is finished, the silhouette goes, and onstage the argument between the two women begins with renewed force, gets to shouting pitch and threatens to become a fight. The speech, coming from that hinterland space silhouetted in the window, clearly has a major impact on these people's lives. But by putting the political activist into the hinterland and the 'ordinary' tenement dwellers onto the stage proper, O'Casey is proposing to us a relationship between, on one hand, the concrete, three-dimensional, lived – but unselfconscious – activities of everyday life and, on the other, the dogma of politics which, however two-dimensional, controls people's consciousness.

This relationship is restated with more force, and more difficulty, towards the end of the act. The stage empties of all except the barman, and in come three uniformed men, fired by the speeches, talking quickly and carrying two flags. Suddenly there is colour, noise, up-tempo rhythm – energy: qualities which make the onstage space very vibrant, and hence attractive. The men pause, to listen to the silhouetted speaker. And then they all quickly leave. The stage empties; a pause; then re-enter Rosie the prostitute with her semi-drunk and embarrassed client. While Rosie sings, troops muster outside. Suddenly the hinterland feels like a space which is not only two-dimensional, but also busy, purposeful and unreachable. The audience themselves become engaged with the hinterland space.

## Significant objects

In the scene that we described earlier from *Serjeant Musgrave's Dance* the central plinth is an object that makes meaning, **signifies**, in its own right. As a sort of market cross-cum-clock tower-cum-lamp post, it is the sort of thing you might see in any small town square. And it is used as such by the civic dignitaries – the first person to speak from it is the Mayor. It continues in this sort of function, albeit with a quiet irony about the connections between civic and military institutions, when Musgrave uses it as a recruiting platform. But when a skeleton is suddenly suspended from it, the object turns into a gallows – without, of course, ceasing to be a part of the civic authorities. When guns are produced it turns into a defensive position, especially with the arrival of dragoons to arrest Musgrave. At the very end of the scene, when the military action is finished, Annie occupies the plinth with the skeleton of her lover on her knees, like the image of the Virgin Mary and dead Christ. After its civic and violent significations, the object is now the place of a pietà, a suffering after violence. That movement from male to female occupation, with the changing significations, is also suggested by careful control of shape and consequent movement. The plinth structure, upward-pointing to Musgrave's heaven, is individual, authoritative, phallic – the sense of height actually grows when the skeleton is hung from it. To give themselves authority, the men mount it. Annie comes into the action by coming down a ladder from a high opening – and ends by bringing the skeleton down to her. The very shape of the movement made necessary by the significant object itself fundamentally structures the logic of the scene.

## Sketching the set, making checklists and making a commentary

Playwrights who specify set are very likely to be constructing such zones, foci, lairs, hinterlands and tensions, and conferring some objects with a special significance. A proper account of a play needs take them into account, which makes a sketch of the scenic space a must when reading a play. The list we have made here is by no means exhaustive: its purpose is to stimulate your own activity of investigating the logic of the stage space. You will doubtless come to carry your own checklist around in your head. Sketching it down occasionally will help you develop your skills of analysis and commentary. Any checklist we make is likely to change – at least in emphasis – as we move from one stage practice to another. What might it look like in the case of Bertolt Brecht's epic theatre, for instance?

Note that even on the relatively bare and open stage of the Renaissance, where no theatrical scene is specified or assumed, the plain distinction between onstage and offstage space affords Webster a powerful structure for articulating Ferdinand's brutality (see p. 152, above) – and perhaps also for making his audience feel complicit with it. The excitement of the radical shifts in *The Hostage* depends on the convention that the stage represents a completely fictional world out of which the performers never step. But this idea only came into existence properly in the middle of the nineteenth century, when theatre architecture gradually removed the acting area in front of the **proscenium** arch – the forestage – and pushed the action back into the 'scene'. The forestage had been lit by the same chandeliers that lit the auditorium, had shared the same space as the audience. Once the action was pushed back, and the proscenium arch painted to look like a picture frame, the audience grew accustomed to looking into a fictional space that was clearly separated from their own world of the auditorium. But almost as soon as the apparently solid, fixed location became the norm for stage setting, long before Behan was writing, dramatists and designers began to explore ways of exploiting this new convention by breaking it. The logic of any one fictional stage space is related to the prevailing conventions of spectating, and these are deeply connected to theatre architecture.

Miller's use of levels and areas in *Salesman* might be likened to Behan's in *The Hostage*, in that there is fluid movement between different areas and periods of simultaneous staging. But note what the movement is between – past and present of the same family in *Salesman*, fictional Dublin and the real stage now in *Hostage* – two very different sorts of contrast. Once we spot such things as simultaneous staging we then need to ask what its *particular* use suggests about people, history, place and time. We hope that, once you have observed the arrangements, you will go on to ask what sorts of attitude are produced in the audience, and what sorts of insight are being formulated. The relationship between people and space ends up suggesting relationships between people and gender, society, time and history.

## How fictional space is established

In the *theatre* fictional space is created by two means, which Pfister (1988: 267ff.) denotes as *verbal techniques* (dialogue) and *non-verbal techniques* (e.g. scenography, props and the movement of characters). Consider that a ship at sea might be established by a character carrying a telescope on a bare stage. The location would be secured more by scanning the horizon with the telescope; by body mime (the ship rolls and pitches); by sound effects; by a sailor-suit. Examples of non-verbal techniques thus include the visual techniques of mime and costume and audio techniques. Howard Goorney (1981: 45) quotes how, in their production of MacColl's *Johnny Noble* (1945), Joan Littlewood's company made the audience feel seasick through body mime and lights.

In the *dramatic text* Pfister again identifies two means, *word scenery* and *stage directions*. Word scenery typically works through **existential** presupposition (see p. 73). Titania invites Bottom to 'sit thee down upon this flow'ry bed' (*A Midsummer Night's Dream*, 4.1.1). No original stage direction specifies the scene. Contrast, for example, the detailed stage direction that heads *A Doll's House*.

What can we make of this difference? First, Shakespeare's script assumes a bare stage in which the establishment of locations is principally by means of verbal technique. Second, those locations are generic: it does not matter precisely what sort of flowers are there, for instance. Third, neither the original script nor its versions published at the time assume production by others than Shakespeare's own company. Any stage object that might be used could be specified directly. The original script – divided into 'parts' – simply told the actors what to say. So the balance between stage directions and word scenery tells us something about the original production conditions.

Word scenery need not be purely for the sake of information. It can be a source of pleasure and display, most notably in verse drama. Spanish drama of the sixteenth century incorporated the poetic form of *gongorismo*, the florid and lengthy description of, say, a city. The flourish might simply contribute to the poetic 'register' of the stage presentation as a whole, but it might also be associable directly with the character delivering it. Thus, in Lope de Vega's *Fuente Ovejuna* (1612–14), the army captain Flores paints a magnificent picture of the scene in which Commander Gomez sits 'upon a sturdy / Stallion the colour of crystallised honey, / With jet-black mane and tail' (p. 42) before the royal city he aims to capture. In some fifty lines like this, Flores stuns the villagers of Fuente Ovejuna into admiration of their master. But Lope simultaneously stuns his audience with this display of word power.

We have already mentioned Enobarbus' barge speech (see p. 101). Part of what he is doing is creating a virtual space. Partly also the speech is a display of composition on Shakespeare's part. But, significantly too, this is Enobarbus' picture of Cleopatra, which he is presenting to Agrippa and Maecenas. It is his *character perspective*: too often it is taken as an 'objective' description of the Egyptian queen and her lover Antony. Flourish or no, word scenery – precisely because it is delivered by characters – always has the potential to allow us into character perspective.

It can also act as thematic carrier. For example, there is repeated knocking at an offstage gate in the porter scene (2.3) of *Macbeth* (1606). As he makes his way to the gate the porter imagines himself admitting various sinners to hell. Since the real gate is not seen, the word scenery transforms it into a sort of hell-gate – which, in a sense, it is, since Macbeth has just murdered the king.

## Signifying and aesthetic aspects of the theatrical scene

We have distinguished between signifying, mechanical, phenomenal and aesthetic functions of the theatrical scene (see p. 139, above). In the following subsections we look a little more closely at signification and aesthetics.

## *Theatre semiotics*

The study of signs in the theatre, their classification and how they work, is the terrain of the discipline called theatre semiotics. There are a number of useful outlines of this area of enquiry, including Aston and Savona (1991) and Elam (1980). Semiotics as a more general field of enquiry into signification predates theatre semiotics, and has a number of different strands and starting places. We might here mention three.

First, at the beginning of the twentieth century, the structural linguist Ferdinand de Saussure asked the question, what is a sign in language? He proposed that we think of the linguistic *sign* as having two inseparable parts – the material mark or sound (the ink on this page, say, in its particular arrangement; or a set of spoken sounds), which he called the *signifier*; and the concept to which this is by custom linked (the idea, say, of a dog or a table or justice), which Saussure called the *signified*. He stressed two things: that the relationship between signifier and signified is totally arbitrary, a matter of pure custom (there is no natural connection between d-o-g and the idea these marks conjure up and communicate); and the signified is a concept, not a thing. The actual thing being referred to in any particular act of language he called – not surprisingly – the *referent*. When we come to describe the working of signs on a stage, the referent is usually in the world of the play – it is a *dramatic referent*.

Second, there is Roland Barthes, who – building on and away from the Structuralist movement of the 1960s – helped extend the application of Saussure's thoughts about language to a whole range of cultural materials – clothing, tour guides, magazine photographs – by understanding each as a text to be read. Theatre semiotics picks up on this development. Of particular interest is Barthes' notion of 'orders of signification'. Thus, for instance – adapting Barthes' own model – a piece of painted card can act on a stage as the signifier for the signified 'crown'. But this crown-sign can in turn act as a signifier for the signified 'monarchy'. And in turn again this monarchy-sign can act as a signifier for the signified 'justice' – or 'tyranny', 'majesty', 'redundancy' and so on (see Barthes 1957, 1993: 114–17).

Clearly, what Saussure has to say about spoken and written language is suggestive in terms of the stage, but limited. For on the stage, a table may signify a table, a dog a dog (or, strictly, the idea of a table or a dog) – as well as actually be a table or a dog. There is nothing arbitrary about this relation. Thus, theatre semiotics needs to think about different *types* of sign, other than but also including the linguistic. And here it has found the work of the philosopher Charles S. Peirce very suggestive.

We look briefly at Peirce next. But, before pressing on with this account, two things need to be said. The first is that it is in itself very selective and condensed. There is much more to the semiotics of drama and theatre than this. The second is that theatre semiotics has itself been very selective with respect to what it takes from its sources. Often, what was originally proposed – and especially its own context – gets lost in the act of adaptation to fresh purposes.

## Icon, index and symbol

Peirce proposed that there are three basic sorts of sign: icon, index and symbol.

An *icon* is a likeness. Russian *ikons* are painted likenesses of saints. The backcloth painted perspectivally to represent a wood is an icon. Indeed, most theatrical signs including scenic ones are iconic: the set looks like what it represents. But some representations are more schematic than others. The tree Beckett specifies for *Waiting for Godot* is not like a real tree in nature, but more like a diagram of one, just as the map of the London Underground is a diagram rather than a picture of the actual tangle of lines. Peirce distinguishes between two sorts of icons: *diagrams* and *images*.

An *index* points to something: our index finger is the one we point with. Smoke indicates that there is fire. An offstage bang indicates that a door has been slammed; a wash of blue light indicates that the moon has risen.

A *symbol* is arbitrary, treating one thing as another with which it has no real connection. A paper banknote stands in the stead of gold, goods or labour. A fish or a lamb stands for Christ. Spoken language is symbolic.

Like all simple schemes, this one gets complicated once you start to think about it. But the complications become interesting, and can again help us think and write about theatre. Consider two things. First, theatre is fundamentally symbolic in Peirce's terms, since it treats all manner of things as if they were others: the stage is not the world. Second, a pine table on stage standing for a gilt table in a queen's chamber is standing for something it is not, but is still a table. It is not only like the thing it is not, but is also the same sort of thing, a table. Much theatre works through *iconic identity*.

So, as Keir Elam (1980: 21 ff.) suggests, Peirce's three categories are best thought of as *aspects* of theatrical signs we meet, rather than distinct species of sign. And it is as aspects that we can most usefully deploy them in our commentaries.

While we shall get most mileage out of Peirce's categories when commenting on actually realized designs, dramatic scripts may nonetheless specify, imply or assume degrees of iconicity. Naturalism values image over diagram. The rationalist Brecht and his designer Caspar Neher favoured diagrammatic stages with a strong indexical impetus: clear abstracted representations point to class struggle and imperialism, for instance.

Note that indices in particular activate the neighbouring offstage space. The knock at the door announces someone's imminent presence. This is the opportunity for dramatic mistakings: misreading the signs is part of the basic stuff of drama.

## Denotation and connotation

A set that stands on stage has a direct representational meaning; but meaning is never purely denotative. There are always connotations, and much theatre depends upon them. Osborne sets *Look Back in Anger* (1956) in a flat within a Victorian house. The original audience might easily connote mild discomfort and shabbiness with such surroundings, but of more thematic importance are connotations of Victorian strictness and old-fashionedness. Jimmy is physically surrounded by reminders of what he is rebelling against.

By careful attention to detail, Lawrence makes it clear to his audience that the protagonist of *The Daughter-in-Law* (1912) has aspirations to rise above her class. The set denotes a working-class room, but one with middle-class pretensions. Connotations as to her character flow from this. In the set for Neilson's *Penetrator* (1993) 'the credibly masculine fights with a softer influence' (p. 62). This innate visual tension around sexual identity produces connotations as to the current and previous lives of the room's male inhabitants.

## Metaphor and symbol

A set may have metaphorical or symbolic significance. The scene Lorca specifies in Act 3 scene 1 of *Blood Wedding* denotes a forest; but its context in the play, what happens there and his short but also precise description – '*A forest. It is night. Great moist tree trunks. A gloomy atmosphere*' (p. 74) – produce such strong connotations of psychic and bodily interiors that the forest scene easily comes to *stand* for either or both of these worlds.

We have here used metaphor and symbol as loosely equivalent terms. Symbol usually carries the sense of an 'outward sign' of something. The bulldog supposed to stand for British strength and determination is emblazoned on clothes, flags, mugs and official programmes. These all suggest that it is emblazoned on Britain itself. Semioticians use symbol in a more precise way, as we have seen.

## Aesthetics, pleasure and meaning

Aesthetics is often taken to mean concern with beauty and value, but is more strictly understood as a concern with feelings and responses. An aesthetic effect can be purely pleasurable, but it can also help convey meaning. We need to be alert to both possibilities as we read.

It matters whether a setting is given as dark or light, blue or yellow, shabby or sleek. Aesthetic details stimulate connotative meanings and help set the tone of the scenes played within the setting. They not only affect the meaning of individual scenes, but also contribute to the rhythm of the stage and argument of spaces (see p. 167 and p. 164, below). The enlarged stages of Covent Garden and Drury Lane theatres helped serve a public taste for spectacle from the late eighteenth century. Partly this is a case of pure pleasure-taking; but wanting to be overwhelmed in the theatre in 1790 was also part of a feeling that life can put us in contact with the 'sublime', the mysterious grandeur of nature which humanity may only glimpse.

Brecht set his face against what he called 'culinary' theatre – art which serves itself up as a feast for consumption. But some of his detractors claimed that his spartan aesthetic was itself just pure artiness. Some influential designers at the Royal Shakespeare and National Theatres in Britain during the 1970s and 1980s, who tended towards minimalist white- or black-box stage spaces, were accused of radical chic, of being 'Brechtian' because it looks cool. Such designs simultaneously connote radicalism and give a direct aesthetic pleasure. As it happens, Brecht was not against enjoyment in the theatre. That is another story, but the sorts of pleasures he wanted his audience to have mattered to him politically. Our own analysis needs always to be alert to how an audience is given and denied pleasure as much as to how it gains information. The setting, conditions of spectating, stage rhythm and features such as transformations all contribute towards this. They work *by means* of pleasure.

## *Intertextuality*

Things have their meaning in relation to others. A sock is not a shoe or a glove. *A Doll's House* is not a well-made play. Consciously or not, we compare any book we read, play or movie we watch with others. The general notion that texts have their meaning principally in relation to other texts is called *intertextuality*. Some texts directly call attention to other texts or textual systems in order to make their own meaning. Bartlett's *Charles III* is fun because it recalls but updates a Shakespeare history, and in doing so plays with our attitude to contemporary royals. Gwynne Edwards (1987) observes how the colours Lorca specifies for *Blood Wedding* mirror those of peasant ceramics. The play relates itself self-consciously *as an artwork* to rural life and culture. In a similar way Neilson invokes early 1930s culture, and specifically film, in his play about the Düsseldorf Ripper, *Normal* (1991). Early on the defence lawyer Wehner waltzes to a 'Weillian nightmare waltz' with a dummy in period dress. The first view of the Ripper is in 'an unnaturally stiff pose', followed by jerky movement (pp. 5,3). One scene is played as silent slapstick movie; in another the stage is bathed in moonlight while a period song is sung. These intertextual references, along with other variations of performance mode, explore the proximity to supposedly abnormal criminality of that which we think of as normal.

# Metaphoric use of the stage and the flexibility of the theatrical sign

The politician who talks about 'the ship of state' is speaking metaphorically. A metaphor treats one thing (a ship) as if it were another (the state or what sustains it). Many plays have metaphoric dimensions. The ship which founders in the first scene of Shakespeare's *The Tempest* (1610/11) could itself be understood as 'a ship of state' – the aristocrats are notably incompetent in understanding or managing it. The scene is acting as a *metaphor*.

But consider now how that scene might be staged. Nowadays we might expect some elaborate scenic arrangement, but the first performances were probably done with none. In either case, actors staggering around the stage floor as if it were the moving deck of a ship are treating one thing (the stage floor) as if it were another (a deck). A famous routine of the Peking Opera involves a sustained body mime in which the performer punts an imaginary boat across the stage as if it were a river. Theatre, then, regularly makes a *metaphoric use of the stage*, even when it is not necessarily making metaphoric figures.

The setting for the original production of Caryl Churchill's *Fen* (1983) was an agricultural field on which were placed various domestic items (a chair, an ironing board) when the scene was an interior. The stage floor moves from one to another, but the field is never – metaphorically – out of the rooms of those who work on it. In the final scene this movement between places is duplicated by a movement across time. The dead Val has reappeared, talking to figures from the past as well as the present. Others from the play's cast come on, in the present, including Nell, walking on stilts, like a fenlander from the seventeenth century; there is also a scarecrow boy there, from centuries ago. The same stage space is treated as if it is inside and out, past and present, living and dead, simultaneously.

That the stage floor can change its **referential** meaning from moment to moment – now a stone floor, next a muddy field – is a particular instance of a general principle that theatre semioticians have foregrounded, the *transformability or flexibility of the theatrical sign* (see Elam 1980: 12ff.). We are prepared by convention to accept two pieces of wood nailed together as a sword, or maybe as a golden crucifix. The ease with which we accept one thing (bits of wood) as another (a sword or crucifix) enables performers and designers to make one sign (wood as sword) transform to another (wood as crucifix) in an instant. The sign itself is flexible. This also means that a stage object can stand for two things even at the same time. The stage is thus a very associative space: it easily brings various referents into relation with one another.

While these are mostly questions of design and direction during a production process, some playscripts clearly make use of this potential.

## Theatre as a syncretic system

A novel works by virtue of the printed word alone. A newspaper cartoon uses words and pictures. In semiotic terms, a novel uses one signifying system (written language), whereas a cartoon uses two. A playtext uses one signifying system – again, the printed word. But it is a script for an activity which is itself a sort of text – the theatrical text (see p. 5) – which employs a large number of signifying systems. These include, for instance, spoken language, costume, lighting, sounds, gestures, movements and scenography. Each of these can make sense on their own: think back, for instance, to the various *different* ways in which a seaborne location can be signified as discussed above on p. 156. Theatre can be thought of as one huge signifying system which contains several others. Semioticians refer to such a system as a *syncretic system*.

Some playwrights – especially in the twentieth century – exploit this fact. A playtext may, for instance, script a transformation which depends on changes in some signifying systems on stage, while others remain constant. At the opening of Howard Brenton's *The Churchill Play* (1974) a catafalque stands on stage, bathed in light shone through a stained-glass window. Silence helps establish the scene as Churchill's sombre and dignified lying in state. But then, while the scenic object remains, lighting, sound and action around it change radically and we are in the company of prisoners who have no respect for the dead man, rehearsing to present an entertainment for official visitors. The catafalque remains a catafalque, but changes its situation and meaning in an instant. The transformation of the scene of which it is a part from state ceremony to inappropriate play-acting brings nationalist ideology and myth-making into sharp collision with ordinary broken lives. The eloquence of the effect involves both the persistence of the denotative meaning of the object and its shifting connotative function.

Transformations can be subtle: the cloak that Nora throws about her shoulders as she contemplates suicide is transformed into a costume element in the world of melodrama she is stepping into. An essay properly attentive to the play as dramatic script would note this. We develop the idea of dramatic worlds below (see p. 164).

## Logics and conventions of the stage

The notion of 'upstaging' someone is part of common parlance. You have taken 'centre stage' in a conversation, for instance, and I say something which undercuts you as the point of interest for your audience. Let's take this back to an actual stage. Centre stage is a strong position. So too is downstage centre. Upstage is less strong; but an upstage entry can disrupt an audience's point of focus from a strong position. These are phenomenological considerations.

Are there other strong positions? Some hold that downstage left is strong – perhaps for right-handed spectators, or because Westerners read from left to right. Certainly, a downstage marginal position is a strong one from which to comment on the action on the rest of the stage. A disruptive upstage entry probably achieves its effect not only because it is behind another's back but also because it takes up the perspectival position.

Strong positions depend not only on position itself, but also on the spectating conditions. Note that our remarks so far are most pertinent to a picture-frame stage; and consider even within this arrangement how the use of **limelight** affects spectatorship. The strength of various positions also depends on what is done at them and what other possible points of focus are being occupied onstage – and on the sequence of their occupation.

Augusto Boal (1992: 150–5) has a game, in which the players successively take up a position of 'authority', that is worth playing as a way of vividly concretizing your sense of all five of these factors. Our concerns here link with the issues of groupings and stage action raised on p. 103.

Different stage conventions focus action in different stage areas and assume different forms of movement about the stage. Some give areas of the stage a symbolic significance. We need to attend to the *assumptions* a dramatic script makes about stage space as well as what it manifestly scripts.

Restoration comedies play downstage in intimate contact with the audiences they ridicule. The players tend to 'cross' the stage, moving from left to right and back again as they speak. Entry to the stage is through the stage doors close to the audience; the character enters the action but the actor 'makes an entrance' too – and perhaps, moreover, the actor is playing a show-off character.

The Elizabethans treated the understage as hell; the innovator Shakespeare has fun with this by having the Ghost of Hamlet's father call up from the 'cellarage' and Hamlet stamp on the stage to attract his attention. The canopy over the Globe's stage was painted to represent the heavens. Up and down have similar associations on secular stages, too.

As we shall see later (see p. 168, below), medieval players frequently had direct contact with their audience. The *platea* is simultaneously audience and fictional space. But in the conditions dominating throughout most of the twentieth century, invasion of audience space by the action could feel threatening or exhilarating. Spectating arrangements are intimately tied up with social norms. Twentieth-century spectators tended to conceive of themselves in general life as private individuals. Invasions of audience space challenged this assumption; but, of course, challenging the assumption can only go on so long as the convention of individual privacy remains dominant.

## Fictional worlds and the argument of spaces

We noted two ways in which the setting of *A Doll's House* is significant. First, the fictional world mirrors the world of the audience. Second, the particular fictional space presented does not change, and this argues something.

Bevington (1987) calls attention to the argument of spaces in his edition of Shakespeare's *1 Henry 4*. Scenes roughly alternate between the tavern world and the world of the court, and a significant shape of the action is Prince Hal's shift of loyalty from the first world to the second. A key feature of the argument of spaces is the value conferred upon each. Hal's movement from the corrupt world of the tavern to the responsible world of the court is a positive one. Bevington points out that there are moments when the tavern scenes are reminiscent of (and even make reference to) medieval depictions of hell and its temptations. Like the hero of a **morality** play, Hal comes to his salvation.

Bevington also demonstrates how Shakespeare complicates this scheme. The tavern world is irresponsible, but also full of warmth; the court is responsible, but personally unrewarding. There are positive and negative aspects to each space. Further, these aspects are associated especially with two characters, Falstaff and the King. Hal's movement to the world of the court and adult responsibility involves rejection of the worst and retention of the best of both worlds and of both father figures. The play argues that Henry 5 – whom Hal is to become – is the ideal synthesis of kingly authority and personal generosity.

Note that particular characters are associated with each world within the play, while others – like Hal – move between them. This is a significant part of the play's design, best discovered by means of French scene analysis (see p. 107).

Significant, too, is the relationship of the audience to each of these worlds. While this is more complicated than for our opening example of *A Doll's House*, it is worth thinking about when commenting on the play. As a start, we could note that the world of courts is remote from most people, but that the Elizabethan chroniclers (like Holinshed) in particular offered a sense of intimate knowledge of historical royal actions and motivations; that taverns are familiar places to most; and that most in the original audience would be familiar with tavern *scenes* in the by-then 'old-fashioned' **morality** plays concerned with temptations of the flesh. Each of these relationships is potentially exploited by the play and so contributes to its meaning.

Within each world there may be a number of scenic locations; in *1 Henry 4* the scenes of highway robbery clearly belong to the tavern world. While we may personally be able to think of school, college or work as one world and home as another, we are less likely to distinguish in this way between the kitchen and the bedroom. Similarly, in many plays individual scenic locations may have particular associations, while not being distinct enough for us to want to call them 'worlds'. Yet they can still contribute on their own account to an argument of spaces. At times in our lives the bedroom may well come to feel like a different world, rather than just another part of home; the line between location and 'world' is blurred. Two things follow. First, we should not worry too much about getting the distinction between mere location and world 'right'. Second, you may find it useful as you get familiar with this work to spot how locations 'become' worlds in the course of a play. Would you say this is true of the Helmers' living room?

The audience will have a relationship to the world of the play as a whole, and this, as much as the subsidiary relationships, will change according to the conditions of production. Shakespeare's audience were witnessing the history of their monarchy: monarchs still mattered. Audiences now probably rather get a sense of English 'heritage' – the world of the stage is to a large extent 'Shakespeare'.

The worlds presented by a play need not all be presented directly onstage. They may be 'virtual' spaces, referred to by characters but not visited by the action. In Chekhov's *Three Sisters* (1901), the young women long to live in Moscow rather than their small provincial town: how they value Moscow and how the audience are made to evaluate this valuing are central to the play's design. Similarly, a world might only have its existence in the mind of a particular character, whom others see as deluded. We have seen how Nora seems at first to live in a world of romance and melodrama. The loftspace in which Old Ekdal keeps his collection of animals in Ibsen's *The Wild Duck* (1885) is visible onstage; but those around him see Ekdal's dedication to this space as a form of delusion, an escape from hard reality.

Clearly, the argument of spaces is tied up with the plot-shape of a play. But they are not the same thing. Consider, for instance, that while Lear and Gloucester in Shakespeare's *King Lear* occupy plot and sub-plot, they are in the same world or set of worlds.

The *relationship* between plot-shape and argument of spaces can be a useful way into a play. *A Midsummer Night's Dream* presents four sets of characters: the fairies; the mechanicals; the lovers; and parents and court. The plot lines specific to the first three groups are made to intertwine in the wood, a world most especially associated with the fairies. The wood is a place of mistakings and magical transformations, a necessary place of processing between the divisions in civil space with which the play opens and the unitings in royal space with which it closes. We might usefully deploy an actantial analysis of the play here (see p. 28). Our attention to the argument of spaces might go further by noting that, at a social level, the world of the mechanicals is greatly distanced from that of the court *and* of any likely audience. The last scene works on this embarrassment. Our notion of 'worlds' is a flexible one, usefully extended, sometimes, from scenic location to world-view. Also, the wood is not only a fairy world, it is also very much a theatrical one: the play self-consciously displays its ability to juggle plots, to our confusion and delight.

We noted how each of the two worlds presented in *1 Henry 4* had contradictory aspects. It is often noted that the 'Absurdist' plays of the mid-twentieth century are designed to make the world of the action seem deeply contradictory to the audience. On the one hand, scene, character type and the superficials of dialogue are very close to the world of the audience. But the dialogue itself, and the **existential** presuppositions it makes (see p. 73), suggest something very different.

By the late twentieth century we see a move beyond Absurdism which creates deep uncertainty as to the worlds on the stage. The non-verbal techniques that usually fix fictional space are either suppressed or made unreliable and inconsistent. Stephens' note to *Motortown* (2006) says 'The play should be performed as far as possible without decor.' Dramas may rely solely on speeches to mark space. For example the second section of Owen's *Love Steals Us from Loneliness* (2010) begins at an event with karaoke, but when Scott begins speaking he is clearly not in the same space. Even where locations are indicated the stage remains unsettled in what it suggests, with a dislocation between action and setting. Although Stephens' *One Minute* (2003) opens with two characters in a clothes shop all the other characters are onstage, where they remain throughout. His note to the play says that 'a character who plays in two consecutive scenes need not wait to arrive in any second setting before playing the second scene'. Thus Catherine finishes a scene in a square in Islington and begins filling up salt cellars in the café where she works. And at five points in the play where solo characters address the audience there is no location but the stage itself. In such work the audience does not so much experience the contradictions of Absurdism as feel that it doesn't confidently know where it is. This uncertainty as to location or reference points for the fictional world allows it to alternate between representing a particular character's outlook – the fantasy or imaginings in their own head – and a world outside them. This sort of blurring of spaces can suggest both the importance of subjective realities and the ungraspability of an objective 'reality'.

## Rhythms of the stage

Closely associated with the argument of spaces is the way in which the stage is scripted to feel enclosed or open, empty or full at various moments (see our analysis of *Macbeth* on p. 17). What the play comes to mean to an audience and the way that it feels (its phenomenal and aesthetic effects) are influenced by this. When reading a play we therefore need to attend both to the number of bodies on stage and to the shape and dimensions of the theatrical set if one is specified.

Shakespeare's *Othello* (1602–4) begins with successive and successively large fillings of the stage with people, culminating in the clash between Brabantio's men and Othello's. His calming of the throng quickly establishes his noble status. The **crescendo** of bodies helps accentuate his ability to command. The opening scenes of *Hamlet* (1601) are contrasted not merely by location but also by body count. From the desolate and relatively empty ramparts of the castle we move to Claudius' self-presentation to his court, which fills the stage.

Act 3 of Schiller's *Mary Stuart* (1800) is the famous 'opening-out' scene, set in parkland, where the stage itself is scripted to become much more spacious than it has been so far. This is the moment when Mary briefly experiences the bliss of freedom from imprisonment. The scene is neither merely an appropriate place for her to be, nor merely a representation of Mary's feelings. It embodies that feeling, exhilarates the audience directly by **kinaesthetic** means. And physical space in the first half of Chekhov's *Three Sisters* becomes progressively restrictive, culminating in the young women being packed into a bedroom while a fire rages outside. The last act opens out as the military prepare to leave for Moscow, an expansiveness which has connotations of loss and desolation in connection with the sisters.

Usually, the sense of the stage filling is pleasurable in itself. The *entry* of the Danish court in *Hamlet* furnishes a direct source of pleasure for the audience, whether or not it is staged with any pageantry. Similarly, as we noted in connection with *A Doll's House*, an emptying stage usually feels sad or cold. *King Lear* ends with the stage direction '*Exeunt with a dead march*' (5.3.326 SD). We have also, however, just noted an occasion when several bodies are chaotically on stage and another when a throng suggests orderliness. In both cases the number of bodies matters, but for different reasons. The tension between full and empty, many and few, is put to productive effect in Neilson's *The Wonderful World of Dissocia* (2004). The first act, when Lisa visits Dissocia, has many characters, doing overstated acting in increasingly bizarre costumes, with scenes flowing into one another. A goat wants to have sex with Lisa and a polar bear sings her a song. The Lost Property Office is a hot dog stand where trays of hot dogs constantly appear, often ending up all over the floor. In Act 2 Lisa is in a hospital bed, which in the original staging was set in a box on a bare stage. The only sound effect is footsteps. Acting is understated, speech is minimal. In several of the short scenes Lisa is simply given medication. The two acts have a completely different physical presence and rhythm, and in that way **articulate** the spaces experienced by Lisa with and without her medication. The extreme contrast suggests that neither space is necessarily more unreal than the other.

Clearly physical rhythms of the stage are intimately tied up with the rhythms of the action, the pace of scenic divisions, the argument of spaces and logic of space. Attention to one consideration calls up others. By swapping our attention from one consideration to another, we enrich our reading of a play.

## Models and maps of theatrical space

The previous section developed various models which can help us analyse how space works on the stage and in theatres. Some worked very locally, others took more of an overview. Using the models depends upon some historical understanding, and we started to develop some historical maps to assist in this.

This last section hints at perspectives you might come to develop at university degree level, by turning again to the larger frame. Are there maps or models that can help us categorize wholesale conventions of space? In order to develop this question, we need first to set out one more important convention.

### Locus and platea

'*Locus* and *platea*' describes a regular arrangement used by Christian plays from the later Middle Ages. *The Castle of Perseverance* (*c*.1440) is a famous example. Players and audience all occupy a circular outdoor space, at the margins of which are erected simple wood and canvas structures called scaffolds. This play has one in the middle of the area, too.

The area within the ring of scaffolds is known as the 'place'. Some scaffolds in some plays may be used by the audience, but spectators more usually walk within the place and sit around its edge. Each scaffold usually represents a significant location, such as heaven, hell or a palace (see Figure 6.4). *Locus* and *platea* are the Latin for 'location' and 'open space', which correspond to scaffold and place respectively. The arrangement is also called 'place and scaffold'.

The action happens both on the scaffolds and between them, in the place. The place is a space of journeying between significant locations which are loaded with symbolic significance. It is also the space of intimate and often playful interaction with the audience. Scaffolds are to be looked up at with some wonder. A figure descending from a scaffold carries a special charge.

## Locus and platea as a general model

In 1987 Weimann showed how Renaissance plays still often work within the terms of the *locus–platea* **binary** even though the stage arrangement is very different. The underlying sense of space and its significance persists because the underlying assumptions of Christian belief persist, too. Believers have a spatial sense of their relationship to the godhead: God is above, deep within or all around. Later, Colin Counsell (1996) attempted to develop Weimann's work into a generalizable tool for analysing Western performance, from Naturalism, Brecht and Beckett to postmodern performance. Even in a predominantly secular culture, there persists a sense of a higher and fixed

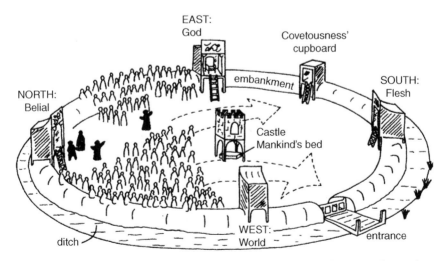

FIGURE 6.4 *Locus and platea (place and scaffold) staging. Illustration by Mick Wallis, based on Southern (1962).*

order of things, and the stage remains a platform on which we encounter
this. Counsell's readings into Western stage practice tease out the interplay
between a 'symbolic order' and illusion (*locus*) on the one hand and
democratic free play and the concrete (*platea*) on the other.

Those readings are very suggestive. But they involve something of a
simplification of what is really going on in medieval place and scaffold
playing. The whole arena, not just the scaffolds, is 'God's space'. God
was felt as an immediate presence; moral values were felt to be concrete,
not abstract things. The very distinction between concrete and abstract
is difficult to apply to medieval Christian belief. This sense of the real
immediate presence of the godhead in everyday life has been called
'theological Realism'.

Models are useful; but we need to use them with care. They can help us
tease out the significant features of specific moments of cultural production
like playmaking: but they can also distract us from important detail. Still, we
understand nothing without bringing some sort of model to it, consciously
or not – so we need to get used to the *activity* of modelling, trying and
testing a number of models at once.

## An abstract and a historical scheme

Let us look at just one abstract model that Pfister (1988: 262–4) introduces
in his exhaustive catalogue of methods for dramatic analysis. Considering
the scenic embodiment of the fictional locale, he distinguishes between:

- *Neutrality* as in the bare stage of classical antiquity and the
  Renaissance
- *Stylization* as in the diagrammatic scenic representations of the
  Restoration
- *Realization*  as in the detailed sets of Naturalism

Pfister rightly warns that, although our examples fall neatly into chronological
order, his three categories must not be taken to suggest a linear historical
development. Stylization and neutrality, for instance, have been regular
features of the twentieth-century stage.

Pfister's work in general and our discussions in this book might still
help us make and develop a scheme relating significant features of playing
arrangements to more general historical features. We could start with:

- *God's universe and concrete experience, theological Realism*
  Medieval *locus* and *platea*;
- *rapid process of change*
  Renaissance flexible variety of space;
  reference to many worlds;

- *theatre as civilized public institution, rational humanism*
  public square in heroic tragedy;
  **Neoclassical** unity of time, place and action;
- *secular and individualist concerns, determinism*
  detailed specificity of Naturalism;
  enclosure.

Our list is concerned with categories of space and the social function of drama. It will not be a neat list, and the important one is the one you come to draw for yourself.

# 7

# Dealing with some newer
# kinds of drama

It is a characteristic of many late twentieth-century playtexts that they emphasize the tension between what we have called the stage's two lines of communication (Chapter 3: theatrical communication), between communication across the stage and communication out from the stage to the audience. By the end of the twentieth century it was quite regular to find texts giving as much attention to communication delivered directly to the audience as communication between the persons on the stage.

The interest in emphasizing that second line of communication may well have started with early twentieth-century political texts, such as agitational sketches, which call for the performers to address their message directly to the audience. The dominant form of theatre seemed to invite the audience to lose itself into a fictional world, and in doing so to absorb false ideas about the real world. Critics of this theatre insisted that performers showed that they were in the same real world as the audience, talking to them directly about real issues rather than offering illusions. Instead of using devices that created a fictional world they often used techniques from traditional popular entertainments where the performer might be acrobat, busker or clown, able to perform wherever an audience gathered. This way of doing things had the additional economic attraction that it was cheaper than building large-scale fictional settings, and could often be done by fewer performers.

This emphasis on the stage–audience line of communication has, in general, two crucial aesthetic effects. The first is that, as in the case of the acrobat or busker, performers show themselves in two different aspects. They give a display of their art, such as singing a song or representing a fictional person, and they also present themselves as performers directly to the audience. Thus an actor may slide in and out of a fictional character. Secondly the space where they act, or sing or juggle, is always merely a platform, although it can be named and treated as any sort of fictional space. These two effects are most obviously noticeable where the written text requires shifts between dialogue across the stage and speech out to the audience. We have observed that these shifts have occurred on a smaller scale in forms of theatre that favour devices such as the aside (see p. 44). In developments from the late twentieth century onwards the alternation between dialogue across and speech out is more substantial and complex. For example, in Simon Stephens' play *One Minute* (2003) at five points in the play each of the characters separately addresses the audience. They talk about themselves moving through London, noting its activities, smells and sounds, and their responses to those. Standing independently of the dialogue and main narrative, the stories **articulate** responses to the city environment which are both idiosyncratically personal and yet connected into, part of, that environment. Note that here, crucially, the alternation between lines of communication does not require that the actors step out of character. Indeed part of its power comes from the sense that the character is trusting you with their personal feelings.

# Monodrama

The desire to communicate directly out to an audience led in the late 1980s to renewed interest in a very ancient form, storytelling. If you look, for example, at Noël Greig's play about HIV from 1988, *Plague of Innocence*, you will find no character names. The text is simply a column of short lines. They tell a story of interactions between a group of people. But while there is a range of different voices the lines are not assigned to named roles. Greig said that he developed this form at a time of drastic cuts to arts funding. His intention was to produce a text which, in the last resort, could be delivered by one person, indeed if necessary by himself. But where it is to be done by a company of performers, the question arises as to how such a text becomes a play as we would recognize it.

Greig said that when he worked with a company on it he invited them to read through as individuals and mark the bits they liked. Then they did a collective read-through, with individuals reading out the bits they'd marked, not knowing what others would read. In this way the text begins to become assigned to different performers. Note that point: the text becomes assigned to performers, not to roles. This has various implications. To begin with, the performer has a more direct relationship with the text. When they start by marking the bits they like, they are responding directly to the text's effect on their own interests and desires. They are not taking on a character to which they have been assigned and then having to find a way to deliver that character's lines. They are thus not limited to, do not 'become', that character. Instead they can range across the text as a whole, delivering it as a part of a group rather than approaching it from the point of view of a single character's perspective. This allows for flexibility in that the performer can speak as a character, speak some narrative, and then speak as a different character. It follows from all this that the final production of something like *Plague* will be shaped according to the way in which the text has been selected and interpreted by a specific group of people, or, to put it another way, its shape will emerge from the specific investment – emotional, political, ethical – that the group have put into it. A different group would then produce a very different production.

Contemporary with Greig's work the British company Forced Entertainment was making work through a process of devising. In the resulting shows the 'characters' seemed to be little more than the members of the company. They did not seem to be pretending to be fictional persons who were not themselves. This illusion – for at some level illusion it is – was assisted by a favourite mode of delivery, the telling of apparently personal stories and in particular the making of confessions. While the work of Forced Entertainment is not, strictly speaking, scripted drama, and thus lies outside the remit of this book, we mention it here because, alongside Greig's work, it illustrates a movement towards a form of theatre that has apparently got rid of 'character' as something which the dramatic text is interested in constructing or needs to use to carry out its work.

In work such as that by Greig and others, the telling of the story can be done by as many people as one wants to involve. But some texts require that the narrative is delivered by one performer alone. It is useful to give these a specific label: 'monodrama', a word used since at least 1803 (Lewis's *The Captive*). The monodrama is explicitly written as a complete piece for performance. Some people might call it a monologue, but a monologue, as the opposite of dialogue, can be one element within something else. It can also be confused with so-called dramatic monologues, written by Victorian poets such as Browning, where the poem is apparently spoken by a specific character other than the poet. These were not written for performance, however. It is the solo nature of the performance in which the efficacy of monodrama resides. All else might be variable. There may or may not be a story as such, it may follow chronological order or it may be a set of juxtaposed episodes. The space may be fixed or flexible, being one or all of: a platform, a single location, multiple locations. The manner might be gossipy, confessional or epic. The solo performer may represent a series of characters or may remain only as one. Such a character may seem to have nothing to do with the author, as in Lewis's *Captive*, or may present him or herself as the author of the text, a tradition which goes back to the medieval poet-presenter. Taken together, all these choices, which we can observe in the written text, construct the underlying relationship between cross-stage and out-front lines of communication. That relationship is shaped in different ways to achieve different ends, as we shall see.

In reading Camilla Whitehill's *Mr Incredible* (2016) we can note immediately that the actor always remains in character and never steps outside it. Straightaway Adam addresses us familiarly, apologizing for his ringtone and for having to rush off for a pee, but he gradually reveals that he has violently abused his partner. The solo enactment works by establishing what feels like a relationship of increasingly claustrophobic familiarity with a character whom the audience becomes uncomfortable about knowing but cannot escape. By contrast in Mojisola Adebayo's *Moj of the Antarctic* (2006) the author appears as herself, and in that role presents a range of characters. In this sort of case we need to be interested in how the characterizations are created. Adebayo's note on the text says, 'All the characters are played by one physically and vocally skilled solo performer.' And certainly there is an acrobatic dexterity to the work of representation. It's the story of an African-American slave who cross-dresses as a white man, escapes slavery and enlists as a sailor. Early on Moj, as a slave, plays the person of May, who taught her to read, and then plays May, the attorney and judge who sentenced the woman who taught May to read. The layering of representations is both a virtuoso performance and a mechanism for setting at a distance – imitated by the imitation of an imitation – the white men in authority. That distancing is combined with explicit mockery when Moj enlists the help of the audience in transforming her appearance into that of a white man. She puts flour on her face, bandages her breasts down, flattens her bottom and has a dough penis constructed by one of the audience. This penis has to be cut in half, however, since the aim is to represent a white man. She then dances to music, out of rhythm, and gets the audience to clap along. The creation of a caricature white man is done by bringing closer the relationship of performer and audience, making them party to the joke. Thus the story of an escaped black female slave becomes at the same time, through the medium of solo performance, a celebration of the potency, skill and anger of the black female performer here and now. The black woman is not contained within a stereotyped identity but instead conjures a whole range of identities, and in doing so articulates a series of repressed voices.

This mode of performing, and celebration, require that the performer-author is always in the central focus. But uncertainty about the slippage between performer and character is itself a highly productive mechanism for the effectiveness of solo drama. One of the most famous examples is SuAndi's *Story of M* (1994). This is a groundbreaking example of monodrama in modern black theatre. Monodrama had been used by Edwardian feminists in order to raise issues around sexual oppression. Here SuAndi uses it to explore the heritage of racism in British culture by telling the story of her mother. It begins with her as a cancer patient in hospital. The performer fully inhabits the character, talking directly to the audience, addressed as 'you'. The situation, and specifically the effects of chemo treatment, are invoked as explanations for the anecdotal mode: 'Now I'm here, two parts dead./ Going over me life/ like you do, /like you all will, / given the chance' (p. 30). Towards the end, the stage gets darker, with the woman asking, unsuccessfully, to have the light put on. At this point the performer ceases being the dying woman; she removes her costume and addresses the audience: 'When my mother died, the world did not/ stand still' (p. 53). She talks of grief giving way to memories, and the realization that though the body dies 'the spirit continues and you carry it/ here, in this place of love' (p. 54). At this moment we see that the imitation of a character was and is a necessary part of grieving and memorialization for the real performer: characterization of another and speaking as the self are both parts of the same necessary, and authentic, process. The theatrical coup at this end-point of the show is the audience's realization that SuAndi's mother was white (although she says early on that she is not 'African'). This leads to SuAndi's assertion of pride in being a black woman and a mixed-race woman, proud of being 'a Nigerian daughter' and 'the daughter/ of a Liverpool woman of Irish descent' (p. 55). The single 'I' that begins the show is revealed to contain multiple ancestry, and to be the richer for its mixedness, both of races and voices. Through its mixing of theatrical elements and performance registers (see p. 31), this moving and inspiring work bears testimony not only to an individual life but through this to black experience and the authenticity of 'mixed-race' identity.

When the solo performer talks directly to the audience, as 'I' to 'you', this produces a closeness of relationship in which an audience is more readily inclined to accept what it is hearing as truth, becoming ethically contracted as witnesses to what is revealed to them here and now. Through the contract between truth-teller and witness, the audience is bound into particular expectations and sometimes behaviours. Actually, however, the appearance of truth-telling is predominantly an aesthetic effect, a 'strategy of authentication' (see p. 81), produced largely by the mechanism of the solo performer acting as a performer and directly addressing the audience: we have no means of knowing that what SuAndi tells us about her mother is true. The scripted devices that construct this mechanism can be seen in the opening speech of Rosie Kellett's *Primadonna* (2016) (this is a show that can be done by more than one performer but this doesn't affect what the opening speech does): 'Hi/ My name is Rosie/ I have ginger hair./ It's not real, although my dad is ginger... .' 'Everything in this story is based on truth./ It all happened in mine or Jamie's actual lives./ We have decided to change some of the names and places/ But that was the only piece of advice my dad's/ lawyer gave us' (p. 95).

Rosie's speech here alerts us to something else which we can attempt to describe, namely the aesthetic convention being used for solo performance. Earlier we talked about formal storytelling. But the mid- to late twentieth century developed a much more widespread solo performance convention: stand-up comedy. Some solo dramas use the stylistic features of stand-up to establish a relationship with an audience, before complicating it (for example *Mr Incredible*). If stand-up is a dominant form, the work of solo storytelling has also allowed for the cultural importation and popularization of non-western, non-dominant, forms of storytelling. Adebayo, for example, begins *Moj* with the figure of 'a West-African female griot (storyteller, historian, singer, mystic)' (p. 23). SuAndi's performance poetry can be seen as a modern version of the ancient poet-presenter who recited their text to an audience.

The invocation of convention is one of the ways the written text shapes the relationship of the solo performer with the audience. The other way is through a device which only readers, rather than audiences, see: the layout of the text on the page, its typography. SuAndi's text looks like a poem divided into scenes each with a simple direction for mimetic activity from the performer. In Stephen Laughton's *Run* (2016) the speech is divided into units of varying lengths, from paragraphs to single words. These seem to work to indicate shifts of pace or mood for the performer. But it is not always that clear. Take this:

And we kiss.

...backwards turns world the and

fuck

I

Don't

Even

Know

Which

Way

And

Everything.

Deep in me.

(p. 239)

This is an example of a more general development in late-twentieth-century theatre writing, to which we shall return. The typography of the written text, its material manifestation, is used as a provocation to the performer. The performer must find an appropriate response to those fractured lines. This response is not specified by the author. What the actor does is a product of their own, personal engagement with the written provocation. And the audience, of course, never see that provocation, only its result. Not since Bernard Shaw's huge stage directions, again invisible to the audience, has the materiality of the text as written object been so important for the creation of performance. Note that in making this provocation the written text does not need to be a fiction, let alone a scripted play. Some theatre makers prefer to work with texts that are not designed for staging, but analysis of those productions lies outside the brief of a book on studying plays. What we need to note now is that, in contemporary playtexts, there is an interest as much in the materiality of the text itself as in what it depicts. So far we have defined this materiality as the manifestation of the text in written form, as a visual object. But it can also include manifestations of the text as something previously spoken and recorded. It is text of this sort that lies at the heart of another major late-twentieth-century mode.

# Testimony and tribunal

The solo drama often features an account about, or told from the perspective of, a particular character and the performance works as testimony to the character's experience or life. Sometimes a dramatic text offers an account of a particular event. Where that event actually happened – an industrial dispute, a terrorist attack – the text works as testimony to that event, presenting the real feelings of those who were witnesses to it. This is also the case where the play pays witness not so much to an event as to an ongoing condition of real life, such as racial or gender discrimination. Such texts belong to the genre of testimony plays, which are plays that derive from accounts of a real event or real experience that is often known to the audience and that invite the audience to consider their own relationship to it. The testimony text will work to represent the full experience and impact of an event without necessarily framing it within a historical context or setting it at a distance for analysis. This emphasis on the accounts of those who witnessed the event, rather than on historical commentary or framing, tends to distinguish the testimony text from documentary drama. But both have political purposes: the testimony text seeks to reveal something concealed or repressed, or to state feelings that have not been heard. An example of this comes in *Guantanamo*, by Gillian Slovo and Victoria Brittain, done at the Tricycle Theatre in May 2004 after five British detainees were released from the prison in February. In Act 3 the lawyer Gareth Peirce asks the audience a question: 'When you have [in front of you] men you're getting to know and they're talking about it, not because you're interrogating them, but it's tumbling out and they're reminding each other, they're telling things that they haven't told anyone ... How do you tell it? How do ordinary words tell it?' (pp. 557–8) These are Peirce's real words, but taken into a theatre they make the audience party to the work of trying to tell it, acknowledging the need to witness it, under ethical, and emotional, pressure from hearing what hasn't been told to anyone.

Where an event is known to be real, and where the text undertakes a social purpose in revealing and/or exploring real responses to that event, it gains ethical authority by insisting on its actuality. There are various ways a text might do this. The most well-known, and influential, is the reproduction of accounts taken verbatim from witnesses. Such accounts are gathered mainly by interviewing those involved but can also, less often, be taken from documents. So important is the method that it is often used as a name for a genre. 'Verbatim' theatre is seen as a development out of documentary theatre, where the process of interviewing enables wide participation in a project. It also comes with problems, however, in that the words of frequently traumatized subjects can be appropriated by actors, silently edited or put to new uses. In these circumstances that which is supposedly verbatim is not necessarily always true to its source, nor even verbatim.

Another way of establishing ethical authority is to base the text on photographic and/or, more often, written documents. Where such documents are records of legal enquiries or courtroom considerations, the text is known as a 'tribunal' play. The distinction between words gathered in interview and words taken from a written document creates different aesthetic practices and effects, a contrast we explore below.

In the case of all plays that deal in testimony, whether they are verbatim or tribunal based, the assumption is that the text originates not in the creative imaginings of a playwright but in words that have actually been said. The words are thus taken to be 'authentic', truthful in that they have been taken from the real world. Andy Lavender reminds us that this apparently 'authentic speaking' is 'a *discursive* realm, a transactional space of meaning-production'. This discourse is itself a theatrical 'mode' that came into fashion at a particular period (Lavender 2016: 37). We have encountered the concept of discourse before (see pp. 55–7). Here the discourse of verbatim and tribunal is marked as true speaking as against fictional speaking. In some cases it is true because it's taken from the record of an event, but it is not delivered by the original speakers. In other cases it is true because it is apparently generated by those who speak it. These are not imitating other speakers: the truth is there in their bodies. But remember that this discourse of true speaking is always a theatrical mode. While in some cases it involves imitation in all cases the discourse is organized on textual principles and uses textual devices.

The written texts of testimony plays suggest their characteristic aesthetic effects. These include, first, a much stronger emphasis on the line of communication out from the stage to the audience rather than across the stage. The audience are treated as those who need to hear the story of the event (as we saw in the example from *Guantanamo* above); in the case of tribunal plays they are often in the position of a courtroom jury. The place inhabited by the speakers tends not to be specified. Thus in Robin Soans' *Talking to Terrorists* (2005), Phoebe enters and then Edward comes in and sits in a comfortable chair. Phoebe speaks about her work with children, Edward talks about people's lives. Phoebe begins, 'It's really difficult for me to talk to you because … well … because what do you say when you return from interviewing children who were abducted by men who raped them, or nailed their knees together to stop them running away….' Edward begins, 'Ninety per cent of the population aren't enormously involved in politics; what are they doing? They're taking the kids to school, they're watching Eastenders ….' (pp. 26–7) Although their subsequent speeches alternate they are not having a dialogue. While Phoebe talks about her sense of helplessness in the face of the horrors, Edward talks about the general disinterest. The juxtaposed speeches delivered to the audience are precisely the device which gets the emotional effect: the audience, seated in a theatre, hears real horrors and experiences incapacity for action. The performers may show more or less strongly marked 'characters': the content of Phoebe's speech has more impact than her character. There may or may not be a narrator or principal witness: in Act 1, Edward introduces a group of young Muslims, and then, later, interjects and comments on the mindset of 'terrorists', but then appears no more. While in some tribunal plays the manner of a witness may be copied very precisely, they are not characterized or given anything to say outside of their moment of examination by the tribunal. The texts of tribunal plays tend not to offer stage direction or instruction to the performers. The texts, even though they depict real historical individuals, can work without characterization as such. Analysis of such plays does not seek to begin with character or story.

Instead we must focus on the arrangement of the spoken words. Although these may have originated in actuality, rather than fiction, they have, nevertheless, been edited into a shape. Dramatists are handling a huge amount of information gathered in interview or documentary record. The power of verbatim and tribunal plays comes from the telling in a couple of hours of a whole story which may have unfolded in a courtroom over months if not years. It gives pleasure to the audience because it enables them to understand how what is often reported in fragments fits together. But that condensation requires cutting, editing and arrangement. The way the original words are handled can produce both new knowledge and emotional effect. We have already noted the effects produced by juxtaposition and direct address. The play based on interview may have a freer hand to do this than a tribunal play, where, as Richard Norton-Taylor says, he is obliged to respect the chronological order of witnesses. Nonetheless here too it can be edited: as Norton-Taylor notes he shifted the order of witnesses to end *Justifying War* with Dr Kelly's widow.

The editing of a tribunal text can be more detailed than this. It can control the lengths of testimony and the rhythm of movement from one witness to another. It can produce focus on key details and specific contrast between different testimonies. In *Justifying War* (2003) the text includes exchanges which identify precise passages in documents: 'There is a passage on page 18.' 'Page 18 of the dossier, DOS/1/73.' It retains a moment when a witness pauses in order to find a page: 'One moment please.' '44.' 'Yes I wish to be very faithful to the witness statement I have given you if I may' (pp. 430, 466–7). Such moments have little function in conveying information from Lord Hutton's inquiry but they work instead to assert the play's closeness to the tribunal documents: they authenticate. Authentication can happen in subtler ways. The witness Andrew Gilligan is asked to read out the text of a broadcast of BBC radio's *Today* programme where he was interviewed by John Humphreys; the lawyer reads Humphreys. While this actually happened in the tribunal, its use in the play has specific effect. The actor playing Gilligan plays Gilligan reading himself. This doubling up, this re-stating of what has been really said, again marks it as true.

Now while the tribunal text is revealing information and using devices that verify its truthfulness, the interview-based, 'verbatim', text works rather differently. In part it often scripts into itself the reminder that the text has been gathered by interview: 'I live in there, in among it all. My home and my car have been held to hostage basically, ha ha that's all I can say, ha, ha, ha.' The silent presence of an interviewer may be used to structure the actor's delivery. 'Let's see them. (*To Alecky*) She won't even let, let me see them. She's a nice black girl isn't she? (*To Jean*) See that young black girl – ' The text meticulously retains verbal tics such as repetitions, half-laughs, broken sentences, and it here has the speaker moving between interviewer and friend. In this play, *Come Out Eli* (2003), the interviewer/author Alecky Blythe has also written herself in as a character. It begins with her on the phone dealing with a prospective interviewee who wants to have sex with her in exchange for an interview. During one of these phone scenes it's clear that the interviewer can be reduced to inarticulateness as much as anyone else: 'Yeah well it's not just – you know it's not – I'm a, I'm a professional.' Quite as much as the telling of a story, the emphasis is on rendering the texture of the telling, the ways that speech struggles. Blythe insists that her actors are as faithful as they can be to the speech patterns of the interviewees, adopting a specific technique which she has her character outline in the play: 'All I require is to get your story, record it, and that's what the actors work from in the show, they hear it playing through earphones and they copy you exactly' (pp. 134, 149–50). This too, then, is a way of marking truth. It works to ensure that we know that the lines delivered still belong to the interviewees. This gets round the problem of performers apparently appropriating other people's words. But it has one other effect. The attention to the difficulties of articulation throws the focus not onto the events but onto the response to events: in *Guantanamo* one character says, 'when you mentioned you were doing this, I sort of thought, well, what do I think, what is my attitude' (p. 550). The interview play is often as much interested in the response to as the facts of events. This of course also requires pretty precise acting.

So, it's worth identifying what sort of play it is and then exploring what effects are produced by the edited story. At the same time we note how the text marks itself as authentic, as truth based. Both elements work to produce aesthetic pleasure – on the one hand the attraction of a story, with revelation of details; on the other the assurance that we are dealing with the real world, being spoken to truthfully. Of course there's a paradox here in that the real world is usually not as tidy, or as interesting, as editing can make it. A student of these texts can attend to this paradox and demonstrate how it operates and what it does.

We stress the point about editing because there is, in some quarters, a suggestion that testimony texts, by making direct use of authentic documents, are able straightforwardly to present actuality and so to sidestep the treacherous theatrical business of representation. Both solo dramas and testimony plays in their separate ways do indeed want to distance themselves from the practices of reproducing a fictional narrative as if it were real, the practice of realism. This is the value of texts drawn, not from fiction, but from interviews or tribunals. But there is very little that is direct about their management of this material. If the stage is apparently presenting, rather than representing, actuality, we have to remain aware that this sense of presentation is carefully textually constructed. Mistaken as it is, the attractiveness of the suggestion about directness often derives from a desire to align testimony practice with a concept that was fashionable in the first decade of the new millennium, to which we now turn.

# 'Post-dramatic' theatre

We have so far been concerned with texts that agitate the tension between the stage's lines of communication, with the attendant slippage between fictional character and performer and between fictional place and stage platform. The texts seem to hover between creation of fiction and refusal of fiction. They begin to distance themselves from theatrical realism. At the same time the stories told by both the solo drama and the testimony play tend (though there are exceptions) to have a coherent shape and organization, even though done on a platform by a non-character. This coherence is specifically disrupted by a third mode of late-twentieth-century playtext. 'This play can be performed by any number of actors. It can be performed in any order,' says the note to Simon Stephens' *Pornography* (2007).

That sort of note sets problems in the path of those who want to study and produce the play. Students of it have always to be aware that what they are looking at is open to change, and the changes may affect how it works on stage. Producers of it know it is their responsibility to take decisions about numbers of players and order of scenes. We began this book by noting that the playtext is always an incomplete object (see pp. 3–6). But, even though many students totally accept that the verbal text is a different thing from what is staged, that acceptance doesn't always prevent the assumption that reliable answers can be found in the text: What is this character's previous life? What is this person feeling here? Playtexts such as *Pornography* find ways of insisting that we notice their incompleteness. Indeed some texts make themselves look as if they should not be on the stage at all, not so much texts designed for staging but texts that obstruct staging. Not only do they refuse to make coherent fictional characters and worlds but they also withhold recognizable narrative shapes and reference points. Breaking so many conventions of realism these plays, going beyond even testimony plays, may be said to be polemically 'post-realist'. Without writing a lengthy essay to explain the rise of this mode of play we might suggest here that it coincides with the rapid growth in information, and particularly personal information, through various forms of social and televisual media. Personal blogs, Facebook friends, tweets and Snapchat promise entry to the feelings and lives of others while at the same time facilitating like never before the creation of fake identities and dissemination of lies. In this world the theatre and its texts start asking questions about the ease with which we are invited to immerse ourselves in communications about people and places that may not be wholly real, about the assumptions we make as to the credibility and reliability of pictures of the real. The post-realist plays insist that reality cannot be separated from our perception of it, that the communication of the real is simultaneously a construction of the real.

Within the wider movement that followed, and rejected, realism, there appeared a series of various experiments and explorations that came to be seen as exemplars of a new genre, the 'post-dramatic'. This term, popularized by Hans-Thies Lehmann in a publication in 1999, rapidly took off in some academic circles as a way of describing a range of productions which started appearing in the last third of the twentieth century. Lehmann suggests these productions all show the following features: 'dehierarchisation' of means, which is to say that any written text by a playwright is not regarded as the main motivation or authority in the staging; simultaneity of sign, leading to 'parcelled' perception in which the audience cannot take in everything at once but has to select for themselves their own object of focus, rather than the production doing it for them; diversity of signs, where the stage refuses to make things coherent, playing contradictory signals off against one another, sometimes giving too many and sometimes not enough; the refusal of formal unity or coherence, with a sense of going beyond limits, which he calls 'plethora'; an interest in the music of words, in the play of languages, rather than their meanings alone; a **dramaturgy** that is visual rather than deriving necessarily from written text, leading to characteristic atmospheres, for example, the cultivation of coolness of tone; an emphasis on physical forms gives an aura of physical presence; instead of inviting and taking pleasure in recognition, the theatre presents that which is not wholly graspable, showing itself incomplete, with signs that refer to no clear deeper meaning but simply offering themselves as surface; that which is real becomes a co-player with the fiction, showing the actors as actors, reminding us that theatre-making is always material productivity; all of this leads to a sense that theatre is never a finished, complete outcome but always unfinished process, never something that can be looked at with shared agreement but instead experienced as social situation and individual response.

The sorts of modes that Lehmann sees as delivering these features emphasize narrative acts, scenic process, cross-art creation, scenic essays, cinematographic theatre, hypernaturalism, ironic distance and disengagement, shared space, theatre solos, choral theatre. Clearly this is a vast range, moving between apparently opposed poles – distanced/shared, solo/chorus, narrative/scenic, cinematographic/hypernatural. All of it, Lehmann says, constitutes work where the traditional paradigm of drama no longer holds sway. Drama may persist but it is not in dominance. The post-dramatic is not against drama, but beyond it, after it. Drama itself works through imitation and 'action', which together produce in an audience recognition and sometimes a shared social bond. 'Dramatic theatre', he says, 'is subordinated to the primacy of the text.' By text he means 'the imagination of a comprehensible narrative and/or mental *totality*'. Although gesture and movement became important the human figure 'was still centrally defined through speech'. The text 'functioned primarily as role script' (pp. 21–2).

The concept of a 'mental totality' is a pretty all-inclusive category, applicable to a lot of material, including perhaps that which is cultivating a generalized atmosphere of coolness or ironic distance, choric organization and musicality, indeed the staging of process itself. Many of the features of the so-called post-dramatic demonstrate their theatre's separation from and disavowal of dramatic theatre. These can be fairly easily grasped as themselves part of a total mental scheme which opposes dramatic to that which is 'post-dramatic'. Like many simple schemes of opposites this one is a bit too simplified to swallow wholesale. It requires that Lehmann gather up together a list of features and a large range of modes that do not always sit happily with one another. Nor do they sit happily alongside diverse practices from the past, where, for example, commedia dell'arte improvised on the basis of a simple list of scenes, which in turn led to the mixed modes of pantomime and melodrama, where an actor's characteristic role shaped and probably took precedence over whatever was in the script. Lehmann is careful to note that one sort of past practice, ancient tragedy, should be called 'pre-dramatic' (p. 34). He also gathers together medieval, Shakespearean and baroque practices as 'impure drama', coming before and parallel to 'pure' drama (p. 48). Excluding the pre-dramatic, that's a period of at least three hundred years. In Lehmann's scheme of pre-dramatic, impure drama, pure drama and post-dramatic, pure drama seems to correspond with a practice of a distinct period of years with a particular approach to script and role. This is the approach associated mainly with theatrical realism. It is for this reason we say that the 'post-dramatic' is but one, rather vocal, element of the contemporary turn away from the phase of realism.

Ours is a minority view perhaps. Lehmann's hypothesis has gained the status of orthodoxy in some quarters. This is unfortunate because, while he is surely right in many of his observations about the shared features of the works he discusses, the rather grander claims of the hypothesis have led to some mistaken assumptions. The 'post-dramatic' tends to be spoken of as a historical rupture with the past. Lehmann is partly responsible for this for despite his assurance in one place that the post-dramatic is not against drama, and that drama persists, he also says, elsewhere, that the transformation of drama has '*mutually estranged theatre and drama and has distanced them ever further from each other*' (p. 30; original emphasis). Yet many plays are being written which show some of the features of Lehmann's post-dramatic but which still firmly characterize themselves as plays, working as scripts for roles and dealing in fiction. Strictly 'post-dramatic' work on Lehmann's terms tends to be a small subsection of much wider developments in writing practice.

Another problem is that Lehmann's claim that the post-dramatic allows for irruption of the real into fiction is interpreted in a banal way to assume that there is an easy divide between fiction and reality. Where in a 'post-dramatic' production the actors show themselves to be actors, taking a break while on stage, becoming exhausted, performance theory would argue that they are still performing – because we all perform: we all adopt different 'faces', roles, for different circumstances. Such 'post-dramatic' actors are **rhetorically** distinguishing themselves from fictional practices. But this is not real life. They are doing it within an aesthetic frame. They are known to be performers, even if only temporarily. Thus, just as with drama, we are dealing with an aesthetic practice which deploys a specific **rhetoric** in order to present us with certain sorts of persons. When we see theatre apparently breaking with representation, it is actually engaged in the business of constructing a sense of that which is directly presented rather than re-presented. This construction may open itself to chance and the unrehearsed, but it is not done without rules, plans and indeed conventions. The interest for the analyst is in the particular shape and effects of this rhetoric of non-fiction, this 'discourse' of truth-speaking as we called it above. And it can be analysed as such.

Thirdly, and perhaps most weirdly of all, there arises an assumption that 'post-dramatic' practice has disposed of the text, where the text is assumed to be a fictional entity which enslaves real actors to its purposes. Again Lehmann is partly to blame for this, because he says the dramatic, which deals in fiction and false coherence, promotes the primacy of 'the text'. As we know, he says the 'post-dramatic' theatre dislodges the playwright's text from its authority, creating space for the ideas of director, designer and actors. When Elfriede Jelinek's *Sports Play* (2012) was prepared for production in London the actors started devising and the designer designing before the German text had even been fully translated. And then, once translated, it was cut down to size, edited, by a dramaturge. But not all production that dislodges the playtext is that collaborative. Within the German theatrical tradition, the director was often the primary shaper of the work. Since at least the 1960s German directors questioned assumptions which regard the written text as sacrosanct. The most spectacular, or scandalous, test-cases early on were the productions which cut up, re-arranged or exploded Shakespeare's plays. In these circumstances the director becomes the primary author, with her or his 'signature' (see p. 57) being more apparent than that of the original author. Indeed in German theatre directors might be given a season of plays, much as one might have a season of Arthur Miller. Thus, for example, in the first production of Jelinek's *Ein Sportstück* (1998) by Einar Schleef the large-scale use of chorus bore the signature not of Jelinek but of Schleef. There is, then, not less, but more text in a post-dramatic production: that of the author, the director-dramaturge, the designer. A student of 'post-dramatic' varieties of post-realism needs to be aware that, when watching them, they are watching at least two texts, the director's perhaps more than the author's, and that any other production of the author's text may well then be a fundamentally different work.

Now Jelinek's text had to be edited down to size because it is huge. Certainly this sort of post-realist text challenges assumptions, as we say above, as to what a 'play' is, presenting neither coherent fictional characters nor an orderly narrative. While Jelinek's text does have named speakers, Martin Crimp's *Attempts on her Life* (1997) has none, simply dashes where the speaker changes. Heiner Müller's *The Horatian* (1968), like Greig's *Plague of Innocence*, looks like a poem rather than a play. Abjuring any illusions that it provides easy access to a fictional world, this sort of text seems to obstruct its own staging. Insisting on itself as nothing more than a written document, it demands intervention from or collaboration with others. This insistence on its writtenness is stated not in what it imagines but in how it is written and appears, in its selection of words, its sound and rhythm, its layout on the page. Earlier (see p. 177) we called this its 'materiality'. This 'material quality of the text' is specifically valued by music-theatre maker Heiner Goebbels: 'I want to draw attention to the physical shape in which a text appears on the page' (2009).

For a student of the post-realist play this materiality is a good place to begin an analysis. What does it look like on the page: great chunks of prose, short lines of poetry, intermittent words? What can we say about its linguistic register, its sounds and rhythm? And then how precisely is it making itself obstructive? What – if anything – do we find strange or unfamiliar about it? Does it specify characters or place, props or activities? Does it have any identifiable dialogue, or are there any contrasts between various chunks of prose, any repetitions or parallels, any rhythmic patterns? A text may have some specifications for performance but not others, and we might be able to see whether its handling of stage spaces or character effects or verbal exchanges have any of the features we have identified elsewhere in this book.

Take for example the opening of Sarah Kane's play *Crave* (1998):

C    You're dead to me.
B    My will reads, Fuck this up and I'll haunt you for the rest of your fucking life.
C    He's following me.
A    What do you want?
B    To die.
C    Somewhere outside the city, I told my mother, You're dead to me.
B    No that's not it.
C    If I could be free of you without having to lose you.
A    Sometimes that's not possible.
M    I keep telling people I'm pregnant. They say How did you do it, what are you taking? I say I drank a bottle of port, smoked some fags and fucked a stranger.
B    All lies.
C    He needs to have a secret but he can't help telling. He thinks we don't know. Believe me, we know.
M    A voice in the desert. (Kane 2001: 155)

We are not told where these speakers are or whether they have any relationship with each other. The lines are, however, laid out as dialogue. This could invite the use of some of the techniques we described on pp. 58–63. A focus on turn-taking, initiation of exchanges and topic control can lead us into different possibilities. A and B seem to comment on lines by C and M, B seems to answer a question by A. C's topic seems to circulate between a mother and a man, M initiates a topic about her pregnancy that nobody else picks up. Now these speakers may all be in separate places, but the sequence which Kane has written, with, as she said, careful attention to its punctuation, automatically, through the dynamics of verbal exchange, begins to set up relationships. At the same time these relationships are provisional and highly transient. It puts itself into a fairly specific linguistic territory and mood (they're not talking about fairgrounds and candy-floss), and replicates the devices of dialogue up to a point, but then leaves them incomplete. Character tends not to be imitation of behaviour so much as expression of consciousness. Taken together these are the elements that begin to suggest an exploration of disconnected communications in psychically alienated lives.

More blatantly provocative perhaps is the one direction from Stephens' *Pornography* which we quote above, which indicates that the scenes may be played in any order by any number. Now unless someone is analysing the play to stage it, they don't need to take a decision about order and number (and the original German director anyway decided to do it the way it was written). The analytic job instead is to accept what is provisional about the text and to note where the play offers itself up for specific intervention by others. From here it is worth inspecting what may be somewhat less provisional, for example, the different elements and texture of each scene, ranging from apparently personal narrative through fragments of dialogue to factual statements, and it may even be possible to conjecture what effects arise from different combinations of scene. Some of these may only be found in the process of production. In the first English production the director worked by orchestrating the different speakers in relation to one another, but at the end of the process one actor noted that there was a line he had not said. He was told to say it right at the end, so this production ended with 'You gonna watch him? You gonna watch him? You watching Snoop Dog?' (p. 226) The placing of it, arrived at by serendipity, gave the play a gently humane finish. In such a repositioning the author's line is treated in the same way as a lighting cue, or an actor's gesture, or a prop. Lehmann is right that this is a break from certain ideas about the fixedness of the author's text, and the student does well to approach the play accepting that the text only ever gets fixed, and sometimes not even then, in particular productions.

What is readily apparent about *Pornography* is that it has a clear topic, the London '7/7' bombings of public transport. While this could have been produced as a 'verbatim' play, Stephens abjures what he regards as a misleading practice, in that verbatim plays often hide the role and function of the researcher in the discovery of their material, a concealment which can be seen as dishonest. He thus opted instead for an imitation of a verbatim play built from imaginary texts. By contrast with this clarity of focus, on a specific time and place and indeed with specific if unnamed characters, Jelinek's *Sports Play* is much more diffuse. Many of its references are indeed to the industry and desires around sporting activity. This provides a metaphor for a larger meditation on issues about appropriate, and supposedly successful, careers, gender roles and bodies. But it is left to us to pick our way through it.

*Sports Play* opens with a lengthy stage direction as to the use of a chorus and possible arrangement of the stage. This all is prefaced by the words 'The author doesn't give many stage directions, she has learned her lesson by now. Do what you like.' The challenge of the stage directions, though, is less their absence than their inscrutability. We are told a woman and young man kick, hit with bats, and throw between them a 'bundle' which is also a person that does everyday tasks and becomes bloodied as a result of the beating. The stage direction has to be more of an image for a certain sort of scene than an operational instruction. Later the text directs that one speaker's monologue is constantly interrupted by another speaker; it also suggests that two monologues may be interwoven at will. Here again there is a great deal of specificity, part of which sets the framework for staging choices to be made by others. We have to learn, then, that even though the stage directions function differently from what we might have expected they still do a job of work. When we try to identify that job of work we note that they establish moods, set frameworks for decisions by others and, perhaps most controlling of all, they present a picture of an author who doesn't have control.

The active construction of this diffident author-figure takes its place among the devices that ensure the play keeps eluding any attempt to pin it down. Having noted the specific but inscrutable stage directions, we then have to ask how the speeches function. Jelinek's scripts are habitually gatherings, montages, of quotations from popular media and high culture: 'You, the mother, are still allowed to wash your son's soul at 30 degrees, it won't bobble, and even after thirty washes its colours will look like new.' (p. 55). Many English-language students will be unlikely to pick up all the quotations at first reading, if at all. But there are other features of what appears on the stage that can be described. For example, an old woman in a pietà tableau, with Jesus on her lap, speaks for seven to eight pages. She describes herself as a killer who is enraged about how she is perceived as a woman. She says such things as this: 'As a woman I should align myself with foreign images, yes, I should allow myself to be constantly described and keep still at the same time. That's not my way. I have to be vaccinated with images with which I never conform. I give up. I prefer to take. My ill-woman cannot break out! Because I won't let her' (p. 86). Looking at the text you'll see that these lines are no more significant than any others: she says the same thing again and again in a variety of different ways. The writing is less interested in creating a recognizable human speech mode and more interested in the proliferation of verbal effects: in associations, repetitions, quotedness, jokes. It produces a sense of surplus, exceeding what is necessary for the expression of character feeling, although of course the sense of surplus is already a sort of expression. Secondly we note that the old woman talks directly to an audience about herself, rather than expressing herself, as a particular individual ('I') and as a generic woman. She describes an image and identity thrust upon her by others, receiving images from the culture around her and sometimes inhabiting them; having an 'ill-woman' inside that the 'I' will not let out. Together with the patchwork of quotations this suggests that a multiple entity is speaking, neither generic nor individual. It constantly describes itself while enacting a refusal to be described by others. In this restlessness, this complicating of single identity, there is political purpose.

Having noted the points of resistance to analysis, the 'difficulties', we could characterize its general range of references – whether to sport, to popular culture and news media, to literary classics. A designer would use this material. We can also pick up on suggestions about mode of performance. Sometimes speakers present themselves as social types: 'We mothers are either silent heroines or louder heroines' (p. 48). Sometimes they quote typical attitudes: 'If I didn't know where it was coming from, this bawling could force me to flee. It's coming from one person alone, namely from you, my lady' (p. 76). Sometimes they speak as if they are spectators of realist media: 'Whatever identity we might bestow upon him, it is not through his deeds that we recognise our favourite sportsman. We have to take his face into account and read his character' (p. 57). All these modes of speaking offer cues, if required, for modes of delivery, like textual stage directions (see p. 13). All of this creates a tension between the fullness of the expressive apparatus, bombarding with words and attitudes, with speaking and movement, and, on the other hand, the unreliability of apparently authentic communication. It's that tension, again, between textual precision and apparent diffidence.

The last major point to note in such a text is how it works at declaring its own sense of itself as text. Achilles asks, 'And you, madam author, why are you so aggressive? We haven't done anything to you' (p. 121). Later, in what might be taken as – possibly ironic – commentary on its mode, the text says, 'We don't need unifying ideas any more, no emotion, no plans. We need dumb pantomime gestures, a slight hand movement' (p. 152). And by way of finally consolidating its own reflexivity the 'Author' comes on: 'Do you have any idea how embarrassed for me people are around here?' (pp. 158–9) Now clearly a production company would have to do much more detailed work than this and come up with decisions of their own in order to produce a text for staging. But for us as analysts we can begin to identify the text's characteristic procedures and its points of reference. From there we can begin to explain how it **rhetorically** produces not only a tension around gender roles but also a tension between overflow of information and diffidence about that information. These tensions may be said to inform its dramatic action.

Jelinek's play can be taken to be exemplary of the post-dramatic mode. Many of the features described by Lehmann (p. 183 above) can be identified in it. At the same time it can be analysed in much the same way that we might analyse any other play. Lehmann would argue that, unlike 'drama', Jelinek's text does not have a primary role to play in the production process. That may be true: it sets challenges for a production company. But it's up to that company to decide how much priority they give to Jelinek's text. They could largely ignore it; but then they could do the same with a play by Shakespeare or Ibsen. The perhaps more interesting task is to be led by Jelinek's text into its own territory, accepting the challenges and games: in short, to let Jelinek's text estrange the company from their own habitual procedures, or, perhaps more specifically, to let Jelinek's text take some priority over the director's 'text', her or his usual way of doing things. Arguably *Sports Play* becomes more properly 'post-dramatic' in feel when Jelinek's dramatic text is given primacy.

Throughout this book, as well as in this chapter, we have seen emerging some of the characteristic features of texts for plays written over the last three or so decades. In the first edition of this book we noted that the new writing then looked rather as if it was intended for TV. By contrast writing for the stage now seems to make TV production difficult if not impossible. Contemporary plays tend to use the tension between communication across the stage and communication out from it. The space of the stage is much less defined, with a blurring between fictional space and simple theatrical platform. On the other hand, there is often a great deal of specificity about speech. There is careful management of both silence and speech noise. There is, perhaps most noticeably, an interest in formalized language, seen in explorations in speech register and uses of different sorts of poetry. Alongside this there is an interest in typography, in the look of the play on the page. Now this last is a very interesting development. A performance in the theatre is not necessarily going to make clear what the play looks like on the page. The audience will have little specific knowledge of its challenges and provocations. Yet those challenges are crucial to the work of the actors and production team. It is almost as if, to understand and engage with the specific creativity of the playtext, reading it has become, once again, a primary activity.

# 8

# Culture and interpretation

When Ibsen's *A Doll's House* was first performed in England the occasion felt very special. Much of this specialness came from the novelty of Ibsen's work, together with his reputation for saying uncomfortable things. But the feeling around the event did not derive from novelty alone: the performance of the play took on the aspect of a deliberate challenge to the status quo. It took on this aspect because the performance was done as a private staging at a commercial theatre, with an audience that included some famous critics of the dominant culture. So, although the play's messages might not have shocked its immediate audience, the performance was done in conditions that implied that it had a combative, shocking relationship with the rest of society. This might not have been the implication if it had been done in a smart West End theatre in front of royalty. Thus the text of Ibsen's play was structurally positioned within contemporary London by its particular theatrical location, its performers and its audience.

The location, the performers and the audience are not things that might immediately strike you when you start reading a play, because as you start reading you enter the world of the play. Nevertheless, in a performance, that world is being represented by one group of real people to another, also real, group. Many playwrights have taken these groups for granted and have written with them in mind: their plays make their meanings within, and because of, this particular context. For us who read plays at some considerable historical and social distance from their moment of writing, it is difficult to identify how this real context helped in making the play's original meaning. Difficult as it is, however, it is still part of the work of exploring how to study a play. The sections which follow give some suggestions about the various issues you might think about as you open the play, and our examples illustrate how meanings derive from and are created by the status of the writer, by location, performers and audience. These examples are taken from across the historical range: if you want to concentrate specifically on the period since 1900 you could consult Shepherd's *Introduction to Modern British Theatre* (2009).

# Writers

## The house dramatist

One of the reasons why Ibsen had a special status in the eyes of contemporary English theatre people was his apparent artistic independence. His plays seemed to express his own serious thoughts about society. This picture of the dramatic writer appealed to those in the English theatre who felt that dramatists were too much under the control of managers. Although a Society of Dramatic Authors had been founded in 1832, to campaign for proper financial payments and professional standing, for most of the nineteenth century writers had very little economic independence. There was no widespread or fair system of royalty payments, nor much protection by copyright. One of the most secure forms of employment was as 'house dramatist', where the writer was part of the production team at a theatre. He or she provided the sort of plays that were required – which might mean anything between pirating a text that had worked well at another theatre, doing an adaptation of the most popular story to hit town that month, producing yet another version of the shows for which the theatre had a reputation and providing a vehicle for the theatre's latest star acquisition (which could well be an acrobat or a performing dog). Clearly, in these circumstances, the question 'What is the writer trying to say here?' is an irrelevance.

It is not just for nineteenth-century plays that the question above is an irrelevance. For most of the history of the theatre, the writer's role tends to be insignificant in terms of their status in the production of plays. Clearly the writer was valued in terms of their particular skill, much as a good stage carpenter or theatre musician might be valued. But there were very few occasions when a writer could insist on her or his creative 'vision' and integrity against the wishes of managers or leading actors. To put the situation like this, however, is to assume that conflict was regular. This assumption is based on a romantic image of the embattled artist fighting desperately to protect her or his vision against the economically motivated forces of commerce. But in fact the separation between artist and businessman is not clear-cut. Shakespeare was a shareholder in his theatre company. His money came from his cut of the profits rather than the separate sale of his playtexts (like many Renaissance dramatists, he did not seek to publish his plays, because to do so would be to make them available to rival companies). It was always within the context of his theatre company that his plays were developed – as we shall suggest later, it is highly probable that the range of talents and interests around him would have had its effect on the sort of thing Shakespeare scripted for them. Furthermore, the company, as a company, had a sense of its own artistic reputation, which it sustained by the sorts of plays that were put on. Shakespeare declares his awareness of the competition between different theatres when he makes Hamlet have a conversation about the fashionable boy actors over the river, a reference which Hamlet's audience would have understood as applying to the Blackfriars theatre, just over the river from the Globe.

## The play gets printed

When Shakespeare's collected plays were officially published for the first time he had been dead for several years: the publication was both a testimony to his memory and a commercial venture by the company. When the collected plays of Beaumont and Fletcher were published the theatres had been closed for five years; the volume was a memorial to a culture destroyed by the Revolution. These two examples suggest that when plays become books they have a separate life *outside* the theatre. Even when individual plays began regularly to be published to coincide with performances, it was not a book as such that the actors and production team worked from inside the theatre. The actors were only given their individual parts, with relevant cues (see p. 38); the prompt copy was a whole text, but not a completely coherent one – alterations, cuts and cues would be written into it. When plays started to become texts for reading, their initial function was as a sort of advertisement for the author or the show. This could only work among the literate – there was much less point in making plays enjoyed by illiterate audiences into books. Towards the end of the nineteenth century the play began to be read more frequently as a book, as a substitute for seeing the show (see p. 13). This appealed to the writers of minority intellectual drama. Once the next step was taken, and plays began to be material for school and university study, then the book apparently became just as important as the show, if not more so. Nowadays study of a play might involve mainly reading it, with visits to a performance or DVD watching as supplements to the book. The play has become a printed object..

## The independent author

The printing of plays had beneficial effects for authors: their work could be separated out from the other creative activities in the theatre and published on its own. When this started to happen regularly in the Restoration, however, the writers already had a status which derived from their social class. Restoration theatre was mainly the domain of a fairly small social élite – actors, writers, critics, audiences moved in the same social circles, addressing one another and making jokes with each other in the plays they performed for themselves. Any individual writer's text functions as a part of this social grouping: the writer may have an independent income, and claim individual responsibility for the text, but s/he is nevertheless structurally positioned by the group. This was particularly true of the woman who sought to achieve independence as an author while being treated as secondary to men. Aphra Behn makes an image of this situation in her play *The Rover*

(1677): the high-class whore, Angellica, talks to her maid on a balcony while down below, outside her house, a picture of her advertises her beauty to customers; men stop and comment on it. While they only respond to the picture, the publicized fiction of Angellica, the real woman has a mind of her own; but she is also separated from the public world of men.

Even the attempt to make the writer's creative role especially important does not necessarily mean that it is the solitary voice of the writer that we hear in the play-book. The Royal Court theatre from the late 1950s onwards aimed to define itself as a 'writers' theatre, showcasing the work of new and challenging dramatists. But alongside this there developed a 'Royal Court aesthetic', a way of designing and lighting shows, a mode of acting; and together with this there grew up a Royal Court audience, expecting radical issues to be addressed, expecting stage language and images that would challenge propriety. Writing with the Royal Court in mind, the playwright has a sense of a particular audience and a particular way of doing plays. In the 1990s plays written for the Royal Court's showcase for young writers often seemed scripted according to conventions mainly learnt from television drama. To put it rather enigmatically, we could say that the theatre (or television) is already in the play – because it is in the mind of the playwright – before the play gets into the theatre.

One way of breaking free of the effect of an elaborate design and production process, with its own inherent values, is for the author to take advantage of economic austerity and re-assert authorial control. For example the author Anthony Neilson often directs his own work and has occasionally acted in it. Authors are perhaps more frequently performers rather than directors. Mojisola Adebayo often performs her own plays and in the five plays published from the Vault festival of 2016 three had author-actors. Even in these circumstances, however, the business of writing is still different from performing. When Neilson played in his own *Penetrator* many of the lines were improvised, but on-stage improvisation tends to be rather more aware of what is working in front of a live audience than what is notionally scripted in a text.

The conclusion we might draw from all this is that the original question, 'What is the writer trying to say here?' is not only often an irrelevance as it stands, but also could be rephrased more usefully to ask, 'What is the *theatre* trying to say here?' and 'To whom is the *theatre* trying to say it?' In short: what does the playtext suggest is being *shared* between theatre and audience? So, in our attempt to get closer to what the playtext might be saying, what it might mean, we need to ask about the location of the theatre, the status of actors and the composition of the audience.

# Location

Where is the performance situated in relation to the community who might watch it? A moment's reflection on performances in modern Western societies will lead to a rather various list, which might include the town's theatre, a circus tent in a field, the back room of a pub, a nearby theme park, a concert hall, a place of worship. Since we are confining our attention to scripted plays, we don't need to bother with most of these – but we still might need to distinguish between the theatre in the smart end of town, where the other 'night spots' are; the performance space in an arts centre; the college theatre; the amateur dramatics club; the community hall in an inner-city residential area – and, in the summer, the main market place in town and the municipal park. Let's take a brief journey through some of the issues around performance location before we look at the impact they have on the playtext.

The various venues listed above differ from one another in two main ways: *where* each venue is and *what* it is.

## Where the venue is

The location of the performance space in relation to the rest of the town tends to influence what it offers to audiences, and what it might be expected to offer. While the theatre at the smart end of town might put on well-made plays, ballets and detective mysteries, the arts centre may show pieces involving physical theatre, video projection and nudity. In each of these cases it is the *cultural* rather than geographical location which matters – theatre as a night spot for a 'good night out', theatre as self-consciously artistic. But, at a time when public transport was less readily available, the *geographical* location might itself suggest something about the range of plays, the dramatic culture. Thus, in the early decades of the nineteenth century, theatres on the south side of the River Thames in London – the 'Surrey side' – had a reputation for roughness, because they were situated much more closely to working-class housing areas than to the rich, fashionable part of town. This roughness amounted not only to large-scale and loud effects but also to stories centred upon working people.

In 1900 a music-hall performer called Ella Shields created a hit with her song 'Burlington Bertie from Bow': this song was a parody of the song 'Burlington Bertie', sung by Vesta Tilley cross-dressed as a fashionable man-about-town. Burlington Arcade is near Bond Street in the wealthy West End of London; Bow was in the working-class East. The Shields song gains its force by articulating a mockery by the lower class of those above them. As we shall see, texts are often designed to respond to, and develop, a sense of location – cultural and geographic – in their audiences; all sorts of character types, situations and jokes gain meaning when we understand this location.

## What the venue is

In the late Middle Ages the townspeople of York could, once a year, watch the religious Corpus Christi plays as they processed through the streets of the city. Only a very few of those same people might be invited to gather in the banquet hall of a local manor house to watch a dramatic entertainment. In the hall the acoustics meant that voices could be used without the limitations that come from addressing a street, so different sorts of line could be written; and the assumption of a more socially homogeneous audience made possible jokes based on shared knowledge and values (see Harris 1992).

## What sort of place is it?

The distinction between streets and hall thus impacts upon the sort of audience and the sort of play that is performed. In the same way, in Shakespeare's London, the large open-air theatres charged much cheaper entry prices, because they had plenty of space, than did the so-called hall theatres located in domestic buildings; so one venue felt very much more select, in social terms, than did the other – the hall theatre was a venue for the wealthy. And if you ever were to get into the royal banqueting house to watch a masque you needed to be something like a minister of state. So even the most basic questions about the performance place – is it open and free to all? is it open with paying entry? is it a large custom-made building? is it part of another building? – carry implications about the audience and play. The dramatist would be well aware of these implications.

## What are its internal arrangements?

Throughout theatre history, plays have generally been written by people who had close associations with particular companies and their theatre buildings – the act of creating a play often has a specific theatre in mind. So the detailed internal arrangements of a theatre building often take a key part in how that play is imagined, how it works, how it makes meaning. A dramatist writing in the Restoration period (1660–90) knew that in each of the two available theatres the area immediately in front of the stage – the pit – was frequented by the most fashionable men-about-town, who showed off both their clothes and their assumed cleverness, through ripostes to the stage. The front of that stage had, on each side of it, tiers of boxes – so an actor standing there was, in effect, in the auditorium, with sections of audience in front and at the sides (see p. 163). Those sections had different sight-lines: so when, for instance, a foppish gentleman on stage was playing to the fashionable wits in the pit, the whole player– watcher interaction was itself a spectacle for those at the sides. Given that the pit was predominantly male, and that women sat in boxes, the interaction of pit and stage becomes an enactment of gender positions, a demonstration of that regular thematic concern of Restoration comedy – the working of masculine privilege.

By the early nineteenth century the pit had become the territory no longer of the rich but of artisans. Over the ensuing years theatre managements tried to attract middle-class audiences back into the theatre. They did so by making alterations to the seating arrangements and furnishings (see Shepherd and Womack 1996). The pit with its shared benches was abolished, and replaced by stalls seats, which could be individually numbered and allocated. These seats were covered to look rather like armchairs, carpets were laid, and the auditorium walls acquired little lamps and lampshades and wall hangings, so that it all began to mimic a wealthy middle-class sitting room. The appearance of a sitting room suggested, and encouraged, sitting-room behaviour: rather than shouting and throwing objects at the stage, audiences began to conduct themselves with decorum. And, as this new auditorium appeared, dramatists supplied it with plays in which characters conducted themselves appropriately to the onstage furnishings, the tables and chairs, cups and saucers. In Tom Robertson's play *Caste* (1867), conflict between characters is expressed not through shouting or weapons, but through the handling of crockery. On this stage, and for this audience, the passionately expressive mode of melodrama felt like a joke, an embarrassment. In 1885, when the seats closest to the stage were regularly stuffed full with the most expensive people, a music-hall singer – Nelly Power – could make a point by studiously ignoring those in front of her, looking over their heads right back to the cheapest seats high up and singing, 'The boy I love is up in the gallery'.

## What does 'going to the theatre' feel like?

For most people, their feeling about the visit to the theatre, and hence their attitude to what they are going to watch, begins to be shaped before they get as far as the auditorium. As we have suggested, the location and mode of the performance place already begin the work on an audience. Then there is the moment of entry – up steps, down steps, carpeted floor, concrete, doormen and ushers, trestle table with tickets, mirrors and chandeliers, a bookstall, a coffee bar with paintings, beer in plastic glasses, gourmet ice-cream. You might regard all of these as entirely irrelevant to the play you are studying. But even playtext readers carry in their heads an image of the theatre space – usually based on their own experience – so that they too make assumptions about the play which depend on their sense of what it means to 'go to the theatre'.

That phrase can imply something different if you are, say, on the annual outing with the gardening club, if you are a professional reviewer, if you are studying the play for an exam, if you are taking your new lover on a treat. Being in the theatre can feel like a magical playground, a workplace, a shop. And then we have to conjecture what it might have felt like in the past – in different spaces, with different relationships with the town. Again, readers make assumptions about 'old' theatres – what it was like seeing Shakespeare, Ibsen, Bond. What it feels like can, in its turn, establish how someone watches: enjoying the presence of glamour, looking for subversive implications, observing the lighting design, noting details of interpretation. And assumptions about what it feels – and felt – like can establish how someone reads. Without knowing it, our attitude to watching is the first step towards looking for a meaning in what we watch: the meaning we find is usually the sort of thing we began looking for. Thus the first audiences of Wertenbaker's play *Our Country's Good* (1988) may well have been influenced by the ambience of liberalism at the Royal Court theatre, just as readers may well be influenced by the letters from prisoners which preface the play, to take it that the play is arguing that, through drama, people may achieve a new sense of self-worth. By contrast, in a different setting, we might see that the play offers a cynical argument as to how the upper class may more subtly maintain its control of the lower class by teaching them to find enjoyment in the drama that was developed for the upper class (rather than enabling them to find their own lower-class 'voice').

# Examples

Much of the direct evidence of location is difficult to find in the written texts that you study. What is invisible is not, however, absent, and you often will need to glance at a theatre history book to check out what the performing place is, where it is situated, what its internal arrangements are. Here are some examples to show the different ways in which location constructs meaning.

## *Medieval*

In York the staging of the plays in the Corpus Christi cycle, which told the biblical story from Creation to Last Judgement, was an annual civic event. The plays were processed around the town on wagons, which stopped and performed several times, following a known route, from dawn to dusk. Audiences gathered at each stopping-point to watch something which was very well known but also special, because it only happened once a year. The backdrop to each play was the familiar, real streets of York, but they were streets emptied of their usual everyday business. For the duration of the plays the town environment is both concretely apparent and yet transported into some domain which is outside daily life, connecting back across the years to each other moment of the cycle's performance. The written text of these plays contains deliberate anachronisms, references to events and phenomena that postdate the supposed time of the Bible story. Far from being disruptive, these verbal references fall into place within, and underline, the sense of double location – the here-and-now city which is simultaneously part of God's eternal scheme.

## *Renaissance*

Between 1600 and 1609 Shakespeare's company of performers were working in their own custom-built theatre, the rebuilt Globe, in Southwark on the south bank of the River Thames in London. It was a sign of their artistic and financial success that they had been able to build this theatre – and although it was an open-air theatre, with entry prices accessible to a wide spectrum of social groups, an opening show – *Julius Caesar*, c.1599 – had signalled a disdain for the taste of the more ignorant. Theatres on the south bank were commonly assumed to offer the clowning and jigs, songs and patriotic history that supposedly appealed to the popular appetite – one of them doubled as an animal-baiting arena. By contrast, when Shakespeare wrote *King Lear* (1605/6) he took an ancient British story, and then removed almost all the history-telling element out of it; he provided a clown, but made the clown's contributions more inscrutable than entertaining; his songs became obscure rhymes. These artistic decisions can be seen as attempts by the company to resist or develop their location. They were, nevertheless, still trapped by it. For when a satirical play – Beaumont's *Knight of the Burning Pestle* – opened at the fashionable Blackfriars theatre in 1607, among its catalogue of jokes was the figure of an old man, Merrythought, who is half crazy and infuriates his family, very like the mad Lear. The principal characters, and targets, of this play are a pair of shop-keeping citizens who fancy themselves as educated playgoers. They are set up as an audience to the play within the play. Where they sit as audience is on stools on the actual stage; since this is the place where really only the fashionable men sat, their inappropriateness is established by their auditorium location. In the eyes of the Blackfriars dramatist these citizens are precisely the people for whom the Globe caters. The Globe's company only escaped from this typecasting by location when they bought the Blackfriars theatre two years later.

## Nineteenth century

In 1829 a play opened at the Surrey theatre, on 'Surrey side', south of the Thames, called *Black-Ey'd Susan*. Its hero, William, is a naval rating; he is almost executed for striking down his captain, who tried to assault William's fiancée, Susan. Very many of the audience at the theatre would have been employed on and around the river; it was among these people too that the naval press-gangs operated, forcibly abducting men to serve on ships. The play's division of sympathy between ratings and officers tends to reflect the majority class position of its audience. If well-dressed middle-class people went to this theatre they had to sit in seats stained by workers' clothes. Nearly 40 years later, in a theatre north of the river, it is the officer (this time in the army) who is the hero of *Caste* (1867). Of the two working-class men in the play, the skilled one, Sam Gerridge, is viewed with patronizing affection as he dreams of setting up his shop for sale of gas and plumbing appliances; the other, Eccles, is unskilled, drunken, greedy and sent off at the end, with the full approval of the audience, to drink himself to death. The stage on which this is enacted is that of the flagship middle-class theatre newly established by Marie Wilton with her partner Squire Bancroft; they had bought a rough venue nicknamed 'The Dust Hole' (in Tottenham Street, in the West End) and transformed it into a smart theatre which they called 'The Prince of Wales'. Here the furnishings implied what the fictional narratives also stated, that the middle class could watch in secure comfort.

# Performers

Marie Wilton and Squire Bancroft were able to make their innovations in the theatre because they had economic power: they were not just performers, they were also managers, employers rather than employees. This gave them an economic status similar to the audiences they wanted to attract. Over a century later, in England it is accepted practice that some leading performers are rewarded by knighthoods, while many go to Hollywood to develop the superstar lifestyles which feature in social media as examples of desirable living. In Shakespeare's time, by contrast, actors were defined in law as 'masterless men', people with the same status as vagabonds. This is one reason why the actors sought respectability and protection for themselves by obtaining patronage from high-ranking aristocrats.

The Elizabethan state felt that it needed to keep a close check on, to licence in advance, the plays that actors were intending to perform. For it suspected that these masterless men were liable to make performances which were subversive, critical of the masters. But when some of these actors gained a reputation for their work they were invited to perform at the royal court – where what was seen to be on display was artistry rather than subversion. So it seems that expectations about, and response to, the performed play depend to some extent on what is assumed about the status of the performers – in relation to the rest of society, to other actors, to their art. Once again, we shall find that these considerations lead us back to our responses to the written text.

## Performers and society

To define performers as vagabonds is to imply that they have no fixed place in society, that they are outsiders. To give them knighthoods is to recognize that they belong among the élite circles of those who more or less own society.

### Lawyers

While throughout theatre history there are examples of successful people who buy into the upper class – usually by acquiring a country house and an art collection – it is the economic arrangements of the profession in general that affect how people perceive the status of performers. Indeed, to call it a 'profession' is a sign of a modern attitude: the professionalization of acting happened alongside the expansion of other middle-class professions (most notably the civil service) in the later nineteenth century (as depicted in Pinero's play *Trelawny of the 'Wells'* 1898). The Royal Academy of Dramatic Art was founded in the early twentieth century, and thereafter acting schools became a recognized route to the stage, a specialized training similar to (if more trivial than) that followed by lawyers or doctors.

## Prostitutes

Prior to this date, the profession most commonly associated with acting was prostitution. From the late seventeenth through to the early nineteenth century there are stories (true and false) of actresses who worked as prostitutes. Seen in this light, acting's social place amounts to illicit or improper work, part of the 'hidden' economy, catering for people's 'undisciplined' cravings. The social place of acting is a big topic but we simply need to recognize here that a play performed by people similar to prostitutes may be treated rather differently from a play performed by people similar to lawyers. The latter may be seen as contributing to serious public discussion – alongside parliamentary speeches, newspaper editorials and scholarly essays – of issues affecting society. That is certainly how the new professionals of theatre in the 1880s wanted plays to be considered. A student with this in mind will be on the look-out for devices that emphasize the shape of argument in the text. By contrast, the 'prostitutes' play is part of the leisure activity of society, an entertainment for public figures who are off-duty. It is seen as a threat to proper work (taking Elizabethan apprentices away from their workshops) and a part of the idle life of the decadent rich (the playground of Restoration fops). More importantly, where acting is like prostitution, a play could be said to have the effect of stimulating the sensual desires of its audience, a form of seduction. Elizabethan opponents of acting said that plays made their audiences undisciplined, sexually aroused, unmanly. If this is your view of how plays work, you will be attentive to the seductive devices in the text. And, certainly, some awareness of this issue can help to explain why so many Renaissance plays want to explore the audience–performance relationship in their plays-within-plays.

## Outsiders

The original Renaissance definition of actors as vagabonds suggests something other than prostitution. It suggests that the professional actors don't really have a place within society, that they are outsiders. What lies behind this notion is the touring troupe – the *commedia dell'arte* clowns, the mummers, minstrels and acrobats, who went from one settlement to another. They worked on village greens, in town market places, in the halls of great houses, always moving on after each show. Although they may carry their staging with them, they are performing on someone else's territory. For the population of a village, the arrival of the players meant a temporary break with the usual daily routine, and, since it was being done by those who had no fixed social place, for the duration of the performance one seemed outside all normal social institutions. This feeling about the performance was strengthened when the routines of clowns deliberately broke social and sexual taboos and made disorderly topsy-turvy a great deal more fun than orderly propriety. The activity of the performing outsiders turned what you might only jokingly imagine into something actually enacted in public.

While very few scripts survive from early travelling troupes we know much more about the actors who toured between the early 1930s and the mid-1980s. If you are reading one of these scripts, you need to bear in mind the image of the outsiders whose performance enables the disallowed to be done in public. The author of the lesbian play *Any Woman Can* (1975), Jill Posener, remembers the excitement of playing to female audiences outside London: 'women would literally come up to us and say "I've never met another one"' (p. 24). The play is structured around autobiographical narratives by its central character. She opens the play by categorizing herself as an outsider: 'You are looking at a screaming lesbian' (p. 15), but as the play goes on we get to know and empathize with her through her narratives. The form of the play invites women to identify with the outsider and, in doing so, to find a new sort of community, and power, as outsiders. The effect is to liberate them from being captive inside alien lifestyles.

So if you are studying a script performed by touring players you might be looking out for the ways it invites its audience to become and enjoy being outsiders – by turning normally authoritative figures into cartoons, by telling 'real' stories, by disrupting sober realism for a song, by calling attention to the genuinely 'deviant' identities of the actors. It is these qualities, rather than realistic character development, which are at the heart of the play's significance for its audience.

## Performers as stars

As we said above, some performers in every period manage to attain a pre-eminence that apparently puts them in a class of their own. That separateness is often marked concretely by their wealthy lifestyle: the actor becomes a star. Again, this is a big topic, so we shall concentrate on the impact that stardom has on a written text.

Many plays are written with a specific company of actors in mind. All Shakespeare's plays were destined to be performed by the acting company in which he was a shareholder: he thus knew, in advance of writing, the physical characteristics and performing styles of the various actors. It is very difficult to establish what direct effects this had on the writing, although it is possible to suggest that his use of clowns was dictated by the talent currently available: Robert Armin did less knockabout than other clowns, so the fool in *Twelfth Night* (1602) is much less slapstick than, say, Launcelot Gobbo in *The Merchant of Venice* (1596–8).

One of the key differences between actors in a company is that each individual may specialize in a particular sort of role. To an extent this is still true today, but it was much more apparent, and necessary, when the same group of performers worked together on a long-term basis. In part this was a way of dividing the labour to ensure that a small group could cope with any new text, but it also allowed for a speedy learning of a new text; so the woman who specialized in virtuous heroines, for instance, would know in advance the general range of sentiments and actions that any heroine would express. An audience learns to associate particular actors with particular character types, and a performer becomes popular not for being individualistic or surprising but for conforming to expectations, doing what the audience want to see him or her do. A writer who is preparing a text for a particular star will arrange the action so that it conforms with the expectations about that star: in the Restoration Nell Gwynn and Charles Hart usually represented characters who fell in love with one another, so, whatever the relationship between their characters at the start of the play, by the end the predicted romantic attachment will have emerged (see Dryden's *An Evening's Love* 1668). The writer can go a step further than this, and construct scenes designed explicitly to display the particular skills of the star – for instance, screenplays for Jean-Claude van Damme incorporate quite a lot of display of muscular body and shiny physical action, but very little philosophical soliloquy. The particular shape of a text we are studying may thus derive not just from the specialism, but also from the starring status, of its performers.

To identify a text as a 'star vehicle' is often to imply that it is moved more by commercial interest than artistic integrity. While this may be so, it does not follow that the text is uninteresting or, indeed, lightweight. Much of its shape and pleasure may be explained by the star's presence. The second part of Marlowe's *Tamburlaine the Great* (*c*.1587) looks like a substantial repetition of the formula of the first play, with its hero going from one conquest to another, without much interesting opposition or character development. It was designed for Edward Alleyn, who scored a hit with the first play. His forte was, as a later writer said, strutting and bellowing – particular forms of physical and vocal production that called attention to the quality of movement and sound, the orchestration of muscles and breath patterns, that made the performer's body larger than life, not bound by the conventions and proprieties of daily activity (see p. 120). To be present at this sort of performance is to be excited by something other than plot or character: for people whose daily lives are spent in fairly routine humdrum activities, Alleyn here – and the same goes for dancers or gymnasts – shows a different way that the human being can occupy space, being centred and powerful rather than just a functionary. To see the star aboard his vehicle is to be thrillingly in the very presence of human potency. This is an aspect of performance which is unique to the medium. Try considering this as one possible explanation for passages of written text that otherwise seem to have little function (see p. 58).

A particular twist on the relationship between star and writing is the case where the writing deliberately subverts expectations about fictional characters which are based on assumptions about the performer. It is now fairly common for film stars to be cast 'against type' – Arnold Schwarzenegger as comic parent rather than robotic action hero. But in the film industry this sort of casting can be little more than an attempt to demonstrate the flexibility of the star and his continued availability for work when robotic action-hero roles have gone out of fashion or his body has aged. By contrast, the casting against type can also work politically, producing a new insight into something that had been taken for granted. When Isabel Mattocks was used for the part of Fiametta in Holcroft's *A Tale of Mystery* (1802) she already had a reputation for playing comically garrulous old women; but in this play Fiametta is the only person who is convinced of the innocence of the hero, a position she maintains even while being put down by her master as a garrulous old woman. Isabel Mattocks' audience this time might realize something about the sexist and ageist assumptions that had inhabited their previous laughter at old women.

## What do we think actors do?

Many modern students of acting assume that the good actor's job is to create a fictional character who is as convincing and life-like as possible – in other words, the actor has to make fiction seem to be non-fiction. This notion governs the actor's attitude to the written text, and the audience's attitude to the performance. But it has not always been like this. As we said above, members of a nineteenth-century company would specialize in stock types – an audience would take pleasure in seeing both the familiar materials and the new elaborations in the role of, say, the elderly mother, much as an audience of jazz or heavy metal like to hear again the already-known, even while enjoying the variants that make it not completely known. There are stories of nineteenth-century audiences protesting when the death of the villain was insufficiently acrobatic; we know he has to die, but the dying has to be a 'turn' – as in the concept of music hall turn, comic turn – in its own right. Although the written text might look fairly thin at this point, the stage would be full of activity.

Actors who specialize in stock types can supplement or build on a written text because they have their own personal repertoire of routines – the range of gestures, facial and physical attitudes, vocal mannerisms that constitute 'business'. Stage business is activity that does not have the status of action (see Chapter 4); it can nevertheless be deeply pleasurable because of its skill and idiosyncrasy. In many ways the invention of 'business' links back to the *commedia dell'arte* clown's use of *lazzi* (see Rudlin 1994). These are units of activity in which the clown allows herself to be absorbed by the physical logic inherent in particular given circumstances; the clown follows through that logic, in all its potential absurdities, to the extent that it continues to 'work' as a stage event. Thus, say, putting your hat on and suddenly finding that it doesn't fit is a situation from which much perplexedly absorbing activity might follow. *Lazzi* can be very pleasurable to watch, because they stage the human body's precarious relationship to a potentially chaotic world of objects. For performers used to *lazzi*, a written text merely needs to set up the basic elements: for those of us reading such a play, we can only spot the possibilities by being alert to the props in a scene, especially those props that seem to move around. In a theatre where actors are trained to be convincing real people, a dramatist who wants *lazzi* has to script them in considerable detail: the opening act of *Trelawny of the 'Wells'* is wholly given over to a large farewell dinner; the waiter attending at the table finds, early in the act, that he has brought two left gloves by mistake; he starts by trying to get the spare glove onto his right hand, but the glove, deprived of its true place in life, ends up in all sorts of wrong places. Also, of course, we could look at the careful scripting of clown double-act business in *Waiting for Godot* (1955).

# Examples

## *Medieval*

The performers of the Corpus Christi plays in York were not professional actors. They were members of craft guilds (manufacturers of nails, grocers, paint makers, etc.). Each guild took responsibility for a particular play and its performance became an 'advertisement' for the guild – not only in the sense that it was appropriate that the water-drawers did the play of Noah and the Flood, but also in that the guild's wealth could be displayed, as the York mercers did in the elaborate decorations and machinery of the Last Judgement. The players, as guild members, were known individuals in the community. This sense of communal familiarity is supported by the everyday contemporary language and anachronistic social references of the plays. Within this context of the 'communal', the religion is the more strongly emphasized, because in their serious performing of holiness the familiar figures seem to be at an unfamiliar distance from their audience, removed by their religious absorption to a higher level of spiritual specialness. Thus the amateur performers of the plays create a double image whereby the community plays to itself and at the same time enacts its capacity to be a sacred body.

By contrast, the mummers in the manor house make a virtue of apparently breaking in from the 'outside', entering through the hall, pushing past people or taking payment for their show midway through it. In a house owned by someone else, they create topsy-turvy. These performers, not guild members but travelling players, are of unfixed social place: the professionals do a show that depends on 'shape'-changing, doubling of roles. The most virtuous figure in *Mankind* (*c*.1470), Mercy, and the devil, Titivillus, were probably doubled by the same actor. This is not the double image of the

Corpus Christi plays, but is instead a tricksy effect that implies, but never states, the blurring of moral distinctions between good and evil.

## Renaissance

The leading actors in *King Lear* were shareholders in their company; *Knight of the Burning Pestle* was performed entirely by boys, who were all employees. In the eyes of the fashionable hall theatre, what was wrong with audiences at the open-air theatres was that they allowed themselves to be imaginatively carried away by the illusion. A major effect of having boys perform is that all the spectacular grandeur – the sheer size – becomes literally impossible; it can be quoted, but in doing so they bring it, so to speak, down to size. So a primary effect of the boys' play is that the theatre displays itself as satiric vehicle – that is its social function.

By contrast, in *King Lear* the audience is offered, and drawn into, a serious and coherent fictional world. The actor who took the lead role, Richard Burbage, was famous for 'becoming' his parts; he made difficult what the boys' theatre made easy, the audience's ability to separate actor from role. This assisted in creating the sense of fictional world. So, too, in rendering the fool difficult and then removing him, the text denies the audience access to a commentary figure who is an intermediary between real world and play world. In making it possible for the audience not only to take seriously but also to empathize with the fictional world, the actors of *Lear* absorb and reverse one of the major criticisms of acting. Their story of an old man who becomes physically embarrassing, who goes mad and in his madness sees visions of copulation, is one that might reinforce the contemporary connections between performance and irrational, unmanning sensuality. But, for the audience of *Lear*, the play's ability to deal with these issues is testimony to the power and importance of drama.

## Nineteenth century

The text of *Black-Ey'd Susan* turned its leading performer into a household name. William the sailor was played by T. P. Cooke, who thereafter specialized in nautical roles. The written script is organized into units that display Cooke's skills: there are moments of dexterous physical combat, storytelling, pathos; the handsome actor was presented as a combination of physical vigour and emotional softness. William's scenes are perhaps better thought of as collections of 'turns' – display pieces for Cooke – as much as developments of the plot. Thus his first entry is with a band of sailors, arriving joyfully to find nobody there to meet them; when the women turn up, William thinks he can see Susan, but she isn't there; when news is brought of Susan the conversation alternates between reassurances and bad news. Increasingly fast emotional reversals are called for. In the next scene William moves from a tearful reunion with Susan into a fight with smugglers into a verbal attack on Susan's villainous uncle. The mode of performance changes in relation to the character(s) addressed. Part of the pleasure in the display pieces, the turns, comes from the rapid transitions between them.

# Audiences

Through our account of playwrights, locations and performers we have continually made reference to audiences. We have, for example, talked about Restoration playwrights as part of a distinct social élite, about working-class spectators at the Surrey theatre, about the citizens of York and their religious plays. Each time we are suggesting that the audience approach the performance with perceptions in their heads about their relationship to writers, to the location of the performance and to the performers. These perceptions form the basis, often unconsciously, of how the audience understand the play and the significances they attach to it. All this we have already suggested through our series of examples.

## The audience's view of itself

What we have not looked at is the audience's perception of itself. This might seem to be as remote as we can possibly get from the study of the written text, and certainly texts don't appear to tell you anything about this. Nevertheless texts are written with an understanding as much about audiences as about performance locations. The audience in the streets of York for the Corpus Christi plays knew that these were special festive occasions during which all normal business was suspended. Furthermore they knew that these were *their* plays, done by members of guilds which had a particular place within the hierarchy and government of the town. When a modern student of these plays is invited to consider the links between them, it can seem like a rather abstract literary exercise. If you were a medieval citizen of York, these plays would link up not only because the Bible story is a coherent whole but also because the plays themselves are a sort of metaphor for the wholeness of the town as a community. Through celebrating Corpus Christi, the body of Christ, the town celebrates its own civic body.

By contrast, the activity of going to a fashionable theatre such as the Blackfriars in 1607, or either of the Restoration London theatres, was a way of displaying your membership of a wealthy élite. You went to the theatre as much to be seen as to see. Part of the performance of being seen is to demonstrate not only your acquaintance with important members of the audience but also your wit and cultural expertise. A student of *Knight of the Burning Pestle* may spend a lot of their time wading through footnotes which identify sources of parody and double meanings. The Renaissance wit would find the parody and puns a delightful opportunity to show off his ability to spot references and pick up allusions. This is especially enjoyable because this play supplies a fictional onstage audience who don't really understand all of what is going on – they are culturally incompetent, and they are of the wrong social class. The fashionable audience's laughter – their display of their own *cultural competence* – is a weapon in a battle between social classes.

Within the general heading of the audience's perception of itself we have encountered two different elements: *the occasion of watching* and *awareness of social difference.*

## The occasion of watching

The occasion of the medieval Corpus Christi plays was important, since it happened once a year; the Renaissance Blackfriars theatre was open throughout the season, but it was socially different from other theatres. The *occasion of watching* can be more or less strongly marked: an annual festivity is strongly marked, an office outing much less so; going to see a play as an alternative to going to a film or restaurant is barely marked as significant. The written text can help to promote a sense of occasion, creating opportunities for solemnity or celebration, but it cannot, in general, invent the occasion (though there have been experiments, most famously by Jerzy Grotowski, where the text is worked on in such a way as to furnish a sense of special occasion, with a special venue and highly restricted audience numbers).

## Awareness of social difference

This again may be more or less strongly marked. Least strong is that of the audience for a television play who, sitting in their own home, are in totally familiar territory with no strangers present. More marked is the awareness of an audience at a 'popular' show – a West End musical, a well-known stand-up comic – since, though they may be a pretty mixed range of people, they are all out for a good time, they are people who like entertainment. The strongest awareness of social difference is that of people who know themselves to be a distinct social grouping before they ever enter the theatre – the Restoration wits, the political activists, the lesbian audience. The written text of a play can promote, indeed create, this awareness much more effectively than in the case of promoting occasion.

## Declaring an interest

The promotion of this awareness by the audience of its own specialness can take three main forms in the written text. First, the play may announce that it is coming from a particular position, *declaring an interest*, rather than assuming it speaks from a position of disinterested objectivity. It may declare itself, for instance, as a gay play (or a play with gay performers). When watched by a gay audience, there is a sense of common language being spoken between stage and spectators. This has the effect of making an otherwise fairly disparate collection of people, who just happen to be gay, feel unified through a shared common quality, their sexuality (see Freeman 1996; Lucas 1994). In the case of political plays, which unite an audience in mockery of political targets, this is often dismissively referred to as 'preaching to the converted'. What is actually going on is that the 'converted' are being brought to an awareness of themselves as a coherent group, distinguished by the fact of their being converts to the cause. This awareness is produced during *The Cheviot, the Stag and the Black, Black Oil* (1973), a play concerned with English exploitation of the Scottish Highlands and toured to Scottish villages by the 7:84 theatre company. The play is structured on the model of a Highland entertainment, the ceilidh, and at points the characters speak in Gaelic; the oppressors only ever talk English. When Doli sings in Gaelic the '*company and audience join in the chorus*' (p. 9): at this point someone who knew no Gaelic would be unable to join in, and those who do decide to join in are consciously using the language which the play sets in opposition to Englishness and oppression. It is through this awareness of themselves as a coherent group, their solidarity, that an audience gains strength to pursue their cause. In this way the play does its political work.

## Creating unity

Second, the play may indeed be assuming that it addresses a mixed audience, the 'unconverted'. The work that the text then does is to make the audience feel unity by sharing responses. This can be done in two ways: first, by producing an object for which everyone can feel a similar affection or hatred – as in the case of the aristocratic villain in a melodrama, or the boasting Herod in a medieval mystery play. Second, there is the use of humour to establish a shared sense of 'us' (who are normal and reasonable) against a strange outsider: thus when the Prince of Morocco arrives as a suitor to Portia in *The Merchant of Venice* he is felt to be inappropriate for her, and so strongly shared is this sense that few people quibble with the overt racism of Portia's remark about his 'complexion' (2.7.79). A slightly different case is that of the disguised Kent's apparently unprovoked attack on Oswald in *King Lear* (2.2): in siding with Kent, we take up the position of the yeoman who assumes that courtiers are always the enemy.

## … and disunity

Often an audience will assume they are among people like themselves, that there is a basic sense of 'togetherness'. Some performers and plays aim to split up this feeling of unity. Many of us have seen the comedian who makes fun of latecomers or who picks on a group of people in the stalls. This splitting apart of an audience can, however, have political effect. Act 2 of Trevor Griffiths' play *Comedians* (1975) is set in a working-men's club, which uses the real audience as the club audience. Three of the turns shape their material to try to please a talent scout, and they start to tell sexist and racist jokes. Much of the play so far has been concerned with the 'politics' of humour. As the jokes continue, some in the real audience stop laughing at what they consider offensive material, while others continue to laugh. At this moment the real political differences in the audience have been brought to the surface.

## Cultural competence

Third, at a very basic level, and often without trying to make any points about unity, the play assumes a certain amount of shared knowledge on the part of the audience. We referred above to 'cultural competence' in the audience. This competence takes the form of recognizing references, allusions, artistic shapes, familiar plot lines. When the mechanicals are rehearsing their play in *A Midsummer Night's Dream*, they get into difficulty because they are not sure how to represent a lion without frightening the ladies in the audience. The real audience find this funny because they know that theatre audiences realize that plays are pretend rather than real. In making their mistake about the rules of watching and performing drama, the mechanicals show themselves to be culturally incompetent. This incompetence is represented by Puck as a sort of ignorance of one's surroundings: 'What hempen homespuns have we swaggering here/So near the cradle of the Fairy Queen?' (3.1.70–1).

Unlike the mechanicals, many readers of this book are pretty competent in cultural terms. If the lines above were quoted out of any context and you were asked about the author, you might suggest Shakespeare (or at least say it was from that period): the language is not modern English, it is shaped into short rhythmic lines – we know in general that Shakespeare wrote plays in verse. We could probably go further, if asked, and suggest that this is taken from one of the comedies – you don't get fairy queens in tragedy. And, if asked what the plot might involve, you might suggest magic, romance and happy endings – things associated with fairies. Finally, it could be that you can guess at the play itself, since *A Midsummer Night's Dream* is commonly known as the Shakespeare play with fairies in it.

## Genre

In spotting that this is poetry, comedy and romance you are recognizing certain familiar features. In making that recognition you are identifying genre: it is poetry not prose, comedy not tragedy. Genre is a word of Latin origin meaning 'kind' – as in grouping, family, species, that kind of thing. To put a work of art into a genre is often a short-hand way of suggesting what its content is: thus in a guide to films on television you will find them categorized as, say, 'thriller', 'comedy', 'horror'. Although the viewer may well not have seen the particular film before, they will know what sort of characterization, language and setting to expect once they know it is said to be a thriller. In the case of Puck's lines here, you know that they have to be from a comedy because tragedies have rules and shapes that make them distinct from comedies (they don't have fairy queens). In recognizing the kind of thing it is, the genre, you make assumptions about how it will work and how it is to be watched, you have expectations about its content.

Quite a lot of critical commentary about different sorts of artwork depends on this process of putting individual works into categories; it is a process that helps to describe, explain or even evaluate the individual work, and it operates by referring individual works to a general type. While this can be seen as an academic imposition, it is also the case that some artworks deliberately advertise their genre category – a television programme might do it through its opening credits or its theme music (and in a culture of channel-hopping it will do this very fast); a play might open with a particular sort of image, as for example a man standing with a skull while courtiers process across the stage, which is the opening to the aptly named *Revenger's Tragedy* (1606). Many artworks declare their genre because audiences derive pleasure from being able to recognize familiar features and from having their expectations fulfilled (see p. 135). Frequently people's experience of real life is that events happen unpredictably, without reason or rule, in a bewildering fashion. Watching a play or film that, for all its twists and turns, follows a basic predicted pattern feels, by contrast, reassuring. Going to see something in a familiar genre, or indeed seeing the same thing twice, is a way of experiencing a world in which what is expected to happen does happen, where you can be given what you desire.

But some plays aim to deny the audience the pleasure of having their expectations fulfilled. In plays which want to challenge assumptions about people and values, a genre category might be suggested, and then deviated from. So, in Shakespeare's *Twelfth Night*, we expect that a situation in which a woman in disguise as a man loves a man who loves a different woman (who in turn loves the disguised woman) will be resolved as soon as the twin brother of the disguised woman appears – the men and women will all pair off in mixed-sex couples in a final, happy last scene. But Shakespeare has not given the twins the same qualities: the brother is much more violent; and the ending has several threads left hanging loose – the brother is loved by a male companion who is then abandoned, the disguised woman never appears in women's clothes, and the happy pairing-up is interrupted by an angry Malvolio who threatens to be revenged on all of them in the future. So our expectations about what makes proper pairing-up, and how it solves problems, are unsettled.

## Critical approaches

When it identifies a genre, an audience develops a technique for understanding the play. Once you recognize something is a murder mystery, the details readily slot into place – a familiar shape is revealed.

But there are other techniques which help towards understanding. These are often more consciously employed, and more consciously learnt, than the knowledge we have of current genres. Such techniques for understanding come from the practice of dramatic criticism – or, rather, practices in the plural. For there are different ways of doing dramatic criticism. The short review of a play in the daily newspaper is not like an analysis written for a college essay. And there have been different emphases over time.

The short review has changed less in its history than the critical essay. Reviews – or 'notices' – of plays originated with the beginnings of a regular weekly, then daily, press in the early part of the eighteenth century. These reviews stated what the play was, where it was on, who the main actors were and sometimes what it was about. The reviewer often noted what worked well and which performers were good or bad. Frequently such reviews worked like a form of advertising, and some were placed in the papers by the theatre managements. Nowadays the review is supposedly more independent, although it still does some of the work it always did – which is to carry out a sort of cultural policing, marking the line between what 'educated' society finds tasteful or valuable and its opposite.

More influential on our understanding of plays – in terms of what they are and how they work – is the critical essay. This has changed in its methods and preoccupations over the years and, although we shall be concentrating on the approaches which most directly affect college and undergraduate study, we shall need to be aware of some of this change. In general, until fairly recently, the critical approaches to plays have tended to derive from what was being done in relation to poems or novels. Drama was taught as a part of literature, and evaluated according to literary criteria. 'Theatre studies' has since emerged as a distinct disciplinary area, only to be overtaken, in its turn, by 'performance studies' (see Shepherd and Wallis 2004 and Balme 2008). But each of these disciplines still has a certain amount of trouble with the written text and with a history of assumptions about the way to approach it. That is why, at the start of this book, we insisted that reading and analysing the written text of a play were very different activities from analysing a written text such as a novel.

## *Character analysis*

A specimen question in a 1990s revision aid for an English Literature exam went like this: 'What do you think of the way Macbeth behaves in Act 5 scene 5?' The candidate was invited to think of Macbeth as a person who can be separated out from the play and judged as a 'real' person. That judging tends to assume he is someone like us, someone who conforms to our notions of what a human being is. Macbeth is not understood as an illusion, a product of a series of fictional devices.

This approach, which can be called 'character analysis', is one of the oldest and most persistent of those currently in operation. It is often linked back to the work of A. C. Bradley, whose most famous book, on Shakespearean tragedy, appeared in 1904. In the book, as part of his analysis, Bradley made conjectures about the thoughts and activities of characters outside of what Shakespeare had written. It was a way of approaching character that was very similar to the exercises undertaken by actors trained in the Naturalist technique, where they develop a past life for their character and try to know how they would respond in situations which are completely outside anything the play sets up. At the time this was radical and unsettling stuff. In the interests of exploring how 'real' characters behave, novelists had been challenging cosy moral platitudes about humanity; Naturalist plays had caused scandal. And alongside this fictional work the early sexologists and psychologists were coming up with a picture of human minds and desires which did not correspond with moral norms. It is within such a contest over beliefs that Bradley was interested in explaining the irrational or obsessive behaviours of Shakespearean heroes.

That view of character as contradictory and irrational was summarized in the idea that the heroes all had a fatal flaw in their character. This idea was then seized on by whole generations of character analysts, who set about identifying fatal flaws without any longer having anything of the context for Bradley's work. From its beginnings as a challenge to norms character analysis itself turned into a norm, imposing fixed and highly limited models of mind onto fictional characters. The fatal flaw came to be used as a single key to explain everything else, leading, for example, to the notion that every single Marlowe hero is an 'overreacher'. This old and impoverished approach got a new lease of life, and considerable enriching, from psychoanalytic critics, who applied the methods of psychoanalysis to fictional characters. Nevertheless, in whatever form, the character analysis approach works off a basic set of rather questionable assumptions: that all plays conceive of people in the same way regardless of the fact that notions about human beings have changed in different cultures and periods; that plays can be reduced to stories about people, leaving them fairly indistinguishable from novels (which aren't just stories, either); and, lastly, that all actors will always seek to play characters 'realistically'.

## Image analysis

The worst aspects of the Bradley approach were satirized in 1933 in the title of an essay by L. C. Knights: 'How Many Children had Lady Macbeth?' Instead of arguing about whether the explanation for Lady Macbeth's conduct was to be found in a frustrated motherhood – which Shakespeare shows no interest in scripting – Knights suggested we concentrate on the words that are actually there in front of us. This approach was refreshing in that it escaped from the world of speculation, where critics can give free rein to their own assumptions and prejudices, and returned to the real thing – the actual written text. In his analysis of that text Knights discussed its images and figurative speech. This attention to word pictures was most often associated with the analysis of poetry. And, indeed, Knights suggested that – in response to the fantasies of the character analysts – *Macbeth* was 'a dramatic poem'. His approach was consolidated a couple of years later with the appearance of Caroline Spurgeon's book on *Shakespeare's Imagery* (1935). This demonstrates how it is possible to identify the major concerns of the plays by analysing their patterns of images. Spurgeon's work was then taken up and developed in the United States in 1947: a book called *The Well Wrought Urn* contains an essay on Shakespeare as a poet which closely analyses metaphors in *Macbeth*. The book's author, Cleanth Brooks, was part of a school of literary criticism called 'New Criticism', which became famous in the late 1940s and on into the 1950s. It insisted that when trying to specify what a poem means it was improper to appeal to anything outside the poem, such as the intention of the author or historical context. The poem's meaning resided only in the words in front of you.

The New Critics based much of their work around fairly élitist forms of poetry, in a world recovering from war. Their somewhat extreme position has long ago vanished. But it left a legacy – the assumption that one of the reliable ways into understanding a play derives from an analysis of its verbal text, and in particular its images. Faced by a question like 'How does Shakespeare create a sense of evil in the play?' a candidate may well have learnt that analysis of images will be required. It would also – of course – be very easy to show how the use of space and the functioning of the bodies can suggest that unsettling quality that's called evil. But a critical approach such as 'image analysis' tends to assume that the play is primarily a verbal artefact which exists on the page as patterns of words; that these words are in no way coloured or shaped by the manner and circumstances of their delivery; and, lastly, that the play has its effect from being read with close attention rather than being heard and watched.

## Reader-response criticism

When the play is read as dramatic poem there is a tendency not to think about the audience. Indeed one of the assumptions of New Criticism was that all readers are the same, that the poem would yield up its meaning to anybody who applied the right approach, that the reader and the writer were more or less the same. One of the reactions against these ideas was to insist more forcefully on the processes of making sense of the artefact. Instead of assuming a community of readers who all had the same literary 'competence', so-called reader-response criticism notes the variety of readers and audiences, who all have their own competences, derived from their own cultural and social positioning. Readers and audiences thus bring with them values and ideas when they approach a text. They bring expectations based on their previous experience and their familiarity with texts' genres and signals. Hence they have a role in contributing to the meaning of, or 'completing', the piece. Against New Criticism, with its historically disembodied reader, the concept of 'interpretive communities', differently positioned audiences, feels much more democratic and concrete. Indeed reader-response criticism made itself felt during that rather democratic decade, the 1970s.

Within college study of drama this emphasis on the audience makes itself felt in a couple of ways. Where there is a stress on the practice of drama, as opposed to literary analysis, one of the regular projects is to investigate how to stage an older text for a contemporary audience. This recognizes that audiences change, and have different values. A decision radically to overhaul an older text can amount to adaptation, or 'translation', of it. Such an activity can be very useful as a form of critical approach, because it is necessary to know in great detail not only how the original works but also how the particular audience, or 'interpretive community', is constituted in order to produce an adequately subtle translation. But this stress on the importance of the audience as maker of meaning can sometimes lead to an individualist stance, which approximates to the declaration: 'That's the way I see it and it's my own response which counts.' The problem with this viewpoint is that it is often unaware of how similar it is to those of everybody else in the same interpretive community, so the person fails to reflect on where their values come from. And it is also a viewpoint which typically ducks out of being challenged by anything that is inexplicable or strange in the text. In this respect it is a form of individualist assertion rather than reader response.

## Historical and cultural approaches

Approaches that elevate the importance of audience response can end up getting fixated on ways in which the play can be made 'relevant'. This can then lead to ignoring those aspects which seem least relevant because they are the most obviously historical. In recent years, however, some of the most exciting critical approaches have based themselves on history.

The exam revision notes that we mentioned earlier advised that if you are studying *Macbeth* it is a good idea to note how many kings there are in the play, and to read up on some late Elizabethan history. Sometimes this is referred to as filling in the 'background'. But that word implies that the history is separate from the great speeches and set-pieces. It is better instead to think of the text within a context, the play as a participant within the culture in which it was made. The relationship between individual text and wider context is likely to be fairly complicated – how, in our own time, might we say that *The Lion King* or *Chicago* related to the early years of the new century? Do they do so in the same way as Franko B's body art?

Reference to historical periods can lead to some very large generalizations – an explanation for the construction of all the women characters in Shakespeare, for example, might refer to the dominance of 'patriarchy'; the treatment of any characters who are not white – or even their complete invisibility – might be attributed to 'imperialism'. But patriarchy – the transmission of power and wealth through male lines – works differently at different periods. Marriages arranged to consolidate landed property require different things from women than does the pursuit of mercantile profit. So 'New Historicism', as it was called, aimed to look in detail at how elements of a society – not necessarily the whole thing – perpetuate or challenge very particular sets of power relations. These Historicists were 'New' not simply because they emerged in the 1980s but because they consciously drew on thinkers and topics that became influential in the modern period. Their work drew in particular on the French historian of ideas, Michel Foucault. Foucault's work showed, by means of many textual examples, how such things as madness and sexuality are produced and controlled through sets of power relations. Plays perform a part in these processes – for example allowing the expression of subversive ideas, or generating a feeling of carnival release from daily affairs, only to close down again at the end and reconcile their audience to dominant power structures.

New Historicism was especially influential in the United States. In Britain there developed a similar interest in detailed accounts of historical cultures. This was known as 'Cultural Materialism', and it derived largely from the work of the Marxist-oriented writer Raymond Williams. In his explorations of the relationship between text and context Williams did work on the institutions and groupings that produced artworks in different cultures. This led to a consideration not just of what a play represents but of how it comes to be there, how it is disseminated in the culture, who owns it. In asking these detailed questions Cultural Materialism was writing a larger history of the state and capitalism. Within this perspective an individual line of a play can be seen to resonate through the history that has brought us to where we are now. The line is historically **determined** and is helping determine the course of history. For example, the first line and a half of Shakespeare's *Julius Caesar* are: 'Hence! home, you idle creatures, get you home! / Is this a holiday?' Historical research shows that this was the first Shakespeare play staged at the Globe, and perhaps was done for the opening of the new theatre in 1599 (see p. 199). Richard Wilson argues, in *Will Power* (1993), that the lines are part of a debate about idleness in popular culture. Their appearance at this inaugural moment at the Globe is an attempt by Shakespeare's company to dissociate itself from London's labouring subculture, and to make itself respectable in class terms. Although they were legally classed as vagabonds, the company operated economically as a preindustrial capitalist enterprise. The opening line and a half enact the new status available to capitalist entrepreneurs.

The presence of Marxism brings to Cultural Materialism an important element which is much less apparent in New Historicism. This element derives from the earliest days of the development of cultural studies, in the 1970s, where the academic work was driven by a sense of the need to change society. Cultural Materialism, at its most characteristic, is trying to use critical approaches to do more than simply read a play. It is hoping to work with its readers to think differently about how society operates – as a first step towards changing that society for something better.

# Interpretation

In looking at genre and its possible pleasures for an audience, we said that a play often needs to be *predictable*, at some basic level, for an audience to feel happy with it. Even where they are not always happy, this predictability is something which is *managed* by the play: it draws on an audience's cultural competence, offers them things they can recognize, and know, and feel secure with – and then makes surprising changes. This assertion of ours implies that predictability and surprise depend on one another for effect: the surprise is shocking because an audience has been led to expect something different, the renewed sense of security is the more profound because the familiar shape is rediscovered after it has been distorted. The surprise of Malvolio's final entry gains from its contrast with the signs of a predictable happy end. The close of *Waiting for Godot* refuses closure: 'Yes, let's go. *They do not move.*'

## Value judgements

In discussions of drama, you can most often hear the word 'predictable' used as a value judgement: 'predictable' drama is bad, surprising is good. This use of these words tends to ignore the fact that they depend on one another for effect in the way we suggest above. It may be that we have to look again at the language we use for assessing plays. For we regularly employ a series of opposed terms in the same way as we use 'predictable'/surprising: for example, caricature/character; flat/round; exaggerated or melodramatic or over-the-top or overacted/realistic; entertaining or escapist/serious. Do these pairs have a similar connection between their apparently opposed terms?

On the matter of caricature versus character, we can note that Hamlet seems to have more inner depth when put alongside Claudius as a type of villain; we get engaged with Serjeant Musgrave's complicated inner turmoil because it feels more real – despite its wordiness – than the cartoon figures of civic dignitaries. By making Claudius and civic dignitaries into types (see p. 28) or cartoons, we attend to them as representatives of positions within a power structure rather than as free-floating individuals. The contrast of caricature and character is *managed* by the text to produce both a sense of depth and an understanding of structural positions. The same might be said of the relationship between flat and round.

If we take exaggerated etc./realistic, we can again see a relationship of mutual dependence. The mechanicals' play at the end of *A Midsummer Night's Dream* is comical because the acting is too large, the verse too simple and the courtly audience mocks it. But most real audiences find the courtiers' wit too obscure to be amusing, and they come across as snobs, alongside whom the mechanicals are fun. The contrast is not only managed but also often works to produce more enjoyment of the exaggeration than the sober realism. In *The Workhouse Donkey* (1963) John Arden made a political point out of the contrast between exaggeration and realism. In the final scene an art gallery is being opened by civic officials and politicians; a commotion is caused by rioters outside; during the commotion a disgraced councillor enters, sits on the table with the buffet on it, pulls down a paper chain to put round his neck and puts the decorative flowers on his head; he then delivers a speech which is based on the Book of Psalms. This presentation alludes to a model of theatre as carnival, as excess; it contrasts with the sober, and hypocritical, realism of the town politicians.

A value judgement that prefers realism to exaggeration is here shown to be one that not only supports hypocrisy, but that makes a political alignment: the sober, and realist, dignitaries want to get rid of their disgraced but theatrical colleague. At this point the audience, or the readers, of Arden's play come to realize that their value judgement has consequences. These consequences have bearing not just on politics, but on the work of theatre: should theatre involve mess and anarchy, or should it restrict itself to tidy and clear meanings?

## Learning not to ask what it means

This question is unresolved by *The Workhouse Donkey*, deliberately. The job of work done by the play is to disturb the audience's sense of easy definitions and clear separations. To try to fix its 'meaning' – to pinpoint in a couple of phrases what the play is saying – is to force the play to become much more simplistic than it is. The strength of *Workhouse Donkey* is precisely that it refuses to allow itself to be pushed around by the question 'What does the play *mean*?' Instead it forces us to ask a different question, which we can phrase in different ways: What does the play start us quarrelling about? What scheme of values does it disturb? What does it set up for debate? So, far from the play yielding up a clear-cut single meaning, it asks us questions. Where do we stand with regard to mess and tidiness, carnival and sobriety, exaggeration and realism?

This point about *Workhouse Donkey* could be made about all plays. Not all plays want to start a fierce quarrel, but most of them refuse to allow themselves to be pinned down to simple singular meanings. If their authors wanted to write such things as this they would have been newspaper editors and journalists, not playwrights. Consequently, we make life hard for ourselves by approaching plays the wrong way. If you come to a play requiring that it tells you what it means, in a neat and tidy way, you will be frustrated and disappointed. It will never quite fit; there will be bits you cannot account for.

## Two simple, and better, questions

The most useful way to begin your approach to a play is to ask a simple question: 'What have we got here?' or 'What is this object like?' This will lead you into a description of the sort of thing it is. That description will, we hope, be more easily done using some of the language and approaches which we have introduced to you in this book. Don't try at this point to interpret it, to fix on a coherent meaning – just describe, as accurately as you can.

Once we have described what is in front of us, we can then ask the second question: 'How does this thing work?' Again we have tried to offer you some examples for thinking about how the activities of the stage are making their effect, how the audience are being placed with regard to the performed material.

## Producing culture

To ask how something works is to assume that it does something, that it works on something. Plays work on their audience – or, to put it more precisely, they work on what is in the audience's heads and in their bodies, on their values, assumptions, beliefs, desires. They sustain these values and they challenge them, they make themselves seductive and they ask questions. In this sense plays are not only made within a specific culture (in the ways we have outlined in this chapter) but they also help to shape, to sustain and transform, that culture.

Let us recall where we started. The playtext co-produces the performance, in the sense that it scripts it. Most of this book has tried to show how that scripting is done. At the same time we have also tried to show how the performance sets up reactions in, uses and challenges the assumptions of, the audience. The performance produces a response in the audience, in the sense that it sets ideas and feelings in play. We are talking here about something bigger than a message from a writer to an audience. The script derives from, and interacts with, ideas and values in the culture around it. The performance is shaped by but can also stretch the various elements that bring it into being. Once script and performance come into existence they become part of the cultural resource on which new productions will draw, against which they will react: they help create the conditions in which the next plays will be able to imagine themselves. Once we understand how plays work, both on the page and then on the stage itself, we can think powerfully about drama as a part of cultural production – and then, of course, we can make powerful cultural productions of our own.

# GLOSSARY

*This glossary defines words and phrases that may be unfamiliar but are not always explained in the main body of the text. We also elaborate on a few words and phrases already defined. But do get used to working with dictionaries, including specialist theatre dictionaries such as Hartnoll 1972.*

**apostrophe** passage of text or speech addressing an absent person (or idea).

**articulate** give shape to an idea, *form* it as utterance, see p. 30.

**binary** system of two linked terms, usually in opposition: e.g. hot/cold, good/bad.

**bourgeois** middle class (from the French); in English, a 'burgher' is a town dweller. The middle class was first formed in towns.

**box-set** stage set depicting the inside of a room, usually constructed with flats, where the audience looks through an invisible 'fourth wall'.

**canonical** a 'canon' of texts consists of those texts deemed by authoritative (and institutional) opinion to be important.

**contingent** dependent on external circumstances, and hence provisional, uncertain.

**crescendo** musical term taken from the Italian, meaning a build-up or steady increase of loudness. Note that, despite its common incorrect usage, it does not simply mean 'loud' – something ending with a *crescendo* ends with a build-up.

**cultural formation** particular and significant shape that a culture takes for a period of time, later to be succeeded by a fresh formation. Involves the relationships between classes and other groupings, their institutions and the dominant ideas. Sometimes also used to mean a formation *within* a culture.

**dénouement** moment of untangling of plot, unravelling of mystery.

**determinations** influencing factors. It is commonly said that what we are and do is determined both by our genetic inheritance ('nature') and by our upbringing and experience ('nurture'). Some use the notion of determination to imply direct production ('this results in only that'), others to imply the setting of limits or frames ('this permits these not those'). We tend to the latter.

**dramaturgy** practice of writing plays. A 'dramaturge' is someone who advises directors and others on the stage interpretation of the dramatic text.

**economy** system of significant differences. That it matters whether we call people by their forenames, surnames or titles according to who they are and when we do it means that there is an economy of naming to be borne in mind.

**eponymous** having the same name. Hamlet is the eponymous hero of *Hamlet*.

**existential** concerning the sheer fact of existence.

**focal economy** way that different points of focus work in relation to one another, and that focus differs from non-focus. See *economy*.

**folio** sheet of paper. Renaissance 'folio' editions, such as the posthumous First Folio of Shakespeare which collected all his plays, were large-format, printed on unfolded sheets. *Quarto* editions of single plays – often published just after first performances – are printed on sheets folded twice, making the pages one-quarter size.

**humanist** originally a mode of thinking that was alternative to 'religious', then a notion of history as human self-development, and now implying a mistaken belief in humans as being separate from the forces (economic, social) of history.

**humours** according to medieval medicine, the four principal bodily fluids – blood, phlegm, choler and melancholy – whose relative proportions determined a person's physical and mental temperament. Hence, for example, 'phlegmatic', 'choleric'. A 'comedy of humours' organizes its characters according to these biologically based predispositions.

**kinaesthetic** sympathetically feeling movement. Usually also implies a bodily reaction: the clown slips on the banana skin; our stomachs turn.

**limelight** introduced around 1816, lime gave a bright white light, much favoured for spotlighting individual actors.

**liminal** at the edge of things (as, say, the tricksy behaviour of the shaman); between states (e.g. neither dead nor alive).

**mediating** relating together two apparently unconnected kinds of activity or thinking in such a way that the interaction alters them. A chorus mediates between the dissimilar activities of performing and spectating. Good writing about a work of art and social relationships will understand each in relation to the other.

**metatheatrical** concerning aspects of theatre that reflect back on the theatre itself, such as jokes in plays about acting (see p. 94).

**monological** having a single meaning.

**morality play** late fifteenth-, early sixteenth-century drama of moral instruction, employing personified abstractions (see p. 41).

**Neoclassical** pertaining to a European-wide intellectual and artistic movement most apparent in the mid to late eighteenth century. Its adherents studied and imitated classical antiquity as a means to discovering and expressing the eternal truths of life. Their aesthetic values had ethical overtones, aspiring to purity, nobility, rationality.

**parabolic** in the form of a parable, like Aesop's fables or Christ's parables recounted in the Bible. Parables are not meant to be taken literally. They abstract general principles from life and their stories and situations are meant to be understood as if in 'inverted commas'.

**pastoral** tradition of writing and art depicting country life which is often idealized, idyllic; it becomes the ornamental play-acting of courtly society, but it also develops towards more realistic comment on agrarian problems.

**proscenium** (arch, stage, theatre) the space in front of the Greek *skena*, or scene, is the *pro-skena*. It meant an acting area. Nowadays it has come to refer to the architectural partition which designates the outer limit of this territory: the proscenium wall separates the auditorium from the acting area. This wall is penetrated by a great hole (to allow the audience to watch the action); the action goes on underneath, and behind, the proscenium arch. A proscenium theatre has this architectural arrangement built into it.

**protagonist** see p. 110: Greek *proto* (first) *agonistes* (actor/combatant); nowadays used for the leading character.

**reception** understanding of a text in reading or performance; the reader/ spectator *constructs* the significant shapes and meanings of the text in the act of reading or spectating.

**reciprocal** two-way.

**referent** actual thing a sign (such as a word and its concept) refers to. 'Fire' makes us think of fires in general. 'Light the fire' sends you to an actual fire; see chapter 6, p. 158.

**rhetorical** of rhetoric, or the art of persuasion, especially at first by the organization and ornamentation of language. A rhetorical effect is not merely eloquence, but a carefully constructed device intended to influence the receiver. Thus, simplicity also can be persuasive. We might, for instance, be persuaded that what we are being told is true – by a 'rhetorical guarantee'.

**semiotics** study of signs. *Semiology* assumes that this study can be a science; see chapter 6, pp. 158–60.

**signifier, signified** a 'sign' consists of two elements: a word or visual image (a red traffic light) and a concept (stop: danger). Without the concept the traffic light is a metal pole with a red light on it: the signifier and the signified have

an arbitrary relationship, but they also depend on each other to make the sign. Performance depends substantially on the use of signs: an audience will understand two armchairs and a small table to signify a living room, or an antique shop; see chapter 6, p. 158.

**stage left/right** to the left or right of a person facing the audience from the stage. *Upstage* is towards the back of the stage, since it slopes.

**syntax** organization of a sentence, or any unit of language.

**tabs** stage curtains.

**Town** the eighteenth-century concept of the Town implied a social group rather than a place; this group was, largely, the literate and wealthy. The Town had its unspoken rules about taste and standards. 'Town' first referred to the area, now the 'West End', between the palaces and the City of London which was developed after the Restoration.

**unities** of time, place and action. First formulated and insisted upon by Lodovico Castelvetro in his commentary on Aristotle's *Poetics* (1571) as rules for proper drama. The rules were that the action should take place over twenty-four hours in the fiction, in a single place, and that there should be a clear and single plot.

**Vice** stage figure from the moralities (*q.v.*) who combined together several personified abstractions (see p. 41) representing vices. The Vice tempts the hero, may sometimes represent the devil, and typically interacts with the audience. The Vice is attractively – though seriously – wicked.

# BIBLIOGRAPHY

## Primary texts

*When we refer to a play in the main text of this book, we give the actual or guessed date of first performance. In the rare cases where this was much later than the play was written, we give the date of its completion. In this bibliography, the second date given is of the printed edition of the play we have used. Where possible, we have used collected editions. Note that various editions – especially of older plays – often present differing versions of the same play.*

## Reference

Adebayo, M. 2006 'Moj of the Antarctic: An African Odyssey', in M. Adebayo, *Plays One*, intro. L. Goddard, London: Oberon Books, 2011.

Anon. *c.* 1440: 'The Castle of Perseverance', in *Four Morality Plays*, ed. P. Happé, Harmondsworth: Penguin Books, 1979.

Anon. 15th century: 'Corpus Christi Play (York)', in *York Mystery Plays*, eds R. Beadle and P. King, Oxford: Clarendon Press, 1984.

Anon. *c.* 1470: 'Mankind', in *English Moral Interludes*, ed. G. Wickham, London: Dent, 1976.

Anon. *c.* 1498: 'Everyman', in *Everyman and Medieval Miracle Plays*, ed. A. C. Cawley, London: Dent, 1977.

Anon. *c.* 1590: 'The True Chronicle History of King Leir and his Three Daughters', in *Narrative and Dramatic Sources of Shakespeare*, VII: *Major Tragedies: 'Hamlet', 'Othello', 'King Lear', 'Macbeth'*, ed. G. Bullough, London: Routledge & Kegan Paul, 1973.

Anon. 1606: 'The Revenger's Tragedy', in *Three Jacobean Tragedies*, ed. G. Salgado, Harmondsworth: Penguin Books, 1965.

Arden, J. 1959: *Serjeant Musgrave's Dance. An Un-historical Parable*, London: Methuen, 1960.

Arden, J. 1963: *The Workhouse Donkey. A Vulgar Melo-Drama*, London: Methuen, 1964.

Beaumont, F. 1607: *The Knight of the Burning Pestle*, ed. M. Hattaway, London: Ernest Benn, 1969.

Beckett, S. 1958: 'Act Without Words 1'; 1960: 'Act Without Words 2'; 1955: 'Waiting for Godot. A Tragi-comedy in Two Acts', in S. Beckett, *The Complete Dramatic Works*, London: Faber & Faber, 1986.

Behan, B. 1958: 'The Hostage', in B. Behan, *The Complete Plays*, intr. A. Simpson, London: Methuen, 1978.

Behn, A. 1677: 'The Rover', in A. Behn, *The Rover and Other Plays*, ed. J. Spencer, Oxford: Oxford University Press, 1995.

Bhuchar, S. 2014: *My Name Is...*, London: Bloomsbury.

Blythe, A. 2003: 'Come Out Eli', in *The Methuen Drama Anthology of Testimonial Plays*, ed. A. Forsyth, London: Bloomsbury, 2014.

Bolt, R. 1960: 'A Man for All Seasons', in *New English Dramatists* VI, ed. T. Maschler, Harmondsworth: Penguin Books, 1967.

Boucicault, D. 1860: 'The Colleen Bawn', in *Nineteenth Century Plays*, ed. G. Rowell, Oxford: Oxford University Press, 1990.

Brecht, B. 1926: 'Man Equals Man', in B. Brecht, *The Collected Plays* II.1, trans. G. Nellhaus, London: Eyre Methuen, 1979.

Brecht, B. 1932: *The Mother*, trans. L. Baxandall, New York: Grove Press, 1965.

Brecht, B. 1943a, 1953: 'Life of Galileo', in B. Brecht, *The Collected Plays* V.1, trans. J. Willett, London: Eyre Methuen, 1980.

Brecht, B. 1943b: 'The Good Person of Setzuan', in B. Brecht, *The Collected Plays* VI.1, trans. J. Willett, London: Eyre Methuen, 1985.

Brenton, H. 1974: *The Churchill Play: As it will be Performed in the Winter of 1984 by the Internees of Churchill Camp Somewhere in England*, London: Eyre Methuen.

Chekhov, A. 1903: 'The Cherry Orchard. A Comedy in Four Acts'; 1901: 'Three Sisters. A Drama in Four Acts', in A. Chekhov, *Plays*, trans. E. Fen, Harmondsworth: Penguin Books, 1959.

Churchill, C. 1983: 'Fen'; 1982: 'Top Girls', in C. Churchill, *Plays: Two*, London: Methuen Drama, 1990.

Churchill, C. 2016: *Escaped Alone*, London: Nick Hern Books.

Cowley, H. 1788: *The Fate of Sparta; or, The Rival Kings. A Tragedy*, London: G. G. J. and J. Robinson.

Dryden, J. 1668: 'An Evening's Love', in J. Dryden, *Works X*, Berkeley: University of California Press, 1970.

Dumas, Alexandre *fils* 1852: 'La dame aux camélias [Camille]', in *Camille and Other Plays*, ed. S. S. Stanton, New York: Hill & Wang, 1957.

Etherege, G. 1676: 'The Man of Mode or, Sir Fopling Flutter. A Comedy', in *Restoration Plays*, ed. E. Gosse, London: Dent, 1974.

Farber, Y. 2008: 'Molora', in Y. Farber, *Plays One*, intr. I. Rowland, London: Oberon Books, 2014.

Frisch, M. 1958: *The Fire Raisers. A Morality without a Moral, with an Afterpiece*, trans. M. Bullock, London: Eyre Methuen, 1962.

Fugard, A. 1982: '*Master Harold*' ... *and the Boys*, Oxford: Oxford University Press, 1983.

Galsworthy, J. 1910: 'Justice: A Tragedy', in J. Galsworthy, *The Plays*, London: Duckworth, 1929.

García Lorca, F. 1933: 'Blood Wedding. Tragedy in Three Acts and Seven Scenes', in F. García Lorca, *Plays: One*, intr. G. Edwards, London: Methuen, 1987.

Greig, N. 1983: *Poppies*, London: Gay Men's Press.

Greig, N. 1988: 'Plague of Innocence', in *Gay Plays: Five*, intr. M. Wilcox, London: Methuen Drama, 1994.

Griffiths, T. 1975: *Comedians*, London: Faber & Faber.

Hazlewood, C. 1863: 'Lady Audley's Secret', in *Nineteenth Century Plays*, ed. G. Rowell, Oxford: Oxford University Press, 1990.

Hodge, H. 1937: 'Cannibal Carnival' (sc. iv and v plus synopsis), in *In Letters of Red*, ed. E. A. Osborne, London: Michael Joseph.

Holcroft, T. 1802: *A Tale of Mystery*, London: R. Phillips.

Hussain, E. 2015: *Blood*, London: Bloomsbury.

Ibsen, H. 1876: 'Peer Gynt' [written 1867], in H. Ibsen, *Plays: Six*, trans. M. Meyer, London: Eyre Methuen, 1987.

Ibsen, H. 1877: 'The Pillars of Society', in H. Ibsen, *Plays: Four*, trans. M. Meyer, London: Eyre Methuen, 1991.

Ibsen, H. 1879: 'A Doll's House', in H. Ibsen, *Plays: Two*, trans. M. Meyer, London: Eyre Methuen, 1980.

Ibsen, H. 1882: 'Ghosts'; 1885: 'The Wild Duck', in H. Ibsen, *Plays: One*, trans. M. Meyer, London: Eyre Methuen, 1980.

Jelinek, E. 1998: *Sports Play*, trans. P. Black, London: Oberon Books, 2012.

Jerrold, D. 1829: 'Black-Ey'd Susan or, "All in the Downs". A Nautical Drama', in *Nineteenth Century Plays*, ed. G. Rowell, Oxford: Oxford University Press, 1990.

Jonson, B. 1606: 'Volpone, or the Fox', in B. Jonson, *Three Comedies*, ed. M. Jamieson, Harmondsworth: Penguin Books, 1966.

Jordan, A. 2015: *Yen*, London: Nick Hern Books.

Kane, S. 1998: 'Crave', in S. Kane, *Complete Plays*, London: Methuen Drama, 2001.

Kellett, T. 2016: 'Primadonna', in *Plays from Vault*, London: Nick Hern Books.

Kipphardt, H. 1966: *In the Matter of J. Robert Oppenheimer*, trans. R. Speirs, London: Methuen, 1967.

Kwei-Armah, K. 2009: 'Seize the Day', in *Not Black and White*, London: A & C Black Publishers.

Kyd, T. *c.* 1587: 'The Spanish Tragedy', in *Five Elizabethan Tragedies*, ed. A. K. McIlwraith, Oxford: Oxford University Press, 1976.

Laughton, S. 2016: 'Run', in *Plays from Vault*, London: Nick Hern Books.

Lawrence, D. H. 1967/68: 'The Daughter-in-Law. A Play in Four Acts' [written 1912]; 'The Widowing of Mrs Holroyd. A Play in Three Acts' [written 1914], in D. H. Lawrence, *Three Plays*, intr. R. Williams, Harmondsworth: Penguin Books, 1969.

Lewis, L. 1871: 'The Bells', in *Henry Irving and the Bells. Irving's Personal Script of the Play*, ed. D. Mayer, Manchester: Manchester University Press, 1980. (Also in Rowell 1990, with different text.)

MacColl, E. 1945: 'Johnny Noble. An Episodic Play with Singing', in *Agit-Prop to Theatre Workshop. Political Playscripts 1930–50*, eds H. Goorney and E. MacColl, Manchester: Manchester University Press, 1986.

Marlowe, C. *c.* 1587: 'Tamburlaine the Great: Parts 1 and 2', in C. Marlowe, *Plays*, ed. J. B. Steane, Harmondsworth: Penguin Books, 1969.

Mason, L. 1982: 'Double Vision', in *Lesbian Plays*, ed. J. Davis, London: Methuen, 1987.

McDowall, A. 2014: 'Pomona', in A. McDowall, *Plays: 1*, London: Bloomsbury, 2016.

McGrath, J. 1973: *The Cheviot, the Stag and the Black, Black Oil*, Isle of Skye: West Highland Publishing Company, 1977.

Middleton, T. 1621: 'Women Beware Women', in T. Middleton, *Three Plays*, ed. K. Muir, London: Dent, 1975.

Miller, A. 1949: *Death of a Salesman*, Harmondsworth: Penguin Books, 1973.
Molière 1666: *Le Misanthrope*, trans. and adapted N. Bartlett, 1988, Bath: Absolute Classics, 1990.
Moraga, C. 1984: *Giving up the Ghost*, Los Angeles: West End Press, 1986.
Neilson, A. 1991: 'Normal'; 1993: 'Penetrator', in A. Neilson, *Plays: 1*, London: Bloomsbury, 1998.
Neilson, A. 2004: 'The Wonderful World of Dissocia', in A. Neilson, *Plays: 2*, London: Bloomsbury, 2008.
Norton-Taylor, R. 2003: 'Justifying War', in *The Tricycle: Collected Tribunal Plays 1994-2012*, London: Oberon Books, 2014.
O'Casey, S. 1926: 'The Plough and the Stars', in S. O'Casey, *Three Plays*, London: Macmillan, 1977.
O'Reilly, K. 2012: 'In Water I'm Weightless'; 2002: 'peeling' [2011 version], in K. O'Reilly, *Atypical Plays for Atypical Actors*, London: Oberon Books, 2016.
Orton, J. 1966: 'The Ruffian on the Stair', in J. Orton, *Crimes of Passion. The Ruffian on the Stair and The Erpingham Camp*, London: Methun, 1967.
Osborne, J. 1956: *Look Back in Anger*, London: Faber & Faber, 1976.
Owen, G. 2010: 'Love Steals Us from Loneliness', in G. Owen, *Collected Plays*, London: Oberon Books, 2016.
Palmer, T. A. 1874: 'East Lynne' (adapted from the novel by Mrs Henry Wood), in *Female Playwrights of the Nineteenth Century*, ed. A. Scullion, London: Dent, 1996.
Pinero, A. W. 1898: 'Trelawny of the "Wells". A Comedietta in Four Acts', in A. W. Pinero, *Trelawny of the 'Wells' and Other Plays*, ed. J. S. Bratton, Oxford: Oxford University Press, 1995.
Pinnock, W. 1991: 'Talking in Tongues', in *Black Plays: Three*, ed. Y. Brewster, London: Methuen, 1995.
Pinter, H. 1958: 'The Birthday Party'; 1960: 'The Dumb Waiter', in H. Pinter, *Plays: One*, London: Eyre Methuen, 1976.
Pinter, H. 1960: *The Caretaker*, London: Methuen.
Posener, J. 1975: 'Any Woman Can', in *Lesbian Plays*, ed. J. Davis, London: Methuen, 1987.
Robertson, T. 1867: 'Caste. An Original Comedy in Three Acts', in T. Robertson, *Plays*, ed. W. Tydeman, Cambridge: Cambridge University Press, 1982.
Rowe, N. 1703: *The Fair Penitent*, ed. M. Goldstein, London: Edward Arnold, 1969.
Sartre, J.-P. 1942: *The Flies*, trans. S. Gilbert, Harmondsworth: Penguin Books, 1968.
Sartre, J.-P. 1944: 'Huis clos [In Camera]', trans. S. Gilbert, in J.-P. Sartre, *In Camera and Other Plays*, Harmondsworth: Penguin Books, 1990.
Schiller, F. 1800: 'Mary Stuart', in *Five German Tragedies*, ed. and trans. F. J. Lamport, Harmondsworth: Penguin Books, 1969.
Shakespeare, W. 1597: *1 Henry 4*, ed. D. Bevington, Oxford: Oxford University Press, 1987.
Shakespeare, W. 1601: *Hamlet*, ed. G. R. Hibbard, Oxford: Oxford University Press, 1987.
Shakespeare, W. 1606/7: 'Antony and Cleopatra'; 1608/9: 'Cymbeline'; 1601: 'Hamlet'; 1597: '1 Henry 4'; 1613: 'Henry 8'; *c.* 1599: 'Julius Caesar'; 1605/6: 'King Lear'; 1606: 'Macbeth'; 1596–8: 'The Merchant of Venice'; 1594: 'A Midsummer Night's Dream'; 1602–4: 'Othello'; 1595: 'Richard 2'; 1592/3:

'Richard 3'; *c.* 1595: 'Romeo and Juliet'; 1592: 'The Taming of the Shrew'; 1610/11: 'The Tempest'; 1592–4: 'Titus Andronicus'; *c.* 1600: 'Troilus and Cressida'; 1602: 'Twelfth Night', in W. Shakespeare, *The Complete Works*, ed. P. Alexander, London and Glasgow: Collins, 1974.

Shakespeare, W. 1610/11: *The Tempest*, ed. F. Kermode, London: Methuen, 1964.

Shaw, G. B. 1902: 'Mrs Warren's Profession. A Play' [written 1894], in G. B. Shaw, *Plays Unpleasant*, Harmondsworth: Penguin Books, 1975.

Sheridan, R. B. 1799: 'Pizzaro. A Tragedy in Five Acts' [after Kotzebue], in R. B. Sheridan, *The Dramatic Works*, ed. J. Knight, London: Oxford University Press, 1931.

Simpson, N. F. 1959: *One Way Pendulum. A Farce in a New Dimension*, London: Faber & Faber, 1960.

Sims, G. 1881: 'The Lights o'London. A New and Original Drama in Five Acts', in *The Lights o'London and Other Victorian Plays*, ed. M. R. Booth, Oxford: Oxford University Press, 1995.

Slovo, G. and V. Brittain 2004: 'Guantanamo', in *The Tricycle: Collected Tribunal Plays 1994-2012*, London: Oberon Books, 2014.

Soans, R. 2005: *Talking to Terrorists*, London: Oberon Books.

Sophocles *c.* 450 BCE: 'Antigone', in *Classical Tragedy Greek and Roman: 8 Plays*, ed. R. W. Corrigan, trans. D. Fitts and R. Fitzgerald, New York: Applause, 1980.

Sophocles 427 BCE: 'Oedipus Rex', in *Classical Tragedy Greek and Roman: 8 Plays*, ed. R. W. Corrigan, trans. K. Cavander, New York: Applause, 1980.

Stephens, S. 2006: 'Motortown'; 2003 'One Minute'; 2007: 'Pornography', in S. Stephens, *Plays: 2*, London: Bloomsbury, 2015.

Strindberg, A. 1902: 'A Dream Play', in A. Strindberg, *Plays: Two*, trans. M. Meyer, London: Eyre Methuen, 1982.

SuAndi 1994: *The Story of M*, intr. D. Osborne, London: Oberon Books, 2017.

Taha, D. 2015: *Fireworks*, trans. C. Naylor, London: Bloomsbury.

Toller, E. 1921: *Masses and Man. A Fragment of the Social Revolution of the Twentieth Century*, trans. V. Mendel, London: Nonesuch Press, 1926.

Vega, Lope de 1612–14: 'Fuente Ovejuna', in L. de Vega, *Fuente Ovejuna and Lost in a Mirror*, version by A. Mitchell, London: Absolute Classics, 1989.

Webster, J. 1612: *The White Devil*; 1614: 'The Duchess of Malfi ', in J. Webster, *Three Plays*, ed. D. C. Gunby, Harmondsworth: Penguin Books, 1972.

Wertenbaker, T. 1988: *Our Country's Good*, London: Methuen Drama, 1991.

Whitehill, C. 2016: 'Mr Incredible', in *Plays from Vault*, London: Nick Hern Books.

Wilde, O. 1895: 'The Importance of Being Earnest. A Trivial Comedy for Serious People', in O. Wilde, *Plays, Prose Writings, and Poems*, ed. I. Murray, London: Dent, 1978.

Williams, T. 1945: 'The Glass Menagerie', in T. Williams, *A Streetcar Named Desire and Other Plays*, ed. E. Martin Browne, Harmondsworth: Penguin Books, 1962.

Zephaniah, B. 1987: 'Job Rocking', in *Black Plays: Two*, ed. Y. Brewster, London: Methuen, 1989.

# Secondary texts

*Here we list critical and reference works that we have mentioned in the main text of this book. Texts marked with \* may well be useful for further reading.*

Aristotle *c.* 350 BCE: 'Poetics' [On the Art of Poetry], in *Classical Literary Criticism*, ed. and trans. T. S. Dorsch, Harmondsworth: Penguin Books, 1983.
Aston, E. 1994: *An Introduction to Feminism and Theatre*, London: Routledge.
Aston, E. and Savona, G. 1991: *Theatre as Sign System: A Semiotics of Text and Performance*, London: Routledge.
Austin, J. L. 1962: *How to Do Things with Words*, London: Oxford University Press.
Balme, C. B.\* 2008: *The Cambridge Introduction to Theatre Studies*, Cambridge: Cambridge University Press.
Barba, E. and Savarese, N. 1991: *A Dictionary of Theatre Anthropology: The Secret Art of the Performer*, trans. R. Fowler, London: Routledge in association with Centre for Performance Research.
Barker, H. 1989: *Arguments for a Theatre*, London: John Calder.
Barker-Benfield, G. J. 1992: *The Culture of Sensibility. Sex and Society in Eighteenth-century Britain*, Chicago: University of Chicago Press.
Barthes, R. 1957, 1993: *Mythologies*, trans. A. Lavers, London: Vintage.
Boal, A.\* 1979: *Theatre of the Oppressed*, trans. C. A. and M.-O. Leal McBride, London: Pluto Press.
Boal, A. 1992: *Games for Actors and Non-actors*, trans. A. Jackson, London: Routledge.
Bradley, A. C. 1904: *Shakespearean Tragedy*, London: Macmillan & Co.
Brooks, C. 1947, 1968: *The Well Wrought Urn*, London: David Dobson.
Burton, D. 1980: *Dialogue and Discourse: A Sociolinguistic Approach to Modern Drama Dialogue and Naturally Occurring Conversation*, London: Routledge & Kegan Paul.
Cima, G. G. 1993: 'Ibsen and the Critical Actor', in *Performing Women. Female Characters, Male Playwrights, and the Modern Stage*, Ithaca and London: Cornell University Press.
Clemen, W. 1986: *A Commentary on Shakespeare's Richard 3*, London: Methuen.
Counsell, C. 1996: *Signs of Performance. An Introduction to Twentieth-Century Theatre*, London: Routledge.
Edwards, G. 1987: *Lorca. The Theatre beneath the Sand*, London: Marion Boyars.
Elam, K.\* 1980: *The Semiotics of Theatre and Drama*, London: Methuen.
Esslin, M. 1968: *The Theatre of the Absurd*, Harmondsworth: Penguin Books.
Ford, A. 1995: 'Katharsis: The Ancient Problem', in ed. A. Parker and E. K. Sedgwick, *Performativity and Performance*, London: Routledge.
Freeman, S. 1996: *Putting Your Daughters on the Stage. British Lesbian Theatre from the 1960s to the Present*, London: Cassell.
Garner, S. B. Jr\* 1994: *Bodied Spaces. Phenomenology and Performance in Contemporary Drama*, Ithaca and London: Cornell University Press.
Goebbels, H. 2009 'Text as Landscape: with the qualities of libretto, even if unsung', *Theatre Noise* conference, Central School of Speech and Drama, London.

Goorney, H. 1981: *The Theatre Workshop Story*, London: Eyre Methuen.

Gorfain, P. 1983: 'Hamlet and the Tragedy of Ludic Revenge', in *The World of Play*, ed. F. E. Manning, West Point, NY: Leisure Press.

Harris, J. W. 1992: *Medieval Theatre in Context*, London: Routledge.

Hartnoll, P. *(ed.) 1972: *The Concise Oxford Companion to the Theatre*, Oxford: Oxford University Press.

Kershaw, B. 1999: *The Radical in Performance. Between Brecht and Baudrillard*, London and New York: Routledge.

Knights, L. C. 1933: 'How Many Children had Lady Macbeth?' in *Explorations*, London: Chatto & Windus, 1946.

Lavender, A. 2016: *Performance in the Twenty-first Century: Theatres of Engagement*, London: Routledge.

Leacroft, R.* 1988: *The Development of the English Playhouse. An Illustrated Survey of Theatre Building in England from Medieval to Modern Times*, London: Methuen.

Loxley, J. 2007: *Performativity*, London and New York: Routledge.

Lucas, I. 1994: *Impertinent Decorum. Gay Theatrical Manoeuvres*, London: Cassell.

Marker, F. J. and Marker, L.-L. 1989: *Ibsen's Lively Art. A Performance Study of the Major Plays*, Cambridge: Cambridge University Press.

Nagler, A. M. 1959: *A Sourcebook in Theatrical History*, New York: Dover.

Pfister, M.* 1988: *The Theory and Analysis of Drama*, trans. J. Halliday, Cambridge: Cambridge University Press.

Rudlin, J. 1994: *Commedia dell'Arte. An Actor's Handbook*, London: Routledge.

Schechner, R. 1988: *Performance Theory*, London: Routledge.

Servos, N. 1984: *Pina Bausch – Wuppertal Dance Theater, or, The Art of Training a Goldfish: Excursions into Dance*, Köln: Ballett-Büchnen-Verlag.

Shaw, G. B. 1957: *The Quintessence of Ibsenism*, New York: Hill & Wang.

Shepherd, S. 1989: *Because We're Queers: The Life and Crimes of Kenneth Halliwell and Joe Orton*, London: Gay Men's Press.

Shepherd, S. 2009: *The Cambridge Introduction to Modern British Theatre*, Cambridge: Cambridge University Press.

Shepherd, S. and Wallis, M. 2004: *Drama/Theatre/Performance*, London and New York: Routledge.

Shepherd, S. and Womack, P.* 1996: *English Drama. A Cultural History*, Oxford: Blackwell.

Short, M. 1989: 'Discourse Analysis and the Analysis of Drama', in *Language, Discourse and Literature. An Introductory Reader in Discourse Stylistics*, ed. R. Carter and P. Simpson, London: Unwin Hyman.

Sinfield, A. 1992: *Faultlines. Cultural Materialism and the Politics of Dissident Reading*, Berkeley and Los Angeles: University of California Press.

Southern, R.* 1962: *The Seven Ages of the Theatre*, London: Faber & Faber.

Spurgeon, C. 1935: *Shakespeare's Imagery and What it Tells Us*, Cambridge: Cambridge University Press.

Taylor, J. R. 1967: *The Rise and Fall of the Well-made Play*, London: Methuen.

Wallis, M. 1995: 'Watching Like Detectives: Othello and the Audience', in *Othello and The Winter's Tale. Essays*, Loughborough: Loughborough Theatre Texts.

Weimann, R. 1987: *Shakespeare and the Popular Tradition in the Theater. Studies in the Social Dimension of Dramatic Form and Function*, ed. R. Schwartz, Baltimore: Johns Hopkins University Press.

West, S. 1991: *The Image of the Actor. Verbal and Visual Representation in the Age of Garrick and Kemble*, London: Pinter Publishers.

Wickham, G.* 1985: *A History of the Theatre*, Oxford: Phaidon.

Wiles, D. 2003: *A Short History of Western Performance Space*, Cambridge: Cambridge University Press.

Willett, J.* 1977: *The Theatre of Bertolt Brecht*, London: Eyre Methuen.

Williams, R. 1966: *Modern Tragedy*, London: Chatto & Windus.

Williams, R. 1977: *Marxism and Literature*, Oxford: Oxford University Press.

Williams, R. 1980: 'Social Environment and Theatrical Environment. The Case of English Naturalism', in R. Williams, *Problems in Materialism and Culture*, London: Verso.

Williams, R.* 1968: *Drama from Ibsen to Brecht*, London: Chatto & Windus.

Wilson, R. 1993: *Will Power. Essays on Shakespearean Authority*, Hemel Hempstead: Harvester Wheatsheaf.

Womack, P. 1996: 'Naturalism', in *English Drama. A Cultural History*, ed. S. Shepherd and P. Womack, Oxford: Blackwell.

# INDEX